Nothing Personal, Just Business

A Guided Journey into Organizational Darkness

HOWARD F. STEIN

QUORUM BOOKS
Westport, Connecticut • London

Library of Congress Cataloging-in-Publication Data

Stein, Howard F.
    Nothing personal, just business : a guided journey into organizational darkness /
Howard F. Stein ; foreword by David B. Friedman.
        p.   cm.
    Includes bibliographical references and index.
    ISBN 1–56720–442–2 (alk. paper)
    1. Organizational behavior—United States.   2. Violence in the workplace—United States.
    3. Job stress—United States.   4. Work environment—United States.   I. Title.
HD58.7.S744   2001
158.7—dc21   00–051760

British Library Cataloguing in Publication Data is available.

Library of Congress Catalog Card Number: 00–051760
ISBN: 1–56720–442–2

First published in 2001

Quorum Books, 88 Post Road West, Westport, CT 06881
An imprint of Greenwood Publishing Group, Inc.
www.quorumbooks.com

Printed in the United States of America

∞™

The paper used in this book complies with the
Permanent Paper Standard issued by the National
Information Standards Organization (Z39.48–1984).

10 9 8 7 6 5 4 3 2 1

Copyright Acknowledgments

The author and publisher are grateful to the following sources for granting permission to reprint from their materials:

Adapted material from Howard F. Stein, "From Countertransference to Social Theory: A Study of Holocaust Imagery in American Business Dress," *Ethos* 28(3), Fall 2000: 1–33, courtesy of the American Anthropological Association.

From "Downsizing, Managed Care, and the Potlatching of America: A Study in Cultural Brutality and Its Mystification" by Howard F. Stein, *Journal for the Psychoanalysis of Culture & Society*, Volume 4, Number 2 (Fall 1999). Copyright 1999 by The Ohio State University. All rights reserved. Pp. 209–227.

Howard F. Stein, "The Holocaust as Trope for 'Managed' Social Change," *Clio's Psyche* 6(3), December 1999: 119–122, courtesy of *Clio's Psyche*.

Howard F. Stein, "Adapting to Doom: The Group Psychology of an Organization Threatened with Cultural Extinction," *Political Psychology* 11(1), 1990: 113–145, courtesy of Blackwell Publishing Company.

Howard F. Stein, "Massive Social Change and the Experience of Loss: A Study in the Cultural Psychology of Mourning in a North American Great Plains Community," in L. B. Boyer, R. M. Boyer, and H. F. Stein, eds., *The Psychoanalytic Study of Society*, volume 19 (1994), courtesy of The Analytic Press. Pp. 273–310.

To the memory of Charles Dignan Stein
(1906–1996)
Father, Teacher, Violinist, Friend

"Without Windows, Without Light"
by Howard F. Stein

This place is without windows,
Without outside light,
Without outside air.
The seasons are changing,
But we would not know.

We work at our stations.
We imagine autumn.
We wear all varieties
Of religious amulets
To simulate the sun.

This place is all brick,
Dark glass, and metal.
It does not have windows;
It does not need windows.
There is nothing to see.

Contents

Foreword *by David B. Friedman*   xi

Preface   xv

Acknowledgments and Roadmap for This Book   xxiii

1. Introduction: "Don't Take It Personally, It's Just Business"   1

2. Countertransference as Tool in Organizational Theory:
    The "Use" of Self to Understand Workplace Violence   21

3. Downsizing, Managed Care, and the Potlatching
    of the Workplace: A Study in Cultural Brutality and
    Its Mystification   51

4. The Holocaust as Trope for Managed Social Change   79

5. Ordinary Brutality at Work   87

6. "How Long Can We Circle the Wagons?": A Study in the
    Sense of Doom at Work   105

7. Rupture and Reconciliation: A Case Study   117

Conclusions   155

Index   161

Foreword

It is a privilege and an honor to have been asked to write the foreword for this extensive scholarly book on a challenging topic. The way in which the request evolved was indeed unusual. Every morning at five o'clock for the past several years I have seen another hardy soul waiting for the bus to go to work. After months of silence we struck up a conversation. I learned that he was a publisher and mentioned that I was a psychoanalyst on the faculty of New York University School of Medicine. We were both fascinated by the other's profession.

One morning he asked me to explain the concept of countertransference and I obliged with a mildly pedantic reply. He was very interested in the subject and told me that he was in the process of editing a work by an anthropologist, Howard Stein, who had published previous works with his firm. In this work one of the chapters focused on the concept of countertransference, and indeed, much of Dr. Stein's new book seemed to be built on that. Since I seemed to be knowledgeable about the concept, he wondered whether I would read that chapter (and maybe the entire manuscript) and offer my viewpoint as a fellow professional and academic. He also inquired whether I would be willing to exchange views directly with Dr. Stein.

The die was cast. After conferring with Dr. Stein he produced a full draft manuscript. I not only read the chapter on countertransference but found myself intrigued by the topic and scope of the entire book. It was shortly thereafter that the author and I were engaged in telephone conferences. I was seduced by the novel ideas he advanced and impressed

by his courage to take a stand that questioned so many of the orthodox-
ies of organizational life. Here was a teacher and scholar who boldly
ventured into hostile territory, a land of desired quick wealth, bounded
by Wall Street, the Internet, and especially television.

While individuals and corporations were caught up in achieving "the
bottom line," he focused his attention on the insidious degradation of
the human spirit *within* corporations. He saw a parallel between what
was going on there and what went on in the Holocaust, an event without
precedent in the history of man's inhumanity to man. The Crusades and
the Spanish Inquisition were but ripples compared to the flood unleashed in the Holocaust. Avoiding the temptation to see it as "business
as usual," Dr. Stein took on the enormous task of plunging into an attempt to understand what was really happening in organizations, and
in fact, to all humankind as well.

He sounds an alarm, calling attention to our alienation from ourselves.
Although others have previously written about some aspect of this, he
utilizes the Holocaust as a symbol to illustrate his perspective and apprehension. He reminds us of the sense of helplessness felt by the
"downsized" workers deemed irrelevant or unnecessary, and equates
them metaphorically to the unwanted victims of the Holocaust genocide.
In one case it was a sense of helplessness. In the other it was actual
helplessness before the gas chambers. Dr. Stein brilliantly makes us feel
the metaphor. In effect, if one senses helplessness, is it not "reality" for
the moment? Are we not often carried away by our feelings? Does this
not affect our thinking and behavior?

I wondered how Dr. Stein became interested in this area. When I
learned that most of his paternal ancestors perished in the Holocaust I
believed that the personal impact played a significant role in the origin
and development of this book.

Dr. Stein cautions us about the power of denial. He alludes to its operation when we are confronted by the unbelievable. We are lulled into
the comfort of believing "business as usual," and we do not believe that
such things have happened and are happening or could happen to us.
For the moment, ignorance is bliss, but the future demands that the piper
be paid.

This is a powerful book, and it promises to be controversial. I urge
the reader to suspend incredulity. If you can do that, you may learn
more about human behavior and attitudes than you ever believed possible. Even more important, you may have a peek into some of your own
unbelievable and unacceptable impulses which were formerly hidden in
darkness. Dr. Stein has forged ahead in his determination and incredible
motivation to educate those of us who would rather imagine that what
is euphemistically described as "progress" may camouflage the destruction of human togetherness, which in the opinion of many people flour-

ished before the "chip revolution." This latest revolution promises to make the degradations of the Industrial Revolution mere child's play.

An area of controversy that I suspect would arise stems from Dr. Stein's ambitious attempts to combine data and inferences from the several disciplines of his training and experience. There is always a danger inherent in that endeavor. Findings in one discipline cannot be applied to another, just as attributing conclusions drawn from one species to another is at best risky. My knowledge and interest in the subject of transference and countertransference was a reason for choosing me to write this foreword. Dr. Stein has made reference to those phenomena which were described by Freud and which today are a cornerstone of classical psychoanalysis. Those findings were drawn from Freud's clinical experience with patients whom today we would label as disturbed. The typical neurotic patient who is in psychoanalytic treatment is not swept up by those emotions and can control and modulate them via patient's judgment and ability to exercise control. Nevertheless, the technique of psychoanalysis permits and encourages the emergence of these repressed and powerful feelings in a way which ultimately benefits the patient. The workplace as described by Dr. Stein is an entirely different arena, where undesirable feelings expressed in raw form are actively discouraged.

The reader who understands and accepts this will benefit by seeing a definite connection between psychological phenomena and the personal impact of "downsizing." However, just as when reading a work of psychohistory, in which conclusions are drawn retrospectively from second-hand data which may not be as reliable as those drawn from personal interaction in a controlled, standard situation ("the psychoanalytic situation" described in an incisive monograph by Dr. Leo Stone), so would it be wise when reading this work to maintain at least some skepticism. It would also be wise to keep an open mind. To shut our eyes to the propositions and conclusions brought forth by Dr. Stein would be distinctly unwise. The important contribution of this book is that it asks questions, attempts to answer some, and provokes the reader to think.

—David B. Friedman
Associate Clinical Professor of Psychiatry
New York University School of Medicine

Preface

There are many reasons to write a book: to contribute to knowledge and to better ways of doing things, to extend a "field" of inquiry or "profession," to inform others, are all good enough reasons. In this book on the workplace, these are among my reasons—but not the most urgent. Here, I wish to bear witness to realities we officially banish from sight. I wish to give voice to the many who have pressed me over the past decade and a half: "Write it, Howard. Write it for us as well as for yourself. Tell them what is happening, even in America, where things like this don't happen. Tell them the stories we have entrusted to you." Whatever else its subject matter, this book is also about having voice, giving voice, and claiming voice.

This book is both sequel and successor to *Euphemism, Spin, and the Crisis in Organizational Life*, published in 1998. If this book contributes to cultural and organizational theory, and to methods for understanding and consulting with people in workplaces, it will be because it succeeded first in bearing witness to the experience of countless organizational workplaces—which is to say, people—in the late twentieth century. These experiences contradict the "all is well" pronouncements from political and corporate leaders about the robust "health" of the American, if not the global, economy. Behind the façade of "business as usual" is an anxiety-driven, brutal world that makes virtually everyone disposable.

People of the United States have long been restless for constant social change (Levine 1999). Vast cadres of experts and consultants now offer services in "managed social change." This book inquires into what the change is *about*. Before we "intervene" and try to "manage," first we need to ask: WHAT *IS*? And why?

The subject of this book is what cannot possibly be happening—yet is. It is a study in seeing what one is looking at—what one beholds—when there is little or no validation that there is anything whatsoever to look at or see. Its task is to reveal what has been concealed. If it is an outer struggle with vision, it is an inner one as well. The suggestive resemblance of the present to the Nazi past that consumed one-half of my family in Europe, was for a long time too close to home for me to recognize it for what it is. How does one find a language for the magnitude of any event made opaque by ordinary language? It turns out that a similar self-blinding language of euphemism has been used for a decade and a half in the United States to twist large-scale brutality into inexorable business logic.

In this book, I argue for the need to reclaim the capacity to attest to the presence of evil in the world, an evil that assumes the innocent and conniving guise of business, "nothing personal, just business." Witnessing, bearing witness, and writing for others to see and hear—these are the beginning of the hope for genuine change. If I cannot alter what I see, I can at least attest to the fact that it happened and is still happening.

When we think of American business in the context of history, words like "enterprising" and "entrepreneurial" come quickly to mind. They correspond to nationally held self-ideals and self-images about human possibility, opportunity, hope, initiative, optimism, personal individuality, autonomy, and restless energy. They are bound up with the "frontier" as both geographic fact and as mental representation. A word such as "atrocity" is ordinarily excised from the American cultural lexicon when applied to organizational—and far wider—life.

The word is reserved, and savored, for "them"—for peoples across borders and oceans—and rarely if ever applied to "us." Names such as Stalin, Hitler, Mao, Pinochet, and Peron "belong" to twentieth-century Russia, Germany, China, Chile, and Argentina, not to here. If these names come quickly to mind, they also come too quickly. For the world of atrocity, of callousness and brutality, has come to be ordinary, and taken for granted, in the supposedly rationally guided world of business decision-making. We now couch brutality in languages of expediency, of practicality, of necessity, even of survival. Euphemism has become coercion in the guise of description, "imperative" in the guise of "declarative" sentence structure. For instance, a common injunction made during a firing or radical job redefinition: "It's nothing personal, just business." We terrorize with our words and with their intentions.

RECLAIMING AND NAMING THE REAL

Whatever else this book does, it gives a name, a label, to what I have experienced in the workplace and that many others share. I hope that I offer a cultural diagnosis that validates rather than discredits the full breadth and depth of suffering (see Kleinman and Kleinman 1991; Allan Young 1996; Kleinman, Das, and Lock 1997—on the use of PTSD [post-traumatic stress disorders] diagnoses to discredit people's stories and feelings by standardizing them into a single narrative- and therapeutic-type).

This book is an "occupational" study in the tradition of Primo Levi's (1988) and Elie Wiesel's (1960) accounts of life in the Nazi concentration camps. One might situate this book within "occupational medicine" or "the sociology of work." The *Lager* or "camps" were, after all, workplaces designed to "produce" work until death. This book is about brutalization and the awakening from brutalization. It is about recognizing and recovering from history.

As I wrote in *Euphemism, Spin, and the Crisis in Organizational Life* (1998), euphemism defines reality. Euphemism becomes and constitutes reality. Euphemism is enforced—both within and without—as the only acceptable reality. Euphemism becomes the only way to bear the deeper reality it denies. This book explores the secrets behind the secrecy. Although it employs theory—ranging from psychoanalytic to anthropological, from organizational to group relations—I hope that the theory will never violate the experience and the voice from which theory must constantly be nourished.

This book stands on the tripod of method, theory, and experience. In the case studies and vignettes, I have carefully reworked the identity of people, places, and times, so as to protect the confidentiality and anonymity of all involved. In a few instances, I embellished an account in order to provide additional disguise.

THE SILENCED WORKPLACE WITHIN

There are legions of books about the workplace. This book is about the workplace from the inside out. It is an account of organizational life from within. Its foundation is the validity of experience in the workplace, and of the vitality of experience as a basis for evoking, describing, and understanding the workplace. It finds meaning in despair: the despair *at* work, the despair *about* work. It conjures a world without windows and without light. It portrays a world of engulfing inner darkness. It studies the death of the human spirit, about the subtle, gradual, and systematic assaults on it. It navigates the unfathomable deeps beneath the supposedly final "bottom line." It brings the unimaginable into the realm of the imagination. In a world in which everyone *has* a number, and everyone *is* a mere number, this book attempts to understand the psychological logic of the "calculus." In a world of the indiscriminate destruction of people, this book restores the reality of *discrimination* behind the illusion of mere (random) numbers.

It is my thesis that an understanding of organizational structure, culture, and identity is incomplete—and impossible—without an understanding of the *experience* of organizational life. In this book, I shall show through vignettes and theory how this experience is part of the organizational structure, culture, and identity itself. The thread of continuity in this book consists of my attempt to bring that experience of the workplace to life: to evoke it, not merely to describe it. A crucial methodological tool of that evocation of this sense of place and of this spirit, is my own emotional response (countertransference, a concept I discuss at length in the following chapters) as worker, observer, and consultant. This source of data supplements the more narrative or qualitative approaches such as naturalistic observation, participant observation, open-ended interview, attention to nonverbal communication, and the study of material, documentary, or "symbolic" culture at work. Throughout this book there is a sustained tension between substance and method.

The book develops or progresses from an elucidation of the scope of dehumanized work life to a consideration of how businesses might become both humane and productive. I cannot and do not apologize for my attention to subjectivity—that of those observed, my own, and the relationship between us. Experience is degraded by relegating it to the realm of the "merely" subjective in supposed contrast with the real, the "hard" scientific data. Indeed, the doctrine of objectivity and rationality, itself driven by factors largely out of conscious awareness, is part of the brutalization and destructiveness in countless workplaces.

The study of "subjectivity" will be my Ariadne's thread through the dark, menacing labyrinth of organizational life. The thread for leaving the labyrinth will be an understanding of how and why we got lost in the dangerous darkness in the first place.

This book inquires into the shared delusion of cultural normality, one created, enforced, and perpetuated by the dialectic of projective and introjective identification: that is, the powerful waves of forcing unwanted parts of ourselves into others, and of taking into ourselves parts expelled by others. It interprets economic explanation as obligatory *mystification* of brutality. It studies the language of atrocity, of atrocity as mere "business" if not "good business." Certainly not everything that calls itself or that goes by the name "business" is of this quality. For many, work is deeply meaningful and personally fulfilling; work is family, work is love, work is even life itself. If in this book I focus on the brutality of work and of the workplace, this quality of the experience is becoming increasingly widespread, not only within the United States, but also worldwide. A "narrow" form of work is broadening.

THE WORK OF RECLAMATION

This book affirms in many ways: *This really happened; it happened like this. It really happened even if it cannot happen here, even if it does not happen here. Even in supposedly rational workplaces. Even in America.* To say it like this sounds off—even odd—as I read it to myself. It is as if I am reclaiming something vital, maybe even claiming it for the first time. I am an anthropologist, trained to observe, and further trained to be self-observant, to listen to my heart and gut as well as to my head. I am supposed to be able to see, to hear, to sense what cultures are about. I expect myself to be able to take notice of all sorts and levels of "data." Yet, how does one train oneself to see what is not supposed to be seen, what is even denied to be "there"?

When I was a child, my mother used to tell me about how, when she was a child, during one of her father's tirades, her mother would gently admonish her: "If Papa says it's raining, it's raining." Survival seemed to mean the preservation of peace at any price, including the outright distortion and denial of reality. My mother was not supposed to trust or to believe her own eyes; someone else's eyes would take the place of hers. That, I suppose, was the exchange rate for security, love, maybe even for existence. The workplace carried on this family tradition, and I brought this tradition—this loyalty to lie—to the workplace.

My struggle for knowledge of workplace and wider social reality is inseparable from the liberation of sight from the bondage of early relationship. My struggle—as ethnographic observer and consultant—for the capacity, the inner permission, to discern light and darkness, sun and rain, for myself is lifelong. It is a part of any "data" that I "collect." Yet, that liberation, that in-sight, is not achieved entirely alone. It is nourished by yet other people ("relationships") who can bear to know what I know, and who can help me to bear to know it as well.

I have spent years overcoming my own disbelief and unwrapping the enforced incredulity many others have imposed on me, as if to calm my outrage: "It isn't that bad," or "What you say is happening isn't happening at all." This book breaks an enforced silence. I have learned to trust my own senses, my own feelings, and to reclaim them as the most vital organizational—scientific and life-giving—data of all. One form the regained trust takes consists of poems I have written in the context of work (Stein 1997, 2000). Organizational "poetics" can take us to the heart of work life (Whyte 1994).

The poet Paul Celan reportedly said of poetry: *"La poesie ne s'impose*

plus, elle s'expose" (quoted by Michael Hamburger, 1995: 34). "Poetry im-
poses nothing, she exposes." The corrective, if not redemptive, place of
poetry—and of all the so-called humanities—in medical, social science,
and organizational discourse is that it exposes, reveals, the heart often
hidden in the din of "rational" and rationalistic debates. For me, poetry
is a way of replying to my own question in, say, a workplace setting:
"What on earth is going on here?" The poem "gives" me an answer I
trust. I have come to accept that organizational poesis—the writing of
"organizational" poetry—helps to make and keep me honest in my scientific, clinical, and consulting work. If it is play, it is earnest play—
work.

When many postmodern writers insist that there is no reality, only
perception and agenda and "spin," I become impatient. I know differently. I cannot refute them within their own language world. I can only
remind myself what an ongoing struggle it has been for me to know,
and to know that I know. This struggle has been the beginning of organizational, and far wider cultural, knowledge.

Whether in narrative account or in poem, my emotional responses are
part of the organizational data themselves. They are an essential part of
my ongoing research project to understand and to help workplace organizations. This *methodology* is crucial to access the *substance*. From this
perspective, my use of countertransference is not an exercise in solipsistic
"navel gazing," but instead it is a tool for comprehending and entering
into the external world. I use and monitor myself as "material" for understanding organizational darkness. The "personal" is thus a technique
or tactic necessary for obtaining organizational data at the depth of participants' experience. Through this use of self, I hope to guide the reader
into the life of organizational culture and identity. It is as if to say, "I
am showing you a way to understand so that you may take this approach and see it for yourself."

ENTERING THE DARKNESS

Most accounts of organizational life in workplaces tend to be told in
such a way as to put distance—emotional safety—between the writer
and the experience of the workplace, and consequently between the
reader and that experience. In this book, I wish to put a personal face
(not façade) on the cruelty organizations can do to people, on the harm
that people can do to one another in the context of the workplace.

Throughout Western culture and history, we have extolled the virtues
of *light*: as in "casting new light on a subject" or "illuminating a topic."
A whole historic era is called the "enlightenment." Here, however, I
draw upon what we can learn from darkness, from entering those places
of the mind and of the workplace where light is shut out and drained

away. Here, darkness will be my companion and guide. I take the reader on a journey to bring organizational darkness into light.

Over the past decade I have written—and participated with others in writing—studies of contemporary organizational life through the specific "lenses" of downsizing, RIFing, rightsizing, reengineering, restructuring, outsourcing, deskilling, corporate medicine, managed care, and other forms of "managed social change." I have written about employees, managers, organizations, and their wider national, even international, cultures. I have discussed the triad of massive change, loss, and grief (including the short-circuiting, even prohibition of grief) in workplace culture, and how experiences and adaptations we once thought were extraordinary have come to be ordinary. The books that have come out of this are *Listening Deeply* (Stein 1994), *The Human Cost of a Management Failure: Organizational Downsizing at General Hospital* (Allcorn, Baum, Diamond, and Stein 1996) and *Euphemism, Spin, and the Crisis in Organizational Life* (Stein 1998). I have published two books of poetry that contain many "organizational" portraits and vignettes: *Evocations* (Stein 1997) and *Learning Pieces* (Stein 2000).

In these earlier works, I have persistently drawn attention to a much overlooked, subtle "psychological" form of human destructiveness in the workplace, one I have called "murder of the spirit" (Greenwood 1995). This book continues that cultural exploration. While not as newsworthy and spectacularly violent as knives, guns, and bombs, it is an even more pervasive form of "violence in the workplace."It falls between the wide gaps of officially recognized harassment: ethnic, racial, gender, and age. It finds expression in intimidation, goading, ridicule, humiliation, bullying, condescension, euphemism, double-talk, mystification, setups to fail, the piling on of demands and expectations, the insistence that the other person is never quite good enough. These degradations that rest upon shame, guilt, and the relentless assault on dignity, are ultimately the breeding ground for subsequent "real" violence. They also wend their way into physical illness, mental illness, accident proneness, marital conflict, alcoholism and drug abuse, and absenteeism. But they usually fail to "count" as "real" violence or even as its precursors.

In this book, I reclaim their reality as violence—as attempts upon the life of the human spirit at work. As children we are all taught the rhyme, "Sticks and stones can break my bones, but names will never hurt me" (or some variant of it). This book explores precisely how abstraction—names, words, numbers, symbols—can wound deeply.

REFERENCES

Allcorn, Seth, Howell S. Baum, Michael A. Diamond, and Howard F. Stein. 1996. *The Human Cost of a Management Failure: Organizational Downsizing at General Hospital.* Westport, CT: Quorum Books.

Greenwood, J. Alex. 1995. " 'Murder of the Spirit' Prevalent in American Work-
    place, Says OUHSC Professor," media release, University of Oklahoma
    Health Sciences Center, 15 February.
Hamburger, Michael. 1995. "Introduction," in *Poems of Paul Celan*, translated by
    Michael Hamburger. New York: Persea Books. P. 34.
Kleinman, Arthur, Veena Das, and Margaret M. Lock, eds. 1997. *Social Suffering*.
    Berkeley: University of California Press.
Kleinman, Arthur, and Joan Kleinman. 1991. "Suffering and Its Professional
    Transformation: Toward an Ethnography of Interpersonal Experiences,"
    Culture, Medicine, and Psychiatry 15 (3), September: 275–301.
Levi, Primo. 1998. *The Drowned and the Saved*. New York: Summit Books.
Levine, David P. 1999. "Creativity and Change: On the Psychodynamics of Mo-
    dernity," *American Behavioral Scientist* 43 (2), October: 225–244.
Stein, Howard F. 1994. *Listening Deeply: An Approach to Understanding and Con-
    sulting in Organizational Culture*. Boulder, CO: Westview Press
———. 1997. *Evocations*. Pittsburgh, PA: Dorrance.
———. 1998. *Euphemism, Spin, and the Crisis in Organizational Life*. Westport, CT:
    Quorum Books.
———. 2000. *Learning Pieces*. Pittsburgh, PA: Dorrance.
Whyte, David. 1994. *The Heart Aroused: Poetry and the Preservation of the Soul in
    Corporate America*. New York: Doubleday.
Wiesel, Elie. 1960. *Night*. New York: Bantam, 1982.
Young, Allan. 1996. *The Harmony of Illusions: Inventing Post-Traumatic Stress Dis-
    order*. Princeton, NJ: Princeton University Press.

Acknowledgments and Roadmap for This Book

This book would not exist without the encouragement and prodding of many people who have been central in my recent emotional—not only narrowly professional—life. They have helped me to trust and to pursue workplace-induced perceptions, feelings, senses, and "intuitions" from which I have often retreated. I am grateful to them for more than they can know: Dr. W. Gordon Lawrence, Michael A. Diamond, Ph.D., Seth Allcorn, Ph.D., Rose Redding Mersky, Ph.D., Burkard Sievers, Ph.D., David Levine, Ph.D., Guy Adams, Ph.D., Shelley Reciniello, Ph.D., L. Bryce Boyer, M.D., Henry Ebel, Ph.D., Melford Spiro, Ph.D., Richard A. Koenigsberg, Ph.D., Harold J. Bursztajn, M.D., Mark Bracher, Ph.D., Peter Petschauer, Ph.D., Harry Moore, Ph.D., and Steven Kernan. My wife, Nance K. Cunningham, M.A., and our son Zev, now seven, lived with the genesis of this book.

Seth Allcorn, Ph.D., read and generously commented on several drafts of this book. My editor and publisher, Eric Valentine, helped me to find the sculpture often hidden in a large block of granite. In that metaphor lies the genesis of this book.

Chapter 1, the Introduction, is partly based on a public lecture made at St. Gregory's University, Sarkeys Performing Arts Center, Shawnee, Oklahoma, on 19 April 2000. It was titled "Waiting for the Trains: A Journey into Organizational Darkness." This chapter introduces the book's method of inquiry, a method that grows out of (at least) two questions: What do we know (or think we know)? and, How do we come to know something? In this book, the "what" or "something" consists of the inner life of workplace organizations. The first chapter inquires into symbols and metaphors as conduits of life.

Chapter 2 is based on a paper published in *ETHOS*, titled "From Countertransference to Social Theory: A Study of Holocaust Imagery in American Business Dress," Fall 2000. This chapter is based on a plenary presentation at the Biennial Meetings of the Society for Psychological Anthropology, Albuquerque, New Mexico, 23 September 1999. I express special gratitude to Philip Bock, Ph.D., and Thomas J. Csordas, Ph.D., for their encouragement and criticism in the earlier article. Editors and reviewers can sometimes see "in" a manuscript a paper that is latent, but not yet fulfilled or realized.

Chapter 2 turns the focus of the process of observation from the outside (individuals, groups, organizations) to the inside of the organizational observer or consultant. Technically, "countertransference" is in fact very ordinary: the observer or consultant's emotional experience as crucial organizational (and larger cultural) data. One studies oneself in the process of, and as a means to, studying and helping the organization with whom one is working.

Chapter 3 is based on a paper presented at the International Psychohistorical Association, Panel on Organizational Psychohistory, Fordham University, New York City, 3 June 1999. A preliminary version of this chapter was presented at the 1998 Fall Colloquium on Organizational Psychodynamics: "Power, Ideology and Change: The Psychodynamics and Politics of Organizational Identity," 25–27 September 1998, Center for the Study of Organizational Change, University of Missouri-Columbia. I wish to thank Mark Bracher, Ph.D., Peter Petschauer, Ph.D., Henry Ebel, Ph.D., Michael A. Diamond, Ph.D., Guy Adams, Ph.D., David Levine, Ph.D., Seth Allcorn, Ph.D., Burkard Sievers, Ph.D., W. Gordon Lawrence, Ph.D., Shelley Reciniello, Ph.D., and Hershey Bell, M.D., for their encouragement in this project.

Chapter 3 explores downsizing, reengineering, and managed care as key governing organizational metaphors. It mobilizes many different kinds of accounts—interviews from consultations, the writer's poems, popular or mass culture—to tell the story of the experience of the numerous forms of "managed social change" and its language. Its story is about the United States and the increasing globalization of its ostensibly economic social forms.

Chapter 4 is based on a paper originally published in *Clio's Psyche*, the journal of the Psychohistory Forum: "The Holocaust as Trope for 'Managed' Social Change." I wish to express gratitude to Professor Michael Diamond and Professor Gary Holmes for their encouragement in this project and comments on an earlier version of this chapter.

Chapter 4 explores a single case or story. The "unit" of study is a person, a corporate executive. She describes the process of ethical transformation: from being one who RIFed people to being one who realized the gravity of what she was doing. In the process, she comes to discover the emotional validity of Holocaust images and metaphors in understanding the experience of much of corporate life. Her account helps to situate organizationally-related Holocaust imagery in personal life history.

Chapter 5 (previously unpublished) explores several vignettes from my consulting experience. Each shows how ordinary the brutalization of work and worker has become in supposedly modern, humanized, corporate circumstances. The observer or consultant must see through the eerieness of language and of work-as-usual to discern the sense of terror and meaninglessness that governs much of everyday relationships.

Some parts of Chapter 6 were originally published as "Adapting to Doom: The Group Psychology of an Organization Threatened with Cultural Extinction." Chapter 6 consists of a longitudinal study of an organization that had been threatened from without for years with dissolution and cultural extinction. It examines "ordinary" organizational brutality that is experienced as coming from the outside, together with its transformation into brutalization within the organization. It is a study in adapting both to doom and to the sense of doom—and the difficulty in distinguishing between them.

Early versions of Chapter 7 were presented at the eleventh annual meeting of the High Plains Society for Applied Anthropology, Northglenn, Colorado, 21 April 1991; and at a Symposium of the International Society for the Psychoanalytic Study of Organizations, New York City, 5 June 1992. An earlier version of this chapter was published in *The Psychoanalytic Study of Society*.

Chapter 7 is an inquiry into whether—and how—organizational darkness might be transcended. It consists of a case study of the transformation of an organization trapped by rage and withdrawal. The transformation occurs at a retreat at which deep feelings over change and loss are given voice in an atmosphere of safety and grace. The chapter gives hope to those economically imprisoned, and self-imprisoned, in today's workplaces.

The Conclusion is less a summary of what preceded it as it is a question posed to the reader—consultant, leader, worker, or organizational researcher: What have we learned about organizational life and about the human condition to help the darkness to lift? I offer neither glib "expertise" nor quick recipes for success, but some thoughts on the reclamation of the human spirit in the workplace.

1

Introduction: "Don't Take It Personally, It's Just Business"

Since Americans first encountered and liberated the Nazi death camps in 1945, we have insisted "That could never happen here," or we have wondered, "Could something that horrible happen here?" In this book, the reader encounters no blood, no firing squads, no gas chambers, no crematoria. But atrocities have been committed, and continue to be committed, here in American workplaces—even in America. We continue to doubt whether atrocities would happen here all the while they are happening before our very eyes and ears. To recognize, to perceive, that something is happening requires that we are emotionally able to bear it in the first place. It has required ten years of work for me to be able to imagine downsizing, reengineering, restructuring, and the long train of euphemisms to be psychologically motivated political oppression in the guise of economic necessity (Stein 1998).

In the United States, more people were laid off in 1998 than in any year since 1993—the year vast numbers of middle management were "downsized." We fail to see the toll because we cannot bear to look. People vanish, disappear—but not like Nazi Germany, Stalinist USSR, or the contemporary Rwanda, Bosnia, and Kosovo of the 1990s or the Latin American countries of the 1980s. We are lulled by the disguise. This book attempts to peer into, and to enter, our self-enforced, self-blinded darkness.

As an inmate of Auschwitz, Primo Levi asked one of his SS guards, "*Warum?*" ("Why?"). The guard replied chillingly: "*Hier ist kein Warum*" ("Here is no [asking] 'Why?' "). Despite the surface sunniness of the

American economy—declared by Federal Reserve Board chairman Alan Greenspan to be the best since World War II—the deeper *ennui* and dread compels the further conclusion, *"Hier ist auch kein Warum"*—"Here is also no [asking] 'Why?' " The very possibility of the question "Why?" presupposes that the social order might be otherwise. The question that haunted Primo Levi the remainder of his life must haunt us if, as workers, as employers, we are to reclaim the humanity which has been ripped from us—and which we have been sorely tempted to discard in order to "survive." The question, and the forbidding of the question, are matters of power: its exercise, its coercion, its intimidation, its perception, and its inner and outer presence. If nothing else, this book attempts to break a spell—and it shows the difficulty in doing so.

THE WATERBOWL

In 1999, following a presentation I had made about downsizing and reengineering, I spoke with a secretary who had worked for many years for a multinational petrochemical firm. First thanking me for validating her own experience during my lecture, she said that she wanted to offer an example of what I had been talking about. A new mid-level manager had arrived and was eager to make his mark on the organization. At a meeting of his supervisees, he admonished them: "We have a lot of work to get done here. Don't think for a minute that you're essential to this corporation. Everyone here is dispensable. There are a hundred people out there hungry for your job. And if you leave, your absence will be as noticed as a finger taken out of a bowl of water. They won't even know that you'd been here."

She and I both shuddered. We briefly mused on its effect for worker morale: inducing, perhaps, an identification with the aggressor, and feverish productivity, accompanied by chronic terror, indifference, and deep rage at such humiliation. We also wondered about the new manager's own sense of expendability, and about the kind of childhood that might have set the stage for such drivenness. Does the conviction of inner worthlessness cultivate worthlessness—and hopelessness—in others? Here, a third managerial philosophy—terror—supplements the traditional distinction between "carrot" and "stick." What, in the workplace, does the threat of homicide look and sound like?

As an organizational ethnographer, I attempt to describe, evoke, portray, and interpret the cultural world of workplace organizations. The image of murder is not hyperbole. Our language requires some way to do justice to the degradation of, and the assault on, human dignity that is never merely "symbolic." Our cultural category of "violence in the workplace" does injustice to the scope and range of workplace destructiveness when we turn a blind eye and deaf ear to everything that *pre-*

cedes and often *provokes* the use of guns, knives, and bombs against people and property. To say that no one is murdered until someone is physically killed helps set the stage for physical violence at work.

KNOWING AND ENVIRONMENTAL INVALIDATION

We are faced with the problem of *knowing in the face of environmental invalidation*: of holding onto the conviction that something truly "is" when others insist that it "isn't" at all—and preventing oneself from succumbing to the belief. One of the most significant, yet—from the viewpoint of empirical science—counterintuitive, discoveries in psychoanalysis' first century is that the emotional response of an analyst, observer, consultant, worker, or leader to another person or to a group provides vital insight into that person or group. Often that "countertransference" offers the only knowledge available. Bion, for instance, made the seminal insight (1959: 134) that the group observer's countertransference response (emotional reaction) is a vital source of data about the group. This book on workplace organizational hatred builds on this discovery and attempts to broaden it.

In the vernacular, often an observer or consultant's "gut feelings" are all the data he or she can "go on," rely upon, that is, can *trust* when environmental—which is to say interpersonal, cultural—*discreditation* are rampant. When others are insisting that "This is not happening," or "It does not matter even if it is happening," how does one affirm the event? How does one reclaim the right to breathe in the midst of so much thick smoke? It becomes an existential as well as methodological issue when we try to write about atrocities against the human spirit as well as against the flesh. A book about the social world turns out to be inseparable from a reclamation of one's senses.

TRAUMATIZATION AND VICTIMIZATION: OR, WHAT'S IN A WORD?

A formulation of Frank M. Ochberg (1997), one of the early formulators of the controversial concept of the "Post-Traumatic Stress Disorder" (PTSD), is especially enlightening (see, however, Young 1995).

There is a considerable difference between the impact of human cruelty, a particular form of trauma, which I call, arbitrarily, "victimization," and natural or accidental events. The generic term for any catastrophic encounter, including earthquake, fire and flood, is, by contrast, "traumatization." When we defined PTSD, we ignored this difference. PTSD was traumatization. But every "victimized" patient of mine complains less about "traumatization" than about "victimization." What are the symptoms of victimization? These include shame, self-blame, feeling lowered in dominance, disgust, paradoxical gratitude (the Stockholm Syndrome), and other stigmata of encounters with evil (see Ochberg, 1988). Victims of cruelty are not just terrified by death and destruction—they are dehumanized and belittled. Primo Levi used the expression "to lie on the bottom" to explain how he and his fellow concentration camp victims were diminished. In some respects, dehumanization is worse than death. Death is biological. Dehumanization is spiritual. . . .

. . . [W]e should attend to assaults on spirit, as opposed to assaults on flesh. We need, in my opinion, to explore the human response to cruelty, because forms of endurance and adaptation perpetuate cruelty. Silence may be merely diminished oxygenation of grey matter. Silence may be unexpressed shame. Silence may be the price of survival in a totalitarian state or a totalitarian family. (1997: 202–203)

Now, to start with, I do not want to overdraw Ochberg's typological distinction between "natural" and "human" assaults. In a similar vein, Volkan (2000: 3) argues that "a closer look suggests that it is sometimes difficult to discriminate between different types of disasters." For example, North American prairie grain (wheat, milo, corn) farmers whose fields are devastated by "severe weather," and who are certainly "traumatized" by storm, flood, tornado, hail, and drought, also highly personalize (anthropomorphize) the destructive event. Further, they often feel a sense of guilt and shame for some dimly-recollected wrongdoing, as though a "natural" disaster was punishment by divine forces.

Consider a second example. During the summer of 2000, a fire raged in and around the Mesa Verde National Park. When the Ute Mountain Ute Indians look eastward to the national park, many do not simply see a natural disaster. "They see spirits that are mad—blazing mad," reporter Nancy Lofholm writes (2000: 7A). Lofholm quotes Terry Knight, spiritual leader of the Ute: " 'The old spirits that are there are not at rest. Their energy is off-balance, and this causes things to happen in the metaphysical world. . . . There is something happening with that tribe within the ground. These spirits are getting back at people for doing this and that' " (7A). Anger is directed toward both the white man and Indians for various metaphysical violations, such as disturbing Indian remains and storing them in museums.

In many Utes' experience of the prolonged, devastating fire, the cataclysm is personal, not purely natural; it is retaliation for people's unexpiated guilt and shame. In short, the experience of being the intended target or victim of hurt seems to be of critical psychological importance in influencing the course of responding to any disaster or trauma. What we might regard as "pure" trauma, others might imbue with the quality of victimization—induced by one's own group and/or by others. If some of our clinical and managerial categories illumine, reveal, they also obscure, conceal. PTSD and Critical Incident Stress Debriefing (CISD) must be included among them.

Clearly, traumatization can be experienced *as* victimization. A personalized, anthropomorphized Nature, even God, can feel cruel. Further, "bad" weather can be blamed on "bad" government and on "bad" cities, as if even natural disasters can be deliberately caused. The experience of being the intended target or victim of hurt seems to be of critical psychological importance in influencing the course of responding to any disaster or trauma.

Ochberg's formulation about victimization rings true to my experience of the "murder of the human spirit" that occurs bloodlessly in American workplaces. His account is not only applicable to those physical forms of human torture and destruction we usually classify as "terrorism." Workers, managers, and executives can terrorize workplaces by intimidation as much as anyone armed with physical weapons. Intimidation and other rituals of degradation can lead to "physical" retaliation in the effort to obliterate shame and the shamer.

KNOWING THE UNBEARABLE

All the sciences, social sciences, and humanities grapple with the question of "How do I know something?" This book likewise grapples with the question: "How do I *not* know something?" or "How do I go about *avoiding* knowing something?" Resistance to knowledge is part of knowledge, my own included. Much of this study is a gradual reawakening to knowing what I could not bear to know about my workplace situation. In a moving essay on "Psychoanalytic Listening to Historical Trauma," Dori Laub and Daniel Podell address the question of knowing and resistance to knowledge:

> What makes an entire nation resist the knowing of atrocities and become perpetrators or passive on-lookers to atrocities? Or, alternatively, what enables an individual, community, or nation to understand the significance of a historical trauma as it is occurring and to act on that knowledge. What are the variables involved in mediating the complex movement between the two poles of the continuum of knowing? (1997: 259)

There is abundant clinical literature on anger and hate in transference, that is, in patients' individual negative emotional responses toward their doctors, analysts, psychiatrists, and other physicians. But, apart from studies of physical violence in workplaces, there is little exploration of the everyday "work" of hatred in organization groups such as work-places, a hatred often shrouded in euphemism. By this I mean the deg-radation, the stripping away of a sense of common humanity and destiny that are far more ordinary than, and as dangerous as, the killings that make the news. Our silence is part of our resistance. This book, then, is about everyday organizational darkness at noon. Seeing, recognizing, the darkness is the beginning of dispelling its blinding hold.

"SUCH SMALL POTATOES": A VIGNETTE

The following example illustrates ordinary interplay between acted-out transference and workplace intimidation. In one high-powered med-ical research institute, a highly ambitious unit head managed and advanced by a combination of intimidation and co-option of subordi-nates' ideas. At division meetings, he would openly express contempt for many of his supervisees' ideas proposed in what he termed "task reporting" meetings. He would ridicule the presenter as well as the ideas, with words such as "That would never fly here," "That's such small potatoes compared to things that would really put us on the map," and "Whoever heard of putting that kind of thing in an organization's mis-sion statement?"

When outside the group, he would test out some of these offerings himself as "trial balloons" or hear them expressed to him in more influ-ential circles. These same ideas would later emerge in grants and con-tracts, in policy statements, in strategic planning sessions, in executive retreats, and on mission statements engraved in official plaques hung in the boardroom—all originating from him. When occasionally confronted privately by a bold employee about the source of the idea, he would utterly deny any connection between his own ideas and the employee's. He would also remind the employee that he was the other's annual job reviewer and evaluator.

Paradoxically, he was a scrupulous advocate of organizational ethics in his own institution. The intellectual property he could not acknowl-edge was the creativity, freedom, individuality, and originality he would not—or could not—recognize in others.

The son of a highly critical and judgmental father whom he could never please, and who openly reprimanded him but offered little praise, this researcher both consciously disliked many company officials and unconsciously did his utmost to succeed. He often treated his subordi-nates as far beneath him, as people who could not do a good enough job.

Transferentially, he "became" his own father to employees who in turn "became" himself in his childhood and youth. There was always more work to be done, none of which could please him. To his superiors he was often argumentative and abrasive, while continuing to try to prove he was advancing the organization. In large measure, transference "up" and "down" the hierarchy drove the work-system in which he functioned as a highly effective and visible, but always dissatisfied, middle manager and researcher. What to others was intimidation was to him "always doing the right thing."

THE BRUTALIZATION OF LIFE AND WORK: FINDING THE RIGHT NAME

The ethical urgency of the hour is a matter of getting the name right for the ordinary brutalization of life, of finding incisive terms for what is happening, terms that clarify rather than deceive. We need the fire, not the smoke. We have too much smoke already.

Ours is a spiritual crisis, not primarily an economic crisis. We produce a spiritual death from an overdose of our own metaphors. Things are not what they seem—or sometimes, what we desperately want them to be. Our flourishing economy is a crusty scab over despair and rage. Behind much of the official, obligatory language of business and economics is the language of the Holocaust: of trains, selections, of sealed death chambers. Sometimes it is the language of the Vietnam War, only now in the corporation: Our "gooks" are those people who we think of as friends, but who (might) turn out to be enemies. Still other times, it is the language of mutilation: hacking by axes, cutting by guillotines, trimming by butcher knives. I have not invented this language of the shop floor, of the corridor, and of the break room. With Wilfred Owen, a great poet of World War I, I say, "All a poet can do today is to warn."

In April 1995, a bomb in front of the Murrah Federal Building shook a city and a nation. For a short time six years ago, scarcity and survivalism gave way to abundance and generosity. Those brief mercies of plenty challenge—or could, if we would permit it—many of our cherished assumptions about what and how much we can and cannot "afford" to do something. For a short time, values other than the "bottom line" ruled many of our lives.

We also live in the shadow of bombs and bombings far less publicly acknowledged. Their craters of human devastation are deep and long-lived. They go by innocent-sounding words that make us think they are only about "business-as-usual," "nothing personal, just business," "economic necessity," and corporate "survival." We all know the words: downsizing, reduction in force, RIF, rightsizing, restructuring, reengineering, outsourcing, deskilling, managed health care, globalization, managed social change. They have become unexamined if not unexaminable social imperatives. Invocation of "the bottom line" stops the conversation. Euphemism creates and regulates reality.

When someone says, "It's nothing personal, just business," the imperative is disingenuously disguised by the declarative. To take exception is tantamount to heresy and apostasy; the consequence is often akin to excommunication. One is not supposed to think, but to accept and believe on the authority of the speaker. Taken further, this, then, is a study in the ordinariness of hell, the masking of brutality as the "banality of evil" (Arendt 1994). If it is about applied social science, it is even more so about bearing witness to atrocity's guise as rationality.

I am sure the reader already notices that I have shifted metaphors, from business to Church. I do so intentionally so that it is clear how dire the cultural consequences can become if one dares to think outside the reigning metaphor. The phrase *Extra ecclesia nulla salus* (Outside the Church there is no salvation) readily applies to supposedly secular economics as well. What I have come to call "The Sacred Shrine of the Bottom Line" has acquired the ecclesiastical status of church if not cathedral. How ironic that in institutions of higher learning, we are prohibited from talking about God and other issues of existential value. Whatever else "the sacred" might be, it is the realm of the nonnegotiable, the non-discussable, the immutable, the—well—the bottom line!

In this book, I situate our economics within culture rather than as its inexorable driving force. I draw upon unofficial language, and upon its associated feelings or affects, to take us deeper than official language. I shall say in many ways that behind the formal language of business frequently lies the informal language of the Holocaust: of mass liquidations, of trains, of selections, of gas chambers. These are "symbolic," to be sure. But these symbolisms can be deadly: if they generate little mortality or morbidity, it is only because we have not bothered to notice or to count the casualties upon our spreadsheets. An understanding of the language of our time is a key both to disguise and to revelation.

Consider in this context the 1947 Nuremberg Code. Today, we might conclude that its concept of "crimes against humanity" could include the symbolic genocide now waged against economically captive populations who, bound by wage, insurance, retirement, and health care to their jobs, are free to disappear if their workplaces wish to dispense with, and dispose of, them. An increasing number of clinicians have examined widespread practices of corporate-based managed health care against the backdrop of the Nuremberg Code, and of the atrocities committed during the Holocaust of 1933–1945. Among these are Harold Bursztajn, M.D. (1997), Jay Katz, M.D. (1996), Karen Shore, Ph.D. (1997), and Jeremiah Barondess, M.D. (1998).

There is an air of unreality to the enforced official reality that the American economy is its healthiest in a half-century. Official optimism masks widespread dread, despair, and rage: by those who have been fired, by those who remain behind to work and wait, and by those upper-level and senior managers who turned people into numbers, only to become numbers themselves.

Ours has become a world, which many characterize as inhabited only by symbolic "Nazis" and symbolic, disposable "Jews," where the arrogant, managerial Nazi of one moment can become the vulnerable Jew of the next. In a metaphorical sense, that very historically condemned and scapegoated group, the Jews, is expanded to include potentially everyone. We have created a world in which everyone could become a disposable, sacrificial Jew.

Now, all this is totally against our usual grain of thinking about terror, terrorism, violence, and kindred words. Our term "violence in the workplace" has long been restricted to physical assault, guns, knives, and bombs. We have an established folklore about disgruntled workers, lone and crazed killers. We speak of someone "going postal," as if the post office is uniquely at risk.

Early in the 1990s, I unintentionally coined the phrase "murder of the human spirit" in the workplace. Many friends and colleagues seized upon it as if suddenly someone had made a diagnosis that confirmed their own experience. This experience included day-to-day insults at work, as well as the large-scale changes rationalized as mere business. I refer to intimidation, harassment, disrespect, callousness, bullying, goading, provoking, discounting, discrediting that can proceed "top-down," "bottom-up," and "laterally" in an organization. Degradation of work, and of people who work, does not require the presence of elite corps of downsizing consulting teams to exercise its power. It can be quite ordinary in the day-to-day life of a workplace. Brutalization can be insidious.

For instance, a manager's "open door policy" can in reality be an invitation to the exercise of humiliation and sadism, if not dismissal. In the spirit of Irving Janis's classic work, *Groupthink* (1982), a worker or executive who, attempting to contribute to the work "team," offers a view contrary to the prevailing consensus is often declared not to be a "team player" and is ostracized. A person who questions a decision or a practice may be characterized as an "uncooperative worker," someone who is "difficult to work with." Harassment in the form of discrediting abounds in workplaces. A manager harangued his colleague: "You keep asking for respect. Don't you understand that you don't deserve respect? What you do is not respected here. And if you tell anyone that this conversation took place, I'll deny it, and you'll really be in trouble."

There are many idols and idolatries in the modern or postmodern wilderness—not the Wilderness of Sinai or of Golgotha, but of a modern world enthralled by the sacred shrine of the bottom line. We have our own Golden Calf. We have discovered that today—entirely apart from anyone's religious denomination or belief—everyone is, or could become, a metaphorical Jew (trains, selections, chambers, disposability,

symbolic death). With an increasingly liberalized, privatized, corpora-
tized, globalized economy, there will be few refuges and many refugees.

Our own shores will, I fear, lead in the caricature of those lofty words
engraved on the Statue of Liberty: "Give me your tired, your poor, your
huddled masses yearning to breathe free." If our waves of immigrants
tended to idealize the "good mother" image inflamed in the American
fantasy, it is more like reality and less than demonology to suggest that
we have become not only a nation of consumers, but also a people consumed.

Amid a moral universe split Manichean-like into categories of metaphorical "Nazi" executioners and "Jewish" victims, there emerges an ethical imperative by which we all are redeemed: *No one in future history
should be condemned to be a metaphorical Jew, that is, to be existentially set up
for disposability and imminent sacrifice.*

Perhaps for the first time in history, the hallowed distinction between
"us" and "them" is blurred at the level of conscious awareness rather
than exclusively at unconscious obliviousness. With the globalization of
the ethos of "managed social change" and of "maximization of shareholder value," every "us" is a potential if not imminent "them": psychologically, ideologically, politically, economically. The prophetic warning
made by Pastor Martin Niemöller about the Nazi era applies to ourselves
as well.

> First, they came for the socialists, and I did not speak out because
> I was not a socialist. Then they came for the trade unionists, and I
> did not speak out because I was not a trade unionist. Then they
> came for the Jews, and I did not speak out because I was not a Jew.
> Then they came for me, and there was no one left to speak for me.
> (Pastor Martin Niemöller [1892–1984])

The *ethical* imperative follows from the new *understanding* we gain (Laub
and Podell 1997).

A NOTE ON SYMBOLISM

Throughout this book, I shall be referring to common American metaphors of organizational destructiveness. Among them, the Holocaust is
perhaps most disturbing and perplexing. How do I suggest that this
image be understood? My answer requires a brief foray into the nature
of symbols, the meaning of meaning, so to speak (Stein 1983; Hook 1979).

In the mind of the person evoking it, who is groping for some *comparison* that can give outer *form* to the present horror, the Holocaust often
functions as metaphor, a fusion of symbol and symbolized, and less often, as simile, a conscious making of likeness rather than identity. In

either case, the juxtaposition is, when viewed from the outside, a symbolic event.

The equation "Downsizing *is* Holocaust" is better understood to be "Downsizing *as* Holocaust," that is, *likened* in some ways to it. Viewed as a symbol appropriated *for current purposes* from history, the use of the Holocaust as a symbol for downsizing does not mean an equation *in reality* of Holocaust and managed social change. One who uses the term now knows it is the 1990s in the United States and not the 1940s in Nazi Germany. The appropriation is not intended to be a preemption (Langer 1998). A present view and use of the past is not meant to be literally the past itself. The symbol is evoked, and when made into a metaphor, it is used to validate the shudder in the face of the current American (and globalized) world. The Holocaust is thus a *symbol* of current horror in the idiom of the past—not a literal reliving of the past itself. If the schizophrenic, in deeply regressed symbolism, would be certain that the present is the living past, that confusion would not be made by most Americans who might today employ the symbol of the Holocaust.

This appropriation of an event-as-symbol is of the same conscious and unconscious genre as, for example, the long tradition of comparing large-scale atrocities and other socially gruesome events with centuries-old Aztec ritual sacrifices of war prisoners. In a similar vein, along with axes and hatchets, the guillotine is today often used as an image for "capitated" (in fantasy, decapitated, that is, mutilating) managed care policy, the "deep cuts" of the Ronald Reagan presidency, and of downsizing. Fears and fantasies of mutilation, death, separation, and castration condense into an image that originated over two centuries earlier with "The Terror" in the bloody aftermath of the French Revolution. A reality of the 1790s in northwestern Europe becomes appropriated as a validating symbol of political and economic strategies.

In the modern business world, chests are not literally hewn open and hearts ripped out; heads are not cut off in bloody public display. One searches history, mythology, and folklore for representations that consciously resemble the destructiveness sensed by the unconscious.

The connotation-ridden symbol comes to stand for the original atrocity, even though it will not be experienced literally. The *choice* of symbolism potentially helps the student or consultant to understand both present and past, one via the other. Still, the researcher or applied organizational researcher must take care not to abandon independent judgment through complete identification with the narrator of the account or with the narrative itself.

CONVERGENCES IN THE LITERATURE

At this point, the deservedly skeptical reader might wonder: Even if the author's argument so far is intuitively plausible, what corroborative data are available to support his position and claims? In this section I attempt to answer that question. In a 1996 review of literature on managed social change, Allcorn et al. noted that "of the *Fortune* 1000 companies, 85 percent report downsizing between 1987 and 1991 with 50 percent downsizing in 1990 (Mishra and Mishra 1994). Of the companies that downsize once, 65 percent will often do it again the following year, and multiple downsizings are not uncommon" (1996: 3). They later argue that

> despite their promise to revolutionize organizations, restructuring and BPR [business process reengineering] encounter many pitfalls. Their success can be compromised by unrealistic expectations for the change process, inadequate resources to accomplish the redesign and implement it, lack of sponsorship, the setting of unrealistically short time frames for the change process by senior management, lack of effective planning, the use of poor methods, defining the wrong scope for the work (often too narrow), and the use of BPR language without understanding it, which can promote a cult-like mysticism around the use of the language that alienates organization members (Klein 1994). (Allcorn et al. 1996: 6)

In their foreword to a longitudinal case study of hospital downsizing, Gilkey and Lieberman similarly point out that

> organizations cannot downsize their way to excellence. In theory, reengineering and downsizing eliminate unnecessary work; in practice these responses eliminate people, implicitly defining them as unwarranted costs and underperforming expenditures. Downsizing is not a strategy, it is a tactic necessitated by a lack of a strategy. It is also a belated attempt to correct errors based on lack of insight and anticipation on the part of top leaders. Similarly, downsizing is not a positive vision; it is the expression of a lack of one. Such failures are based on an inability to anticipate the need for change, which always diminishes options and erodes opportunities. . . . (1996: vii)

Based on a wide variety of experiences, theories, and independent data sets, an increasing number of organizational theorists, consultants, and journalists are coming to question the wisdom behind, and assumptions governing, the many forms of managed social change. In virtually automatic, lockstep use in organizational revitalization, these forms are rife with magical thinking. Beginning on 3 March 1996, the *New York Times* published a seven-part series on "The Downsizing of America: A National Heartache." Authors Uchitelle and Kleinfield supply abundant organizational demographics and vignettes to support their argument that downsizing and its cognate terms (RIFing, rightsizing, etc.) have produced demoralization more than they have revitalized workplaces.

In a 1995 *Washington Post* essay, Grimsley describes "The Downside of Downsizing: What's Good for the Bottom Line Isn't Necessarily Good for Business." Roth (1993) speaks of downsizing as a "dangerous ploy." Preston (1992) examines the demoralized aftermath of downsizing, while Byrne (1994) writes of "The Pain of Downsizing" in the cover story of *Business Week*. Gertz, a vice-president of Mercer Management Consulting Inc. (Boston), writes of the consequences of downsizing: "The best managers and workers, tired of the turmoil, begin to jump ship, while the remaining employees, disheartened and distracted, become ever less productive. Ultimately, downsizers find that they've cut the muscle from their companies, not just the fat." (1996: 11A).

Downsizing often fails to deliver on the vast expectations made of it (Cameron 1994). Productivity, trust, and morale, among other factors, often suffer with downsizing. The anticipated reduction of expenses and dramatic increase in profit are far from universal (Cameron 1994). Downsizing and its related forms of social change have virtually redefined work and employment. The social contract between employer and employee, even between executive and company, has been cancelled (Uchitelle and Kleinfield 1996), and a cascade of downward mobility—real and feared—is the result.

The cover story of *Newsweek*'s February 26, 1996, issue is titled "Corporate Killers." A large hatchet-head accompanies the article's listing in the table of contents. Indeed, images of axes, hatchets, and guillotines have been commonly drawn by editorial cartoonists over the past decade to depict the experience of downsizing, managed care, reengineering, and restructuring. The *Wall Street Journal* and the *Washington Post* now regularly publish articles that question the claims of managed social change.

Micklethwait and Wooldridge (2000) argue in *A Future Perfect* that the long-term advantages of economic globalization far outweigh the temporary destruction of jobs. By contrast, William Adler (2000) closely examines the disrupted lives of the three women who occupy an assembly-line job as the job—and its company—moves from New Jersey to rural Mississippi and to Matamoros, Mexico, across the border from Brownsville, Texas, in search of productivity and profit through globalization. In a recent book, *The Working Life: The Promise and Betrayal of Modern Work*, ethicist Joanne Ciulla (2000) describes how organizations cultivate and exploit workers' loyalty, only to discard them by the thousands with no sense of reciprocal obligation. The work ethic of intimidation and fear induces only the pressure to work harder for a future that is always in question. Diamond (1997) explores how management and leadership by intimidation constitute forms of "administrative assault," and in turn constitute workplace violence. He later (1998) explores the psychological regression of organizational members into paranoid-schizoid defenses against anxiety, and the widespread use of splitting the social world into all-good and all-bad parts.

Journalist Susan Faludi (1999) explores the consequences of downsizing and reengineering in *Stiffed: The Betrayal of the American Man*. Faludi documents over and again how these induce vulnerability, anxiety over loss, dread of futurelessness, that derive from American workers' shared social predicaments and mutual identifications. The social production of meaninglessness and rage are the outcome of the assault of the prevailing American business ethic on masculinity. One wonders what quiet despair or volatile rages, what disappointments, what impenetrable silences and sullenness, their children witness and unconsciously identify with—even among the most outwardly adaptive and resilient parents. The future envisaged by those who bear the brunt of globalization and its many strategies is far from "perfect."

SUBSTANCE AND METHOD

If the "substance" or "content" of this book consists of the exploration of organizational darkness—that is, the emotional brutalization of the workplace—the "method" consists of the exploration of two related concepts: countertransference and metaphor. All *substance* of understanding is circumscribed by the *method* of coming to that understanding. Simply put, what we know (or assume that we know) is related to how we come to know in the first place. Looking with the observant, naked eye, with the microscope and with the telescope, reveals different universes of the known. It is not different with organizational understanding (or broader, cultural understanding) and consulting. *This book is about "looking"(not only visually) into the experience of workplace culture via metaphor—and, further, "looking" into the meaning of workplace metaphor via observer countertransference.* I want to say a few preliminary words about these terms, then I shall rely on the remainder of the book to convey how they can be useful.

Metaphor is a universal linguistic and symbolic practice of speaking of one phenomenon in terms of another. In the process of substitution, one thing comes to be personified by, identified as, the other (e.g., calling another person a "dog" or "angel"). It is simultaneously a way of organizing, articulating, expressing, and communicating how one experiences and feels—or is supposed to experience and feel. "This work situation is *hell*," says one employee; "We are all one *family*," says a manager; "The CEO thinks he is the *sun and moon* of this place," complains a junior executive. These are instances of metaphor. The figure of speech called *euphemism* takes metaphor even further by specifically directing attention *away* from one thing by directing it *toward* another—a point I have made at length in my earlier study of organizational euphemisms (Stein 1998) that fall under the rubric of "managed social change."

These terms, and their distinction, will recur throughout this book. It is as if—if the reader will allow me to try to situate much of our organizational language on an imaginary "graph"—there is a bimodal distribution of words and phrases about the changes taking place in American workplaces. One set of metaphors consists of the official, formal language, governed largely by euphemism: downsizing, RIFing, rightsizing, reengineering, restructuring, deskilling, outsourcing, and the like. These all embody and reflect belief in the rational, enlightened-self-interest model of business decision-making. A second, nonoverlapping set of metaphors consists of an unofficial, informal language, governed by imagery of the Holocaust, of the Vietnam War, and of images of mutilation and destruction ("dead meat," "dead wood," "head count," "cut out all the fat," "cut to the bone"). All these designate targets of reduction. This phenomenological world is filled with dread, destruction, and catastrophe. It is a malevolent world governed by selections for life or death, trains to transport people to death camps, sinister Doctors Mengele, closed chambers in which people are eliminated, of gooks who cannot be trusted, and so on. It is as if the second set of images illumines what the first set disguises if not conceals. From the viewpoint of a cultural worldview or ethos, they are, of course, inseparable. They are both ways of speaking about, and speaking to, the same social universe.

Now, a question might immediately arise in the reader as to the nature of the comparison being made in the metaphor. If "downsizing" or "restructuring" embody dramatic understatement, are not comparisons with death camps, with the blurring of friend and enemy in war, distortions beyond overstatement? Do they not violate reality in the guise of trying to do justice to experience? Just as I left the answer to the reader in my book on *Euphemism, Spin, and the Crisis in Organizational Development* (Stein 1998), I must do likewise here. My central methodological point is that *the organizational darkness is not the fact of the "symbolic" equation of the American workplace and the Holocaust, but the emotional experience of the workplace that makes the metaphor—and certain recurrent others—plausible and, for many, emotionally apt or "right."*

One may justly argue that the Holocaust and downsizing or managed care cannot, even must not, be compared. For instance, consider the following approach, as one colleague put it:

> You can recover from being fired from a job; you can't recover from being fired in an oven. The Holocaust is the final "downsizing"

from which there can be no return. People who are fired—even brutally fired—can still get another job; they are still alive. Why, then, do people choose this metaphor? People grab the most powerful analogy they can find. Perhaps they use the Holocaust to explain to themselves and to other people their terrifying feelings. People may exaggerate for effect to validate how badly they feel. They may exaggerate to make their own feelings real. Still, getting caught in downsizing is not the same as getting caught in the Holocaust, unless someone goes out and commits suicide over the despair. Perhaps the Holocaust is too big a metaphor, and as a result trivializes the experience of downsizing and reengineering. In this framework, to use the Holocaust metaphor is to give a false experience of reality to the person who has been fired or who cannot obtain health care. It is an inappropriate metaphor.

A related argument against the equation of the American corporate workplace with the Holocaust is the distinction between *reality* and *feeling*. The argument goes as follows: In the Holocaust, the instances of resistance notwithstanding, Jews were totally at the mercy of the Nazis. In American corporations, people have choices over employment, even if they are fired. Even though people could find other employment, they feel at the mercy of bosses and executives. Feeling is not reality or fact. Abject helplessness is not the same as the sense of helplessness. The American workplace does not exercise the same kind of total control over people's lives as did life under Nazi domination.

Thus, as a metaphor of the American workplace, the Holocaust is simply too full of connotations to be appropriate. The weight of American business events does not add up to the weight of the Holocaust. At best, there are similarities between American corporate experience and the Holocaust, but certainly not identity. Again at best, the Holocaust can be seen as a symbol many people draw upon today to articulate their present experience. But the *sense* of helplessness in the present must be distinguished from the Jewish *reality* of helplessness during the Holocaust. At most, one might concede that lower echelon workers, those with few skills, occupy that kind of dire, vulnerable reality in the United States. (I owe these two paragraphs from a discussion with David B. Friedman, M.D., 14 August 2000, phone conversation.)

This book, in a way, is an attempt to formulate an answer to these thoughtful objections. The recurrent use of catastrophic images point to the question of the *specificity* of metaphors. What are the kinds of experiences in organizations that lead people to choose one symbol over another? And of all the symbols available, why a specific choice? Answers to this question take us away from debate over World War II or the Vietnam War images to the basic emotional experience of change in organizations—and of how people cope with "social suffering" (Kleinman, Das, and Lock 1997).

The remainder of this book explores American corporate workplace *experience* and the *symbols* to which that experience gives rise. It is my hope that this effort in comprehending American work experience will map the uses and limitations of the Holocaust—and any other—metaphor.

If I may draw from a different era, I am reminded, for instance, that as recent as the late twentieth century, Poles and some of their Polish American descendants would use the word "Cholera!" as a curse word—that is, as a way to put a curse on another person. The infectious disease that had long ravaged eastern Europe and that was now gone, was succeeded by a word that would magically mean its deadly assault. In the transformation, dread disease becomes curse. Certainly, the person invoking the word has appropriated the word, and transformed the disease, far beyond its original descriptive usage. Perhaps to label the word-use as "appropriate" or "inappropriate" is too limiting to aid in our understanding.

It is my hope that in this book, the reader will be immersed in the world of the corporate workplace and will gain a sense of the context in which metaphors *arise* and are *used* in workplaces. I hope the reader will constantly ask: In addition to what an outside observer or consultant might think of the "choice" of metaphors, what does the world feel like to people who select certain metaphors to evoke their workplaces?

REFERENCES

Adler, William M. 2000. *Mollie's Job: A Story of Life and Work on the Global Assembly Line*. New York: Scribner.

Allcorn, Seth, Howell S. Baum, Michael A. Diamond, and Howard F. Stein. 1996. *The HUMAN Cost of a Management Failure: Organizational Downsizing at General Hospital*. Westport, CT: Quorum Books. Pp. vi–x.

Appelfeld, Aharon. 1993. Quoted by Hana Volavkova, ed. *I never saw another butterfly: Children's Drawings and Poems from Terezin Concentration Camp, 1942–1944*. Expanded second edition by the U.S. Holocaust Memorial Museum. New York: Schocken Books. P. ix.

Arendt, Hannah. 1994. *Eichmann in Jerusalem: A Report on the Banality of Evil*. New York: Penguin. Orig. 1963.

Barondess, Jeremiah. 1998. "Care of the Medical Ethos: Reflections on Social Darwinism, Racial Hygiene, and the Holocaust," *Annals of Internal Medicine* 129(11), 1 December: 891–898.

Bion, Wilfred R. 1959. *Experiences in Groups*. New York: Ballantine.

Bursztajn, Harold J. 1997. "Medical Necessity, Managed Health Care Denial of Benefits, and the Nuremberg Code." Panel: "Medical Ethics: Who Gets the Care?" Moderator: Professor Uwe E. Reinhardt, Ph.D., Princeton University 250th Anniversary Symposium, Princeton, NJ. 29 May.

Byrne, John. 1994. "The Pain of Downsizing," *Business Week* 3370: 60–68.

Cameron, Kim. 1994. "Strategies for Successful Downsizing," *Human Resource Management* 33(2): 189–211.

Ciulla, Joanne B. 2000. *The Working Life: The Promise and Betrayal of Modern Work.* New York: Times Business.

Diamond, Michael A. 1997. "Administrative Assault: A Contemporary Psycho-analytic View of Violence and Aggression in the Workplace," *The American Review of Public Administration* 27(3), September: 228–247.

———. 1998. "The Symbiotic Lure: Organizations as Defective Containers," *Administrative Theory and Praxis* 20(3): 315–325.

Faludi, Susan. 1999. *Stiffed: The Betrayal of the American Man.* New York: William Morrow.

Freud, Sigmund. 1910. "The Future Prospects of Psycho-analytic Training," in *The Standard Edition of the Complete Psychological Works of Sigmund Freud.* Volume 11. James Strachey, trans. London: Hogarth Press. Pp. 139–152.

———. 1912. "Recommendations to Physicians Practicing Psycho-analysis," *Standard Edition.* Volume 14. London: Hogarth Press. Pp. 109–120.

Gertz, Dwight. 1996. "Growth, Not Downsizing, Leads to Greatness," *USA Today*, 7 February. P. 11A.

Gilkey, Roderick W., and Gary R. Lieberman. 1996. "Foreword," in Seth Allcorn, Howell S. Baum, Michael A. Diamond, and Howard F. Stein, *The HUMAN Cost of a Management Failure: Organizational Downsizing at General Hospital*, Westport, CT: Quorum Books. Pp. vi–x.

Grimsley, K. D. 1995. "The Downside of Downsizing: What's Good for the Bottom Line Isn't Necessarily Good for Business," *Washington Post National Weekly Edition*, 13–19 November. Pp. 16–17.

Hook, R. H. 1979. "Phantasy and Symbol: A Psychoanalytic Point of View," in R. H. Hook, ed., *Fantasy and Symbol: Studies in Anthropological Interpretation.* New York: Academic Press. Pp. 267–291.

Janis, Irving. 1982. *Groupthink.* Boston: Houghton Mifflin.

Katz, Jay. 1996. "The Nuremberg Code and the Nuremberg Trial: A Reappraisal," *Journal of the American Medical Association* 276: 1662–1666.

Klein, Mark. 1994. "The Most Fatal Reengineering Mistakes," *Information Strategy: The Executive's Journal* 10(4): 21–28.

Kleinman, Arthur, and Joan Kleinman. 1991. "Suffering and Its Professional Transformation: Toward an Ethnography of Interpersonal Experience," *Culture, Medicine and Psychiatry* 15: 275–301.

Kleinman, Arthur, Veena Das, and Margaret M. Lock, eds. 1997. *Social Suffering.* Berkeley: University of California Press.

Langer, Lawrence. 1998. *Preempting the Holocaust.* New Haven, CT: Yale University Press.

Laub, Dori, and Daniel Podell. 1997. "Psychoanalytic Listening to Historical Trauma: The Conflict of Knowing and the Imperative to Act," *Mind and Human Interaction* 8(4): 245–260.

Levi, Primo. 1988. *The Drowned and the Saved.* New York: Summit Books.

Levine, David P. 1999. "Creativity and Change: On the Psychodynamics of Modernity," *American Behavioral Scientist* 43(2), October: 225–244.

Lofholm, Nancy. 2000. "Utes See 'Spirits' in Calamities" [Fire in Mesa Verde National Park], *Denver Post*, 28 July. Pp. 1A, 7A.

Micklethwait, John, and Adrian Wooldridge. 2000. *A Future Perfect: The Challenge and Hidden Promise of Globalization*. New York: Crown Business.

Mishra, Aneil, and Karen Mishra. 1994. "The Role of Mutual Trust in Effective Downsizing Strategies," *Human Resource Management* 33(2): 261–279.

Noer, David. 1993. *Healing the Wounds: Overcoming and Revitalizing Downsized Organizations*. New York: Jossey-Bass.

Ochberg, Frank. 1997. "Introduction: Twenty Years After Defining PTSD," *Mind and Human Interaction* 8(4): 201–203.

Preston, Paul. 1992. "Downsizing: The Aftermath," *Administrative Radiology* 11(9): 21–25.

Reich, Robert. 1993. "Of Butchers and Bakers: Is Downsizing Good for the Company," *Vital Speeches of the Day* 60(40): 100–102.

Roth, William. 1993. "The Dangerous Ploy of Downsizing," *Business Forum* 18(4): 5–7.

Shore, Karen. 1997. "Don't Let Them Take Your Mind and Spirit: On Being Called a 'Provider,' " American Psychological Association, Acceptance Speech, "Distinguished Psychologist of the Year."

Stein, Howard F. 1983. "Psychoanalytic Anthropology and the Meaning of Meaning," in Bruce Bain, ed., *The Psychogenesis of Language and Human Conduct*. New York: Plenum. Pp. 393–414.

———. 1997. *Evocations*. Pittsburgh: Dorrance Publishing Company.

———. 1998. *Euphemism, Spin, and the Crisis in Organizational Life*. Westport, CT: Quorum Books.

———. 2000. *Learning Pieces*. Pittsburgh: Dorrance Publishing Company.

Uchitelle, Louis, and N. R. Kleinfield. 1996. "On the Battlefields of Business, Millions of Casualties," first of seven articles on "The Downsizing of America," *New York Times*, 3 March. Pp. 1, 26, 28.

Volkan, Vamik D. 2000. "Traumatized Societies and Psychological Care," Opening paper presented at the "Crossing the Border" Dutch Adolescent Psychotherapy Organization, Amsterdam, 18 May.

Wiesel, Elie. 1960. *Night*. New York: Bantam, 1982.

Young, Alan. 1995. *The Harmony of Illusion: Inventing Post-Traumatic Stress Disorder*. Princeton, NJ: Princeton University Press.

2

Countertransference as Tool in Organizational Theory: The "Use" of Self to Understand Workplace Violence

INTRODUCTION

The first methodological concept—organizational symbol and metaphor as key to organizational life, discussed in the first chapter—brings me to a consideration of the second, allied methodological concept, *countertransference*. If metaphors offer a "window" on a workplace or the wider culture, an observer's or consultant's countertransference in turn offers a "window" on understanding the meaning(s) and feeling(s) associated with metaphors. The observer is a crucial instrument of both distortion and of clarification of the culture being observed. Paradoxically, perhaps, one learns to look "inward" as a way of looking "outward" (toward the organization, the client, the nation).

Scientists, consultants, physicians, and even many psychoanalysts emphasize the need for the disciplined, systematic collection of exclusively "external" data. Much as they might publicly disparage reliance on "gut reactions" (abdominal tightening and other self-monitored physical responses) as instructive about where and how to proceed next in decision-making, many nonetheless rely on it as a guide.

To explain how this process works, it is necessary to examine— briefly—the history of the concepts of transference and countertransference. Part of my rationale for brevity early in this book is that the relationship between the self of the observer, the process of observation, the observer's relationship with others, and the process of interpretation of organizational metaphors, constitutes the central subject matter of this book. It is the task of the book—not this section—to explore thoroughly this process.

The earliest discussions of transference and countertransference dichotomized between two types of projective processes, depending upon who was doing it, the patient or the therapist (analyst). Transference consisted of unconscious feelings from the *patient's* childhood past, which the patient projected in the present onto the therapist. Countertransference consisted of unconscious feelings from the *therapist's* childhood past, evoked by the current relationship with the patient. Countertransference consisted of those "transferential" feelings evoked in the therapist by someone else. Transference was viewed as primary. Countertransference was secondary, derivative, a reaction.

Thus understood, both forms of unconscious response, and subsequent communication, were equally distortive of the other person in the clinical dyad. Further, though, the clinician's transference was seen as counter to, in response to, the patient's transference, which was regarded as the primary problem. From the outset, Freud was ambivalent toward the analyst's unconscious, alternately viewing it with suspicion and in need of monitoring and control (1910), and as the "organ" upon which the very understanding of and helpfulness toward the patient depend (1912). In more recent years, many analysts, and many social scientists and consultants who draw upon psychoanalytic thinking, have come to broaden their understanding of both transference and countertransference. In a word, things are far less simple than we had thought nearly a century ago.

EXAMPLE: THE POLICEMAN AND THE DRIVER

Let me use a homely example to illustrate this "evolution" in understanding. Consider the situation in which a highway patrolman pulls over a driver for speeding and issues a ticket. Although the patrolman is polite and businesslike in his demeanor, the driver becomes incensed, flies into a rage, and protests that he is unjustly accused, and accuses the policeman of picking on him. One might argue that this is an instance of "pure" transference, of an emotion in which the driver inappropriately displaces feelings he had in relation to early male authority figures onto the hapless highway patrolman. Put differently, these feelings are unprovoked. If anything, they are "provoked" by the situation (of being caught, stopped, and symbolically punished), rather than specifically by the person of the policeman who, after all, represents the authority of the community. "Pure" transference, or countertransference, is thus inherent in the character of the person responding rather than in the current ebb and flow of the relationship.

Still, *something* unleashes the driver's wrath. The policeman is not a pure screen. In either case, the projection is "good for" only projective knowledge of the other person. Feelings of guilt, shame, and anxiety are replaced by feelings of blame and self-righteousness. The driver "knows" he is being picked on, if not persecuted, even when he is not. He, the driver, might be construed as trying to "provoke" the patrolman with his own rage—thus "confirming" his perception. This latter twist will transform "pure" transference into a relational product. Perhaps no transference or countertransference is entirely "pure," that is, purely subjective rather than intersubjective, purely internal rather than attuned to reality.

Consider now a variation of the original scenario that would allow for a broader understanding of countertransference. Let us assume that here, the highway patrolman is loud, haughty, that he thumps the hood of the culprit's car with his hand, that he delivers a moralistic diatribe against the driver, that he berates him as he writes the ticket. The driver in this situation becomes enraged, incensed, resentful, as in the earlier scenario. Let us further apply the concept of countertransference to the driver of the stopped vehicle, and the concept of transference to the highway patrolman, and explore the emotional dynamics of the arrest.

Here, the highway patrolman is overreacting, or at least acting inappropriately obnoxious toward the person he pulled over. The driver, sensing that the officer's rudeness and rage are out of proportion to the reality of the driver's speeding, examines his own emotional response to the officer to obtain from the relationship between them crucial data about the officer. Rather than verbally exploding at the officer, he "looks at" how he feels and formulates a hypothesis: "I feel as if he is beating up on me as if I am a bad boy and he is a frightened, maybe ashamed, maybe guilty father. Maybe there's a little of the reverse. Maybe he'd love to drive as fast as he wanted, but instead has to go hunting for people who speed in order to punish himself. That way, he can have his cake (his impulsive speeding) and eat it (that is, have his conscience)." The driver keeps his composure and does not take the tirade personally.

The policeman in this second scenario would be considered by modern psychiatry to be "acting out," which is a common behavioral feature of people diagnosed as having borderline personality disorder. We all have transference and countertransference issues; it goes with being human. But people mostly have these issues under control; that is, they do not act them out. The unrestrained transference that Freud discovered among some of his patients also characterizes the policeman in this scenario. He could have issued the ticket at any time. He had the authority to do so. For him, however, this authority was insufficient, and it is here that his transference "bled through," so to speak.

He was behaving like patients diagnosed with borderline personality disorder rather than as simply embodying the authority of a policeman.

Instead of experiencing inner conflict and emotion, he acted them out. His threatening gestures and pounding showed a lack of restraint and a lack of judgment. He is very much like bosses who abuse their position and power by berating and intimidating those whom they supervise. They need to make their subordinates feel powerless—which is also to say that, like the policeman in this scenario, they need to act out their transference toward others.

Such a circumstance in reality can induce feelings of helplessness that come to be rooted countertransferentially not "merely" in the inner subjectivity of the driver but in the intersubjectivity of the relationship. Such a confusion-ridden relationship with reality makes its menace difficult, if not impossible, to assess. In the least, *feelings* of helplessness in the face of authority add to the confirmation of the *reality* of that helplessness—aided by a defense called "identification with the aggressor." (I owe many of the ideas in the past three paragraphs to a conversation with David B. Friedman, M.D., 14 August 2000.)

For the sake of my present argument about countertransference, it does not matter which of these explanations (or which combination) is "right." Rather, the point is that the driver's emotional reaction to the officer's emotion can become—with careful exploration—crucial information about the officer and not be "pure" projection or "pure" transference.

The use of observer or consultant countertransference for emotional sensitivity draws upon this second variation of the scenario. It will become the foundation for understanding organizational metaphor and organizational life. Further, instead of resting on inappropriate *extrapolation* from clinical dyads and relationships to large work groups, the exploration of countertransference in cultural observation and consultation will itself become a (not the) foundation for understanding those organizational groups.

IMAGINING A CULTURAL DEATHSCAPE IN THE WORKPLACE AND BEYOND

This chapter brings the observer and consultant's countertransference—the emotional experience as part of the "work" itself—to the very center of the subject. It is the ultimate source and font of organizational and cultural knowledge. In a sense, the focus of this chapter is methodology rather than substance—or rather, methodology and the kind of organizational substance to which it gives access. Put metaphorically, the "first person" turns out to be a precursor to the "third person." In even the most austere of the sciences, there is always present an observer, which is to say, a "first person."

For many years, in that cluttered "surround" of my office or study, I have kept a tattered, yellowing copy of Arthur Koestler's novel *Darkness at Noon* (1941) within arm's reach of my typewriter, and later computer. I house it with my English, French, German, and Hebrew dictionaries, with my thesaurus, and assorted other essential reference material I draw upon constantly. Not only does it sit "there," but I will also occasionally leaf through it, find a page or passage, read it, and put the book back. I now, finally, know why. Often the act comes first, then the realization much later. I have been telling myself about "organizational" darkness all along via the constant presence and reminder of the ghastly Stalin trials in the Soviet Union during the late 1930s. *Darkness at Noon* is an historical link with a different place and time, but it is also a metaphor of the dimly dawning light I have gained upon the present: here not only there, an enforced darkness amid the blaze of noon.

There is a second "literary" image that has seized me during the writing of this chapter: the beginning and ending of Herman Melville's novel, *Moby Dick* (1851). As if out of nowhere, one day as I wrote, I walked up to the wall of books in one part of my home and reached up for *Moby Dick*. I did not know why, nor did I know what I was looking for. I found it immediately: Ishmael's opening soliloquy, then, over five hundred pages later, Ishmael's epilogue as survivor of Captain Ahab's obsession, the whale's rage, and the Pequod's destruction. The epilogue is prefaced with a quotation from *Job*: "And I only am escaped alone to tell thee." I immediately identified with Ishmael: here is the character I had "become" in the raging sea of social change, participant observer, fortunate survivor, and chronicler. Ahab's calculation and fury at sea merged into Rubashov's trial and execution under Stalin. They were, and are, both about an impenetrable darkness—and about the effort to enter it, to survive it, and to comprehend it. This chapter is no different.

The thesis of this chapter is that countertransference is the foundation of much understanding, that all perception passes through the self of the perceiver. It is the central issue in all knowing, including the understanding of organizations. All methodology rests upon its work. There is a crucial, and often denied, link between our inner emotional life and our ability to know. Following W. R. Bion (1959: 134), I shall take the observer's emotional response—his or her countertransference—to be at times the only reliable measure of social reality. At the abstract level, countertransference consists of nothing less than thinking about how we think, an approach taken by such writers as Bion (1959, 1962), Boyer (1999), Laub and Podell (1997), Stern (1997), Tansey and Burke (1989), and Lawrence (1997, 1999).

What one knows is inseparable from what one can bear to know— what one can first incorporate, then examine—about oneself, about others, about the world (Coleman 1968). This chapter is thus a study in the dialogue between knowing and known and not-knowing, and in the role of unconscious processes in that dialogue. As social science, it is a general

inquiry, not a narrowly "psychological" one. This chapter explores countertransference—the totality of emotions, fantasies, and body sensations
evoked within the observer—as a methodological tool of ethnographic
study (organizational and wider), that is, as a path to the understanding
of self and "otherness."

One may think of countertransference in terms of *embodied knowing and
disembodied (not-) knowing* (Csordas 1994). When one learns via countertransference, one is including, incorporating, and examining something
within oneself; when one does not learn via countertransference, one is
excluding, expelling, ridding something from oneself. The former leads
to greater integration, the latter, to greater fragmentation. It turns out
that the "what" (content) of knowledge is inseparable from the "where"
(location) in which the knowledge is perceived to reside. Embodiment
and disembodiment are about both.

More broadly, this chapter addresses abiding issues in organizational
studies and in anthropology: among them, the nature and experience of
the self, of identity, of adaptation to political terror, of the relation between work, workplace, and interior experience in a capitalist society,
and of the increased globalization of the U.S. economy and its ideology.

With respect to ethnographic or organizational content, this chapter
describes and interprets a cultural deathscape—one that is founded upon
a clustering of euphemisms in the American landscape, for example,
downsizing, reduction in force, RIF, rightsizing, reengineering, restructuring, outsourcing, surplusing, separating, deskilling, vertical integration, organizational flattening, managed care, acquisition, and merger
(Stein 1998a; Allcorn, Baum, Diamond, and Stein 1996). The corporate
business ethos is distilled in that ubiquitous imperative phrase, "The
Bottom Line," a denotation that has been widely adopted from the ac-
countant's ledger sheet and made connotatively into the signature of a
civilization.

When invoked, "The Bottom Line" is a conversation stopper and the
final idiom of appeal—a kind of secular Aristotelian prime mover or
juggernaut. It is an obligatory discourse beyond which—within the culture—there is no appeal. To those who experience it as ideologically
compelling, it is the *only* way. Within its grasp, there is no suffering, or
suffering is explained away: "It can't be happening," or "It can't be *that*
bad," or "We *had* to do it to save the corporation."

I illustrate the methodological and theoretical value of countertransference via concrete ethnographic data that come from American workplace participation, observation, and consultation. I show how the
Holocaust (the Nazi effort to exterminate the Jews) is a frequently invoked metaphor for organizational downsizing and its related catastrophic organizational changes that have pervaded American society
since the mid-1980s. I study the experience of suffering in the workplace

and employ my *countertransference as a way to access that suffering*. My resonance as a Jew with the subject of downsizing and managed care has led me to a sense of the uncanny, and in turn to further insights into the experience of American workplace culture.

If I claim that the Holocaust is a trope for organizational downsizing and other forms of "managed" massive social change, I also recognize that my identity as a Jew provided the experiential foundation for wondering what the nature of the connection might entail. Why would people talk *that* way? I listened to "field" and "workplace" experience via my own life. What I heard was as spooky as it was uncanny. When I am asked about my "family tree," "genealogy," or "kinship system," I have a vivid sense of absence on my father's side. Except for three relatives who emigrated from Romania early in the twentieth century, all the rest disappeared during the Holocaust. A lively transatlantic exchange of letters before World War II was followed by utter silence.

This gaping "hole" in my family tree (which is also an ethnic-religious one) has made me especially attentive to similar organizational and cultural "holes" such as have occurred in the form of ethnic, national, religious, and organizational atrocity. (The reader will find a further biographical "hole" in the vignette later in this chapter.) As colleagues and organizational clients with whom I consulted began to use Holocaust imagery in describing the experience of American "managed organizational change"—from downsizing to managed care—my attention became riveted. I began paying keen attention to disappearances and to people who were made invisible. "What was happening in America?" I asked myself with urgency and alarm. I came to pay as much attention to the Holocaust-laden language of the corridors and photocopy rooms as I did to the business language of the conference rooms and journals.

Substantively, this chapter explores how American workers progress in their understanding of what is happening to them in their workplace, and in the United States in general, as they move from thinking "This is happening" (recognition) to "Is this happening?" (questioning), finally to "This cannot be happening" (denial). It is about a world in which the work of atrocity assumes the cloak of business. The *methodological* focus on countertransference derives from the observer's difficulty—unconscious resistance—in recognizing what is present (primarily in himself or herself, which affects his or her perceptions).

Such recognition is not a simple matter of recording and interpreting cultural data. It is not enough to recite the professional shibboleths of fieldwork (from participant observation to open-ended interviewing), and to claim that these methods magically lead to insight (Philip Bock, personal communication, 1998). It is first a matter of being able to hear, to listen, at all. For data, I begin with my countertransference. I end with a portrait of the American workplace and of the culture of which the workplace is an institution. I begin with what we often label observer subjectivity; I end with a deeper understanding of political oppression. *A study of the workplace that begins with my own inner darkness becomes a vehicle for a journey into organizational darkness—a place of secrecy and dread often expressed in the idiom of the Holocaust.* I serve the dual roles of ethnographer and ethnographic specimen or "key informant."

Consider the following eerie scenario as a point of departure in this exploration of the evocative and interpretive power of countertransference. In 1995, after Seth Allcorn, Howell Baum, Michael Diamond, and I had completed the manuscript of the longitudinal study of a hospital downsizing (1996), we took a walk through the large hospital in which interviews with managers had been conducted the previous year. We wanted to see for ourselves *now*, after the "terminations," what it looked like.

We entered at night through a door near the administrative offices. We walked through many corridors of this hospital, passing many executive suites, all dark inside now. As we walked, we remarked to each other how calm and clear and orderly everything looked. The halls were well lit; offices had nameplates, bulletin boards were filled with the latest announcements. We were surprised that everything was so tidy. We were all uncomfortable being there, yet we needed to be there, if only to affirm the reality that we knew had taken place. It all felt uncanny. Something seemed to be missing.

Almost in a single voice, we wondered aloud how it could look like *this* after what everyone had been through: "Where was the blood? Where were the bodies? Could it have been cleaned up so well?" Now, we knew full well that no one had been killed, no blood had been spilled on the walls or the floors. There had been no bodies. But our collective fantasy and horror as we walked—that *something* present and vital was now missing—constituted vivid data in understanding the fate of the organization after multiple downsizings.

Only by identifying with the injury that had taken place could we realize that injury had occurred there. Only by feeling our own suffering as we walked through the walls, could we sense that suffering had taken place there. Our *passive* suffering was a clue to the *active* violence that had occurred. That moment, all we had to go on was our countertransference: what we "saw" was in the mind's eye of the unconscious—a consensual validation based on autonomy. The darkness within was a clue to the darkness outside.

COUNTERTRANSFERENCE AS KNOWING VIA THE SENSES

There is increasing precedent within and outside anthropology for trusting all one's senses as a guide to social data. Paul Stoller has championed this argument in *The Taste of Ethnographic Things: The Senses in Anthropology* (1989) and in his more recent book, *Sensuous Scholarship* (1997). From his longitudinal study among the Songhai of Niger, Stoller concludes that the reigning anthropological and postmodern metaphors of "text" and textuality are not all; often they are narrowly and misleadingly visual. The other senses are often more important in ethnographic comprehension of the "other." How we represent people in ethnographic accounts depends on how we allow ourselves to experience them in the first place. Stoller argues that we can learn via our inner experience and not only, or even primarily, via disembodied vision.

If Stoller literally comes to his senses and learns from them in anthropology, Morris Berman does likewise in history. In *Coming to Our Senses: Body and Spirit in the Hidden History of the West*, Berman (1998) argues for trust in one's "gut" feelings as a methodological tool. We understand, not by emotional distancing, but through allowing the history we study to become a part of us, a point Berman first enunciated in *The Reenchantment of the World* (1981). Embodied feeling, bodily—pre-emotional—sensibilities, inform the researcher about deep, elusive, social realities.

In a similar vein, Weston La Barre (1978: 267) noted that ethnography is in large measure a species of autobiography. What we can and cannot know proceeds from who we are. Just as ethnographic knowledge can be hopelessly projective, "All intelligence draws its strength from and is flawed by defects in feeling" (1972: 530). Field experiences trigger personal feelings and recollections that in turn can inform the current situation.

In a recent interview, psychiatrist and psychohistorian Robert Jay Lifton (2000), who had interviewed Nazi physicians and studied the survivors of the atomic bombing of Hiroshima, emphasized:

> In all good psychiatric or psychoanalytic or clinical psychological work you have to give of yourself, and your self has to be available and attentive, and, therefore, in some ways, vulnerable. When you study very painful events that derive from highly destructive behavior—mass killing and dying, as I have—the self touches some very painful areas, but you have to let it be open to them. Otherwise you do not learn everything very much [sic]. *The self is one's instrument and has to feel pain to work on painful issues.* (2000: 21, emphasis added)

In different ways, these writers embody Blaise Pascal's wonderfully proto-Freudian aphorism that "the heart has its reasons of which reason knows nothing" ("*Le coeur a ses raisons que la raison ne connâit point,*" *Pensées,* 1670, Section 4, No. 277). "How" we know anything ethnographically is always implicit in the "what" we know or think we know. And if these are manifestly intellectual, cognitive processes, they never cease to be emotional, affective, physiological, embodied issues as well—issues that direct attention to the "where" or locus of knowing. If Pascal's "heart" of knowing can be abstractly metaphorical, it can be palpably sensate as well. Our heartbeat can teach us much about what we feel and what we know.

This is the point Melford Spiro (1979) emphasized when he asked "Whatever happened to the id?" in anthropological study. He noticed the violence in folklore that structuralist anthropologists had ignored. In our common language, we might say: "It takes one to know one." That is, one must have access to knowledge of one's own aggressiveness in order to recognize and study it in others. Spiro could learn about the folklore he studied because he could first bear to learn about himself— to sense via his own countertransference the feelings that "charged" the words of myth. Part of the symbolic power of language (Bourdieu 1993) comes from the power of conscious emotion and of unconscious affect— and of defenses against acknowledging their very presence and power.

Two types of countertransference are frequently identified: "concordant" and "complementary" (Racker 1968; Boyer 1999). The former leads to insight, the latter to resistance and to the effort to control the other person and oneself. In concordant countertransference,

> the analyst [observer, consultant] identifies with the corresponding part of the patient's [informant, client] psychical apparatus, that is, ego with ego and superego with superego, and can behave empathically because he experiences as his own the central emotion experienced by the patient [Other]. In complementary countertransference, the analyst identifies with the internalized transference object of the patient. (Boyer 1999: 28)

In the latter, for example, a powerful counteridentification with a terrifying father or mother might prohibit insight into another person.

Countertransference clearly involves feeling, not disembodied thought. The kind of knowing conferred by countertransference is one informed by emotion—or distorted by emotion. Arnold Modell (1984), for instance, referring to the intersubjectivity of the psychoanalytic situation, addresses the issue of meaning, and draws attention to the importance of the emotion behind the words people use.

> Meaning in the psychoanalytic situation depends not so much on words as on affects. . . . [A]ffects are at the heart of the problem of psychoanalytic [and, I hasten to add, cultural] language. Words do not by themselves constitute the primary data of psychoanalysis. . . . What endows words and other symbolic structures with signif-

icance is the communication of affects. It is the analyst's response to communicated affects that forms the basis of what is called empathy. Empathy cannot be present without the communication of affects. (1984:172)

The communication of affects lies at the basis of ethnographic knowledge as well. Anthropologist and psychoanalyst George Devereux's book, *From Anxiety to Method in the Behavioral Sciences* (1967), is an encyclopedic study of countertransference in doing and interpreting fieldwork. It is devoted largely to documenting the many sources of contamination, distortion, and partial insight that derive from the unconscious use of method to allay the observer's anxiety, and which thereby create all varieties of scotomata (that is, "blind spots," metaphorical holes in perception, understanding, feeling, and knowledge). Emotional reactions may profoundly distort our awareness and understanding of others. This view is the "classical," admonitory position on countertransference, enunciated by Freud in 1910.

Countertransference *may* also be helpful in knowing others; it *may* heighten understanding. In his emphasis on the reverberation of the patient's unconscious in the analyst's unconscious, and in the examination of the latter as a datum about the former, Devereux also adumbrates the later, "totalistic" understanding of countertransference (1967: 303–304). Freud himself (1912: 115–116) had urged that the "therapist turn his own unconscious like a receptive organ towards the transmitting unconscious of the patient . . . so that the doctor's unconscious is able . . . to reconstruct the patient's unconscious."

Just as the observer or analyst seeks to *control and diminish* that facet of countertransference that would distort, the observer or analyst seeks also to *give freer reign* to that facet of countertransference that would reveal (Boyer 1993, 1999) a position with which Devereux would concur. Greater access to one's unconscious, together with increased capacity to hold onto anxiety and examine the unconscious contents it signals (Tansey and Burke 1989), would seem to be key ways of distinguishing countertransference that reveals from countertransference that further conceals and purely "acts out" the fantasy and wish.

CONTRIBUTIONS OF MELANIE KLEIN, WILFRED BION, AND W. GORDON LAWRENCE

Melanie Klein, Wilfred Bion, and W. Gordon Lawrence have helped to further crystallize my thinking about the culture-revealing dimension of countertransference. Bion and Lawrence emphasize the nature of "embodied" knowing with specific reference to the pioneering work of Melanie Klein (1946, 1955) on the dialectic of projective and introjective identification. Klein first defined projective identification as "a combination of splitting off parts of the self and projecting them on to another person" (1946: 108). Later, she described it as "the feeling of identification with other people because one has attributed qualities or attitudes of one's own to them" (1955: 311). What one seeks to destroy or to exalt, one also seeks to retain. Through the confusion of boundaries, one attempts to control in another disavowed or idealized, but unattainable, facets of oneself.

Projective identification enacts and embodies self-in-other quite literally (Apprey and Stein 1993). Denial of separation and separateness lies at the heart of the "work" of projective identification. The behavior induced in the attempt to *control another person* is an indispensable part of the attempt to *regulate the self*.

Projective and introjective identification complement one another. In the former, one attempts to force a part of oneself into another person, and identifies with it as if it were an inherent characteristic of that other person. The other person becomes identified with the projected parts of the self and perceptually "becomes" those parts. In the latter, one identifies with a part that has been introjected from another person, a part often cast off by that other person and projected into oneself. One takes it into one's very self-identity; that is, what was introjected "becomes" part of one's very self.

In an influential essay, Zinner and Shapiro (1972) propose that the concept of projective identification can bridge intrapsychic and interpersonal dynamics within the family:

> Projective identification is an activity of the ego which, among its effects, modifies perception of the object and, in a reciprocal fashion, alters the image of the self. These conjoined changes in perception influence and may, in fact, govern behavior of the self towards the object. Thus projective identification provides an important conceptual bridge between an individual and interpersonal psychology, since our awareness of the mechanisms permits us to understand specific interactions *among* persons in terms of specific dynamic conflicts occurring *within* individuals. (523)

In earlier works, I have utilized the concept of projective identification in exploring a wide range of social behavior, from Slovak American ethnicity (Stein 1974) to American-Soviet relations (Stein 1985).

Having said this, I hasten to add that the concept of projective identification is at the center of long-standing, often bitter controversy within psychoanalytic circles, specifically between the so-called "schools" of Anna Freud and Melanie Klein. For those of the Anna Freud school, the claim of the "reality" of projective identification (projecting *into*) is itself evidence of projection (projecting *onto*): that one is blaming another for one's flaws or predicament. Yet, in her discussion of "altruistic surrender," a variation on projection, Anna Freud approximates the internal and interpersonal dynamics of projective identification. She writes that projection "disturbs our human relations [as] when we project our own jealousy and attribute to other people our own aggressive acts" (1936: 133). In "altruistic surrender," we seek and find in other people a "proxy in the outside world to serve as a repository for the self's own wishes" (1936: 136). Gratification of a projected impulse is achieved in and by another person; an interpersonal relationship performs an internal defensive function (Sander 1979: 12). This process of "extension of the self" (Klein 1955: 313) can expand to subsume entire groups (Hall 1977).

Just as organizational and ethnographic writing often projectively construct the Other, projective identification from those whom one is studying also constructs the self of the observer and interpreter. Social construction—which draws upon various forms of projection—goes both ways: it is intersubjective. The ethnographer's task is to *feel* the projection, to recognize it, and to examine it.

Wilfred Bion addressed this issue in his study of small group dynamics. Bion (1959: 134) argued that the analyst's emotional reaction is a vital source of data about the group. Often "countertransference"—the emotional sensations in the observer or therapist—offers the only knowledge available. Although Bion wrote from the context of group treatment, his insight extends to the far broader horizon of all understanding of other people. In the following passage, he is inquiring into the evidential basis for interpretations and directs the reader's attention to "interpretations for which the strongest evidence lies, not in the observed facts in the group but in the subjective reactions of the analyst" (1959: 134). He continues:

> In group treatment many interpretations, and amongst them the most important, have to be made on the strength of the analyst's own emotional reactions. It is my belief that these reactions are dependent on the fact that the analyst in the group is at the receiving end of what Melanie Klein (1946) has called projective identification, and that this mechanism plays a very important role in groups. Now the experience of counter-transference appears to have a distinct quality that should enable the analyst to differentiate the occasion when he is the object of a projective identification from the occasion when he is not. The analyst feels he is being manipulated so as to be playing a part, no matter how difficult to recognize, in somebody else's phantasy—or he would do if it were not for what in recollection I can only call a temporary loss of insight, a sense of experiencing strong feelings and at the same time

a belief that their existence is quite adequately justified by the objective situation without recourse to recondite explanation of their causation. . . . I believe ability to shake oneself out of the numbing feeling of reality that is a concomitant of this state is the prime requisite of the analyst in the group. (1959: 134–135)

This ability is equally a prime requisite of the organizational consultant and anthropologist. I have come to rely on these uncomfortable, often terribly frightening, experiences as crucial guides to interpersonal and organizational reality, and in turn, to culture "itself." I refer specifically to my experience of frequent (1) "temporary loss of insight" accompanied by (2) "strong feelings," and (3) my belief in an objective, external source of these feelings. I come to feel as if I am "going crazy," "possessed" by alien thoughts and feelings that are not mine, that at such moments of invasion I am literally "gone out of my mind."

Because many of those with whom I interact (as coworker, supervisor, subordinate, or consultant) disavow that they are doing what I sense they are doing, I must rely on my often-violent internal physical and emotional responses as a guide to what is taking place. I must learn to watch myself and listen to myself not only *while* I watch and listen to another person (or to a group), but *as a means of* doing so. In the process of doing so, I learn that my embodiment is, via projective and introjective identification, others' disembodiment. From the viewpoint of theory, projective identification functions as a powerful (if also pernicious) link between person and group, between symbol and symbolized, between inner experience and social role (Stein 1986).

Bion (1962) emphasizes that projective identification is not only a *defense* mechanism, but is also a mode of *communication* with others. In particular, it functions as a means of communication "in learning from the patient what he [or she] cannot think consciously" (Boyer 1999: 8), a formulation that holds far more broadly in human affairs than psychoanalytic therapy. One can *feel* (sense) what another person cannot *say*.

Bion's formulation of group experience and understanding has methodological and theoretical implications about the "site" of dreams, pathology, enactments, and the unconscious, and of how they function. In their exploration of "social dreaming," consultant-theorists Gordon Lawrence, David Armstrong, and others (Lawrence 1998a) extend the work of Bion in making sense of unconscious facets of workplace organizations. Just as Lawrence and his collaborators build explicitly on Bion's foundation, they also build implicitly on Freud's notion (1921) that all individual psychology is ultimately group psychology, since there is no human organism without a family (La Barre 1954).

Lawrence, for instance, writes, "there are dreams in search of dreamer" (1998b: 8). He hypothesizes that in social dreaming, "the dream [belongs] to the matrix and not the individual" (8). David Armstrong likewise envisages "the sense of the dream as 'Other': a kind of visitation, something wider than a personal construct, which is giving voice to an experience that is not of oneself alone" (1998: xx). Further, "there is no privileged location for emotional experience: it is not always and perhaps not ever the property of the individual alone" (xx).

Lawrence writes that "social dreaming does not question the use and value of dreams in the classic, psychoanalytic tradition but, like Bion's work on groups, affirms that dreams have also a social dimension, though there needs to be a dreamer to give expression to them" (1998c: 125). Finally, W. Gordon Lawrence, Marc Maltz, and E. Martin Walker suggest that "there is ample evidence that dreams are not solely the property of the dreamer but belong to the greater context of which the dreamer is a part—the place that the dreamer holds in her or his daily life and personal and work roles" (1998: 180). The first step in knowing this is to awaken from one's *organizationally and culturally obligatory dream and its dreaming* (La Barre 1972).

Awakening from the dream of workplace life is part of understanding what and whose it is. Under the spell of projective identification (that is, unconscious embodiment), even to awaken is forbidden. I dream a dream that is and was not entirely my own—but is an obligatory dream I am expected to mistake and act upon as exclusively my own. In coming to my own senses (to borrow from Paul Stoller) in ethnographic studies, organizational and otherwise, I first allow myself to have the dream—to allow it to be put into me and to contain it. Then I awaken from it to understand it and to use it in my—and our—work. This is the same process that Ogden (1989, 1997a & b) and Boyer (1999) describe for their use of "reverie" in individual psychoanalysis. In the following section I illustrate this often intensely disturbing process.

VIGNETTE: A DISTURBANCE OF MEMORY

From Sigmund Freud (1936) to Thomas Ogden (1989, 1997a &b), many psychoanalysts have examined their pathologies as conduits to insight. *The pathology of the self-observant observer becomes as much a "royal road" to the unconscious as is the dream of the patient* (Erikson 1964). In this section, I offer an incident from my own pathography as a signifier of cultural, not merely personal, psychodynamics. I describe the experience of my own derealization (the making of reality unreal). This vignette illustrates the methodological theme of this chapter: the interior experience of a culture (organization) on the part of worker, consultant, and observer alike provides a crucial guide to that organization or culture "itself."

Stated differently, what might appear (from the outside) to be the writer's self-indulgent "self-involvement" turns out to be self-involvement *for* a research purpose. The "self" of the observer or consultant is part of the (external) subject of research. Thus understood, the researcher is *obligated* ethically and substantively to talk about himself or herself as part of the organizational or cultural material. Exploration of the self by the observer or consultant is part of the way one can understand the darkness of workplace life. One comprehends the darkness via immersion in it and by examining its reverberations within the observer's own self.

In March 1998, I was typing a reference list for the bibliography of a manuscript I was completing. An early entry in the alphabet was *The HUMAN Cost of a Management Failure: Organizational Downsizing at General Hospital* (1996). It was coauthored by four people. I could only remember three: Seth Allcorn, Howell Baum, and Michael Diamond. As I typed, I felt a dreadful panic. I was flooded with terror. I felt as if I were going to die immediately. The feeling was dire. "Emotional" was entirely "physical." I turned quickly from my computer, and without consciously thinking, I picked up the telephone and called Michael Diamond, a fellow organizational consultant, a psychoanalytically-oriented theorist, and dear friend. He quickly completed the reference. I was the "missing" fourth author whom I could not remember. I had disappeared to myself. Out of breath, I asked him to help me understand what was happening.

I felt confused, "crazy." What Michael Diamond and I pieced together was that my temporary lapse of memory (a parapraxis of derealization) coincided with the intolerable realization (1) that I was already, in fact, dead, at least symbolically; (2) that my experiences with several near-firings and constant job self-reinventions and justifications of my own in recent years did indeed feel like constant death-in-life; and (3) that I felt at some level, or in some part of myself, I had already disappeared. I was already dead, missing—even to myself.

At another level, in response to living and working at the brink of being dead, I made myself dead, killed myself off, first. At least I would be in control of the fatal moment and of the final deed. At least in that last act, I would destroy myself. I would perform the execution. I would master the terror of passive victimization by actively becoming the aggressor against myself (Freud 1920). I would turn years of harassment and private Jew-baiting upon myself.

In my own symbolic action, I fulfilled—embodied—an organizational wish: to make disappear, to kill off, an entire way of thinking and working, and to replace it with one that negated it (Erikson 1968). My individual, personal symptom consisted also of the institution-in-me. I was its container, the embodiment of intolerable wishes, fantasies, and defenses. I became the battleground of metaphorical Nazi and Jew. My symbolic death would kill off intolerable organizational thought about the experience of workplace life.

Whatever else my symptom discloses, it *also* discloses the process by which projective and introjective identification operates. Organizational deadening "lived" in me as a "foreign body" I could neither keep nor rid myself of.

In my daily work as clinical teacher, group process facilitator (seminar leader for groups based on the work of Michael Balint), internal consultant, and organizational consultant, I frequently serve as temporary "container" (Bion 1959, 1962) and "holding environment" (Winnicott 1958, 1965) for others' fantasies, wishes, hatreds, and ambivalence—which we together attempt to understand. In this episode, however, I suddenly could not contain *myself*—which included everything and everyone I housed. I felt myself dissipating, disintegrating, falling apart (Ogden 1989). I could not contain alone within myself my dread, my horror of being a living death. With no forethought as to whom I should call, I knew that I needed to talk with Michael Diamond, to be *contained* by him—by my conversation with him—in order to get my own self and skin back, and thereby to understand the "social" dream of which I was the dreamer.

I realized at that moment that, though I had long continued to "function" (work) effectively and to "produce" abundantly in my workplace, a core and split off part of me had disappeared in the relentless onslaught of close calls with termination, marginalization, and a constant questioning of my value to the organization. I also came to realize that enactment is often an essential part to insight (as precursor), and how insight is often achieved intersubjectively. We not only *contain* or house one another, but we also help one another to become more *complete*, more whole, more integrated (Searles 1975, Boyer 1999).

My phone conversation with Michael Diamond (an emergency consultation) convinced me, now as before, how powerful—often frighteningly so—an instrument of understanding our own unconscious responses are. This episode gave me unwelcome access to the interior experience of what researchers and consultants, including I, study mostly in other people: downsizing, reengineering, restructuring, outsourcing, surplusing, deskilling, and similar contemporary business strategies.

"Who, then, is this Stein?" I ask myself ("I" to "me") in the objectivized third person, as ethnographic specimen and social cynosure (La Barre 1946) in the drama I describe, and of which I am also a cultural part. "Who is Stein?" turns out to be the same question as "Who is a worker-manager-executive?" As a metaphor, the purpose of "Stein" is to make the known both thought and unthought: that is, a compromise formation. It is to allow thoughts to exist with no thinker but "Stein." Projectively, "Stein" replaces thought. "Stein" embodies the social dream.

At a symbolic level, "Stein" is a personification of what the Nazis saw in "Der Jude" (*the* Jew as abstraction, a reification, a social cynosure [La

Barre 1946]). In the cataclysmic world of downsizing and managed care, where everyone is a potentially symbolic "Jew" destined for annihilation, everyone is likewise a potential symbolic "Stein." That dim realization is the point from which others in the workplace flee into dogmatic not-knowing. To share a common fate with "Stein" would be the ultimate insult and danger. It would be to become consciously identified as a metaphoric Jew. It would place others squarely in the experience of psychotic anxiety. The creation of symbolic social distance creates the illusion of safety.

Many colleagues' conscious differentiation from "Stein" is a sustained emergency defense that disavows the unconscious recognition of affective kinship. The conscious recognition that "we all are potentially (metaphorical) Jews" is replaced with the dream of "Stein-the-Jew." Projectively, "Stein" cannot be a person, so long as he is required to be a living metaphor, a personification of group disavowal: that is, so long as his identity is, *via projective identification, an embodiment*. I cannot be a distinct subject ("I") if I must be only an object ("me," "him").

During the past decade, many colleagues and friends in organizations—educational, medical, corporate, and military—have given me accounts (stories, narratives) similar in spirit and form to my vignette. As workers, as administrators, and as executives they spoke of daily psychological brutality and brutalization in their workplaces—from mass dislocations such as firings to day-to-day intimidation and degradation. They spoke of inner and outer pressures to "forget" and "get on with work," and of the sudden eruption of memory and feeling when some later event (similar in form to the original) triggered the reawakening (see Freud 1900, "identity of perceptions").

Much of what they said—as ethnographic "informants," as "clients" in consultation, as university colleagues, as film crews while videotaping interviews with me—became my official data. Further, out of the blue, some people—strangers—sent e-mail letters and made long-distance telephone calls to me, saying that they had just read some paper of mine "on the Internet," or a certain book I wrote, and they thanked me for validating their horrific workplace experiences.

My own story is also cultural, organizational, data. It begins as something we label as "personal," "individual," and it ends as being a sample or microcosm of organizational and national culture. My "slip"—my frightening memory loss—was intersubjective. It was about me, my-self, and it was also about the workplace group (and its history) in me. My countertransference was also profoundly *cultural* knowledge. It instructed me about "otherness" as well as about "me." I learned about them via myself. My embodiment was a crucial way station toward cultural knowing. In a sense, "wearing my heart on my sleeve" was an early step in penetrating the heart of organizational darkness. At least in this carefully scrutinized instance, my "personality" was about our (including their) "culture," which was in turn about intersubjective psychodynamics. I shall return later to this methodological point.

Let me now put this vignette in more technical, theoretical terms. My case of "countertransference"-enactment (Hirsch 1996) was not entirely a personal "dream." It was also a specimen of what Lawrence terms "social dreaming at work" (Lawrence 1998a). It was others' dream-in-me (a presence I had introjected). It offered vital organizational and broader cultural knowledge. My fantasized deed was their "unthought known" (Bollas 1989). It could only be (recurrently) known in (my) action. With the self-confidence of a repetition compulsion, I had enacted toward my-self (introjected) the projective identification with which I had been targeted. Doing (action) and feeling (emotion, affect) are often a way station to knowing. I shall return to this point later.

Organizational (cultural) scapegoating is one manifestation of embodiment and disembodiment, which are in turn about the languages and processes of inclusion, exclusion, and expulsion (De Vos 1980) and their projective/introjective equivalents. To further complicate methodological issues of organizational ethnographic validation, I was the only one who could "prove" that what I sensed was in fact taking place, because it could not be thought, let alone spoken. When I would try, even tactfully, to inquire into terrifying facets of organizational life that I experienced, many colleagues took offense; they thought I was crazy, or at least profoundly mistaken. They felt angry, hurt, misunderstood. How could I think these things of them? Are we not colleagues who work side by side—sometimes for years—in conferences, in clinics, in classrooms, in committees? How could I think that they somehow imagined me to be two dissociated beings, one ordinary, the other sinister, malevolent, dead (Lifton 1986)? Yet I did. I felt as if I had been split, as if one, then another, of these two were being "addressed." Both of these were supposed to be "me," but both felt equally unreal.

To be organizationally (culturally) acceptable, I had to radically mistrust myself, my senses. My madness was the price of their stability. Only lately have I learned to trust my countertransference as virtually my only reliable form of reality testing under these circumstances. Countertransference became a vital bridge to (disavowed) social reality, and thus to social theory (Stein 1994, 1998; Allcorn, Baum, Diamond, and Stein 1996). My countertransference reactions led me to "use" the metaphor of the Holocaust as a way to describe and comprehend the violence done to workers in contemporary America.

By listening via my own unconscious, I can comprehend and hold on to others' projection of Holocaust imagery and experience onto contemporary workplace cataclysm. To draw upon Stoller (1989) and Berman (1998), I can *sense* the presence of a "total institution" (Goffman 1961;

Rosenhan 1973) through its work. My countertransference is essential to hearing and validating their transference to the workplace and to me.

There is a more general methodological point about organizational understanding to be drawn from this. In their seminal work, George Lakoff and Mark Johnson (1980) discussed the "metaphors we live by." If I may borrow their metaphor, observer countertransference directs us to explore both the metaphors we distort and comprehend by. The Holocaust is—whatever else it might also be—my own metaphor, one that stems from my emotional reactions. Other observers, if tuned-in to their own emotional reactions to fieldwork or to "applied" situations, might have other equally apt metaphors to characterize the brutalization of American workers, or whatever group or subject they are studying. For instance, another consultant, who is an American veteran of the war in Vietnam, points out that people are often seen as "gooks" in the American workplace. In contemporary corporate culture, as in Vietnam during the 1960s and 1970s, it is almost impossible to know if some people are friend or foe, enemy or ally (Seth Allcorn, personal communication, 1998).

The point here is not the Holocaust metaphor per se, but its mental function in bridging observer and observed. The metaphor occupies a transitional space between self and other, between not-knowing and knowing (Winnicott 1965).

COUNTERTRANSFERENCE, TEXT, TEXTUALITY, AUTHORSHIP, AND IDENTITY: WHO ARE WE TALKING ABOUT?

I have come to believe that the exploration of countertransference while "in the field," ethnographically or as an organizational consultant, can offer insights into core issues in organizational understanding and far wider: for instance, the nature of selfhood, aggression, culture, and adaptation (and the relation between them), to mention only four. That is, one can study these *in the light of* countertransference to deepen what one learns by other, more established methods.

This chapter has methodological implications that reach beyond the contemporary U.S.A. They concern the issue of "the interpretation of cultures" (Geertz 1973), the nature of cultural knowledge, local and beyond (Geertz 2000), and the question of linking individual and large group (from workplace to nation-state). They address issues that "culture and personality" and "national character" studies less than persuasively attempted to resolve—yet which persist even after their schools have been abandoned. If culture is not "personality writ large," what links the layers of, say, a person, workplace organization, national culture, and even beyond?

A datum about the observer's self, derived from the observer's unconscious, *might be* a datum about the *implicit culture* of those under study or those requesting organizational consultation. This is not to leap to the culture-and-personality or national-character conclusion that culture is simply personality writ large. Rather, the link between individual psyche and large group process (conscious and unconscious), symbolism, and act is complex. What links the layers or levels and is not an artifact of the interpreter's slippage between them?

If a datum about individual "personality" is not automatically generalizable into a datum about "culture" or "organization," I am arguing nonetheless that a datum from the observer's countertransference, adequately inspected and calibrated against data from other sources, can be interpreted *also* as a datum about the organization or larger culture under study. Dundes (1984), for instance, recognized the presence of hostility and anality in a large collection of German folktales, from which he reconstructed, in turn, their central role in parent-child, individual unconscious, and cultural symbolic structure.

To my pleasant surprise, many of "my" poems about Euro-American Great Plains culture—wheat and cattle farming, family life, illness and medical treatment, landscape, and religion (Stein 1996, 1997, 2000)—have been recognized by prairie friends and colleagues as accurately evoking and validating "their" culture. People native to this region thank me, often with both gratitude and astonishment: "How could you know us so well when you're not even from here?" To whose culture(s), then, do "my" poems belong? Who, exactly, *embodies* the culture I attempt to portray in my poems? Whatever else my Great Plains associates and I are doing, are we not *also* engaging in creative, reciprocal projective and introjective identification, an ingredient in empathy and recognition, as well as in control and destruction? It would appear that at least sometimes the Geertzian "text" of "local knowledge" can be supplied by the ethnographer (or applied anthropologist) as well as by the "native" group member. If we look over natives' shoulders at their texts, we also do much more. Even "text"—organizational, ethnic—is an intersubjective project.

The relationship between ethnographer and Other becomes transformed into the observer's unconscious "subtext" (to continue the metaphor) that can be a useful tool for illumining and interpreting the manifest text of the Other under study—provided that the observer also studies oneself in the process of observation. One may thus carefully negotiate both between the layers of culture and between the boundaries between the cultures of the observer and the Other. Knowing via the senses is especially powerful when it takes the observer by surprise if not by ambush. It is not so much a matter of generalization as it is one of intense *aperçu*. One knows not with disembodied thought, but with one's entire body—one's whole being. Further, one may study the anthropology of emotion (Jenkins 1994) via observer countertransference, that is, via the emotional response of the observer to the Other (Devereux 1967) in workplace organizations and beyond.

I admit that the fact of countertransference further complicates the issue of perception, inference, interpretation, and generalization in fieldwork. Text, textuality, and even authorship come to be intersubjective projects—and much of that subjectivity is out of conscious awareness and control. When we go to the field, whose "data" are we collecting? Whose text is text in "local knowledge"? Others'—but others' through our own. What we might label as "our own" data can tell us about others. If we sometimes know others' metaphors *despite* our own, we sometimes know them *through* our own. This chapter is a study principally in the latter.

CONCLUSIONS AND IMPLICATIONS: COUNTERTRANSFERENCE AS METHOD IN ORGANIZATIONAL STUDIES

In this chapter, I have argued that, as organizational and wider cultural observers and consultants, countertransference can prevent us from seeing, help us to see, help us to bear what we see, and help us to understand what we see. I have discussed how countertransference is a very part of "gathering" and making interpretive, theoretical sense of the data. Countertransference is another name for "sensing" and making use of that sensing. Under some circumstances, countertransference is a vital tool for restoring to sensibility what has been driven into insensitivity. In the idiom of the widespread cultural distinction between "hard" and "soft" science, observer and consultant countertransference, which on the surface seems invisibly soft, turns out to be implacably hard. Upon its workings rests what we can bear to know, and what we cannot.

At the level of *content*, this chapter has presented a study in core institutional processes in contemporary American society. At the level of *process*, this chapter has studied how one goes about learning—which is to say first emotionally bearing—the macabre beneath its thick veils. The link between knowing and known is the knower: here, to be able to contain—first to embody, then to work through the embodiment—the atrocity and terror behind the smokescreen of euphemism. I have learned more about selfhood and otherness than I bargained for: otherness contaminated with disavowed parts of self is no distinct other. It is an embodiment of disembodiments; a personification (embodiment of projective identification), not a person; an "it," not a "Thou" (Buber 1958).

Today, the workplace (one "corporate" business unit or another) now vies with, if not supersedes, the nation-state as the unit of ultimate dependency and vulnerability, an "omnipotent symbolic object" in the internal and intersubjective worlds. In business logic as in nationalist doctrine, individual lives are sacrificed (and expendable) for the sake of the vitality and symbolic immortality of the corporate social unit. Economics is the medium and language of the sacrifice. Economics is often rationale for political terror. I think again of Arthur Koestler's 1941 novel, *Darkness at Noon*, and of the source of his title, a line from John Milton's "Samson Agonistes": "Oh dark, dark, dark, amid the blaze of noon." But now the blindness, self-inflicted, is our own.

My—and others'—countertransference experience of organizational terror and atrocity can clarify prevailing social theory. Consider but one example: the issue of naming or labeling. From labeling theory and its understanding of stigma (Goffman 1963; Rosenhan 1973), we know how destructive impressed names and labels can be. They can be used to foreclose knowing, to distract attention from deeper, more painful knowing (Laub and Podell 1997). They, too, are part of the dance of projective and introjective identification, and in turn, of embodiment. To diagnose, Devereux argued (1980), is not merely to name, but to distinguish the diagnoser from the diagnosed, not only to make the diagnosis. It is for the clinician, for instance, to say: "You are the one who is sick, or polluted, not I." In this facet at least, diagnosis is a projection-driven ritual of self-reassurance—and, by extension, a reassurance to all those others who identify themselves as culturally healthy, clean, or good. Diagnosis is an arm of dominion and control.

Less explored is the crucial role of naming—of the ability to symbolize—as a means of reclaiming the real from the secret, the real self from the dominion of the false self (Winnicott 1965). Naming can serve the process of destigmatizing, at least to a degree. Diagnosis, naming, can also serve the purpose of *declining and withdrawing from projections*. It can be an act of differentiation and integration, a boundary-defining and -establishing event that attempts to halt boundary violation. It can be a way of saying, simply, to oneself: "This, I know." In an essay on trauma and therapy of American soldiers who survived combat in Vietnam, Chaim Shatan (1997: 220–221) quotes Adrienne Rich on entrapment by the unnamed and unnamable:

Whatever is unnamed, undepicted in images, . . . omitted from biography, censored in . . . letters, . . . mis-named as something else, made difficult-to-come-by, whatever is buried in the memory by the collapse of meaning under an inadequate or lying language—this will become, not merely unspoken, but unspeakable.

Countertransference becomes the foundation for this emancipation of words (and worlds) from worldviews. Countertransference becomes a potentially powerful tool of consultation—and in turn of organizational self-liberation. Access to feelings here includes the ability to harness one's paranoia for methodological purposes (an idea I owe to Thomas Csordas, 23 September 1999, personal communication). The observer's and consultant's openness to the uncanny allows the experience of intense fear, anxiety, and threat to become part of the data that are "gathered." The prize, as it were, for the effort is finding words that correspond to one's own genuine feelings generated in and by the field.

Workplace organizations—no less than the ethnic, national, or multinational organizations of which they are a part—can become ruled by the prohibition of the creative making of meaning and its substitution by enforced meanings surrounded by walls of enforced silence. Self, countertransferentially understood, is intimately connected to the capacity for culture creation and adaptation, and for the breaking of inwardly-as-well-as-outwardly-enforced silence. Cultures—our own included—can learn only if their members can have the heart (the courage) to admit they are wrong. The study of countertransference is part of that cultural awakening.

In the following chapter, the observer and consultant's "subjectivity" is used as a tool in understanding downsizing, reengineering, restructuring, managed health care, and other forms of managed social change.

REFERENCES

Adams, Guy B., and Danny L. Balfour. 1998. *Unmasking Administrative Evil*. Thousand Oaks, CA: Sage.

Adams, Scott. 1996. *The DILBERT Principle: A Cubicle-Eye's View of Bosses, Meetings, Management Fads and Other Workplace Afflictions*. New York: HarperBusiness (HarperCollins).

Allcorn, Seth. 1998. "Foreword," in Howard F. Stein, *Euphemism, Spin, and the Crisis in Organizational Life*. Westport, CT: Quorum Books. Pp. ix–xiv.

Allcorn, Seth, Howell S. Baum, Michael A. Diamond, and Howard F. Stein. 1996. *The HUMAN Cost of a Management Failure: Organizational Downsizing at General Hospital*. Westport, CT: Quorum Books.

Apprey, Maurice, and Howard F. Stein. 1993. *Intersubjectivity, Projective Identification and Otherness*. Pittsburgh: Duquesne University Press.

Armstrong, David. 1998. "Introduction," in W. Gordon Lawrence, ed., *Social Dreaming at Work*. London: Karnak. Pp. xvii–xxi.

Barondess, Jeremiah H. 1998. "Care of the Medical Ethos: Reflections on Social Darwinism, Racial Hygiene, and the Holocaust," *Annals of Internal Medicine* 129: 891–898.

Berman, Morris. 1981. *The Reenchantment of the World*. Ithaca, NY: Cornell University Press.

―――. 1998. *Coming to Our Senses. Body and Spirit in the Hidden History of the West*. Seattle: Writers Guild.

Bion, Wilfred R. 1959. *Experiences in Groups*. New York: Basic Books.

―――. 1962. *Learning from Experience*. New York: Basic Books.

Bock, Philip. 1998. Personal communication.

Bollas, Christopher. 1989. *In the Shadow of the Object: Psychoanalysis of the Unthought Known*. New York: Columbia University Press.

Bourdieu, Pierre. 1993. *Language and Symbolic Power*. Cambridge: Harvard University Press.

Boyer, L. Bryce. 1993. "Countertransference: Brief History and Clinical Issues," in L. B. Boyer and P. L. Giovacchini, eds., *Master Clinicians on Treating Regressed Patients*. Volume 2. Northvale, NJ: Jason Aronson, Pp. 1–24.

―――. 1999. *Countertransference and Regression*. Northvale, NJ: Jason Aronson.

Buber, Martin. 1958. *I and Thou*. Revised edition. Ronald Gregor Smith, translator. New York: Scribner's Sons (orig. 1925).

Bursztajn, Harold J. 1997. "Medical Historical Perspectives Regarding Managed Care and Medical Necessity: True and False," paper presented at the American Psychiatric Association Annual Meeting, Symposium on Ethical Issues in Managed Health Care, San Diego, 19 May.

Bursztajn H. J., T. G. Gutheil, and A. Brodsky. 1998. "Ethics and the Triage Model in Managed Care Hospital Psychiatry," *Psychiatric Times* 15(9): 33–38.

Coleman, Jules V. 1968. "Aims and Conduct of Psychotherapy," *Archives of General Psychiatry* 18 (January): 1–6.

Csordas, Thomas. 1994. *Embodiment and Experience: The Existential Ground of Culture and Self*. Cambridge: Cambridge University Press.

Davidson, Ronald H. 1986. "Transference and Countertransference Phenomena: The Problem of the Observer in the Behavioral Sciences," *Journal of Psychoanalytic Anthropology* 9(3), Summer: 269–283.

Devereux, George. 1955. "Charismatic Leadership and Crisis," in Gézà Róheim, ed., *Psychoanalysis and the Social Sciences*. New York: International Universities Press. Pp. 145–157.

―――. 1967. *From Anxiety to Method in the Behavioral Sciences*. The Hague: Mouton.

―――. 1980. *Basic Problems of Ethno-Psychiatry*. Chicago: University of Chicago Press.

DeVos, George A. 1980. "Ethnic Adaptation and Minority Status," *Journal of Cross-Cultural Psychology* 11(1) March: 101–124.

Dundes, Alan. 1984. *Life Is Like a Chicken Coop Ladder: A Portrait of German Culture Through Folklore*. New York: Columbia University Press.

Ebel, Henry. 1999. Personal communication, letter, 16 May. Quoted with permission.

Erikson, Erik H. 1959. *Identity and the Life Cycle: Selected Essays*. New York: International Universities Press.

―――. 1963. *Childhood and Society*. Second, revised edition. New York: Norton.

―――. 1964. *Insight and Responsibility*. New York: Norton.

―――. 1968. *Identity: Youth and Crisis*. New York: Norton.

Freud, Anna. 1936. *The Ego and the Mechanisms of Defense*. New York: International Universities Press.

Freud, Sigmund. 1900. "The Interpretation of Dreams," in *The Standard Edition of the Complete Psychological Works of Sigmund Freud*. Volumes 4–5. London: Hogarth Press, 1953. Pp. 1–627.

———. "The Future Prospects of Psycho-analytic Training," in *The Standard Edition of the Complete Psychological Works of Sigmund Freud*. Volume 11 James Strachey, trans. London: Hogarth Press. Pp. 139–152.

———. 1912. "Recommendations to Physicians Practicing Psycho-analysis," in *The Standard Edition of the Complete Psychological Works of Sigmund Freud*. Volume 14. London: Hogarth Press. Pp. 109–120.

———. 1914. "Remembering, Repeating and Working Through," *The Standard Edition of the Complete Psychological Works of Sigmund Freud*. Volume 12. London: Hogarth Press. Pp. 147–156.

———. 1920 (1955). "Beyond the Pleasure Principle," *The Standard Edition of the Complete Psychological Works of Sigmund Freud*. Volume 18. London: Hogarth Press. Pp. 7–64.

———. 1921 (1955). "Group Psychology and the Analysis of the Ego," *The Standard Edition of the Complete Psychological Works of Sigmund Freud*. Volume 18. London: Hogarth Press. Pp. 69–143.

———. 1936 (1964). "A Disturbance of Memory on the Acropolis," *The Standard Edition of the Complete Psychological Works of Sigmund Freud*. Volume 22. London: Hogarth Press. Pp. 239–250.

Freud, Sigmund, and D. E. Oppenheim. 1911. *Dreams in Folklore*. New York: International Universities Press, 1958.

Gay, Peter. 1998. "My German Question," *The American Scholar* (Autumn): 25–49.

Geertz, Clifford. 1973. *The Interpretation of Cultures*. New York: Basic Books.

———. 2000. "From the Native's Point of View: On the Nature of Anthropological Understanding," in *Local Knowledge: Further Essays in Interpretive Anthropology*. New York: Basic Books (1983). Pp. 55–70.

Goffman, Erving 1961. *Asylums*. Garden City, NY: Anchor.

———. 1963. *Stigma: Notes on the Management of Spoiled Identity*. Englewood Cliffs, NJ: Prentice-Hall.

Hall, Edward T. 1977. *Beyond Culture*. New York: Anchor Books/Doubleday.

Hirsch, Irwin. 1996. "Observing Participation, Mutual Enactment, and the New Classical Models," *Contemporary Psychoanalysis* 32: 359–383.

Hollander, Nancy Caro. 1999. "Inner Persecution and Outer Reality: The Individual and the Transitional Space of Authoritarian Society," *Mind and Human Interaction* 10(2), Fall: 98–109. Special issue on Hypernationalism and Xenophobia.

Jenkins, Janis H. 1994. "Culture, Emotion, and Psychopathology," in Shinobu Kitayama and Hazel Rose Markus, eds., *Emotion and Culture: Empirical Studies of Mutual Influence*. Washington, DC: American Anthropological Association. Pp. 309–335.

Klein, Melanie. 1946. "Notes on Some Schizoid Mechanisms," *International Journal of Psycho-Analysis* 27: 99–110.

———. 1955. "On Identification," in Melanie Klein, Paula Heimann, and Roger Money-Kyrle, eds., *New Directions in Psycho-Analysis*. New York: Basic Books. Pp. 309–345.

Koestler, Arthur. 1941. *Darkness at Noon*. New York: New American Library, 1961.

La Barre, Weston. 1946. "Social Cynosure and Social Structure," *Journal of Personality* 14: 169–183.

———. 1954. *The Human Animal*. Chicago: University of Chicago Press.

———. 1972. *The Ghost Dance: The Origins of Religion*. New York: Dell.

———. 1978. "The Clinic and the Field," in George D. Spindler, ed., *The Making of Psychological Anthropology*. Berkeley: University of California Press. Pp. 258–299.

Lakoff, George, and Mark Johnson. 1980. *Metaphors We Live By*. Chicago: University of Chicago Press.

Lamphere, Louise. 1987. *From Working Daughters to Working Mothers: Immigrant Women in a New England Community*. Ithaca, NY: Cornell University Press.

Laub, Dori, and Daniel Podell. 1997. "Psychoanalytic Listening to Historical Trauma: The Conflict of Knowing and the Imperative to Act," *Mind and Human Interaction* 8(4) Winter: 245–260.

Lawrence, W. Gordon. 1997. Centering of the Sphinx for the Psychoanalytic Study of Organizations, 1997 Symposium, International Society for the Psychoanalytic Study of Organizations, Philadelphia, June.

———. 1998a. *Social Dreaming at Work*. W. Gordon Lawrence, ed. London: Karnac Books. Pp. 169–181.

———. 1998b. "Prologue," in W. Gordon Lawrence, ed., *Social Dreaming at Work*. London: Karnac Books. Pp. 1–8.

———. 1998c. "Social Dreaming as a Tool of Consultancy and Action Research," in W. Gordon Lawrence, ed., *Social Dreaming at Work*. London: Karnac Books. Pp. 123–140.

———. 1999. Thinking as Refracted in Organizations—The Finite and the Infinite/the Conscious and the Unconscious, Plenary paper presented at the 1999 Symposium of the International Society for the Psychoanalytic Study of Organizations, Toronto, Canada, 25 June.

Lawrence, W. Gordon, Marc Maltz, and E. Martin Walker. 1998. "Social Dreaming at Work" (concluding chapter), in W. Gordon Lawrence, ed., *Social Dreaming at Work*. London: Karnac Books. Pp. 169–181.

Levi, Primo. 1988. *The Drowned and the Saved*. New York: Summit Books.

Li, James T. C. 1996. "The Physician-Patient Relationship: Covenant or Contract?" *Mayo Clinic Proceedings* 71: 917–918.

Lifton, Robert Jay. 1986. *The Nazi Doctors*. New York: Basic Books.

———. 2000. Interview: "The Advocacy and Detachment of Robert Jay Lifton," *Best of Clio's Psyche, 1994–1999*, Millennial edition. Franklin Lakes, NJ. Pp. 20–21.

Lotto, David J. 1998. "The Corporate Takeover of the Soul: The Current State of the American Health Care System," *Journal of Psychohistory* 26(2), Fall: 603–609.

Melville, Herman. 1851. *Moby Dick, or the White Whale*. New York: New American Library, 1961.

Modell, Arnold H. 1984. *Psychoanalysis in a New Context*. New York: International Universities Press.

Morrow, Lance. 1993. "The Temping of America" [temporary employment], *Time*, 29 March. Pp. 40–47.

Ogden, Thomas. 1989. *The Primitive Edge of Experience*. Northvale, NJ: Jason Aronson.

———. 1997a. "Reverie and Interpretation," *Psychoanalytic Quarterly* 66: 567–595.

———. 1997b. "Reverie and Metaphor: Some Thoughts on How I Work as a Psychoanalyst," *International Journal of Psycho-Analysis* 78: 719–732.

Pascal, Blaise. 1670. *Pensées*. Section 4, Number 227. Wheaton, IL: Christian Classics Ethereal Library, 1999.

Paul, Robert A. 1987. "The Question of Applied Psychoanalysis and the Interpretation of Cultural Symbolism," *Ethos* 15(1), March: 82–103.

Racker, Enrique. 1968. *Transference and Countertransference*. New York: International Universities Press.

Rosenhan, David L. 1973. "On Being Sane in Insane Places," *Science* 179(20), 19 January: 250–258.

Sander, Fred M. 1979. *Individual and Family Therapy: Toward an Integration*. New York: Jason Aronson.

Searles, Harold F. 1975. "The Patient as Therapist to His Analyst," in Peter L. Giovacchini, ed., *Tactics and Techniques in Psychoanalytic Therapy, Volume 2, Countertransference*. New York: Jason Aronson. Pp. 99–151.

Shatan, Chaim. 1997. "Living in a Split Zone: Trauma and Therapy of Vietnam Combat Survivors," *Mind and Human Interaction* 8(4), Winter: 204–222.

Shore, Karen. 1998a. "Don't Let Them Take Your Mind and Spirit: On Being Called a 'Provider,' " Inter-Divisional Mid-Winter Conference, February 1998, Division 42: 1997 Distinguished Psychologist of the Year, Acceptance Speech at Awards Reception, La Jolla, California.

———. 1998b. "A Death Knell for Clinical Psychologists as Psychotherapists," National Coalition of Mental Health Professionals and Consumers, Inc. www.nomanagedcare.org/Knell.html.

———. 1999. "The Need to Replace Managed Care with a Better System of Health Insurance and Health Care Delivery," Speech to Wurzweiler School of Social Work, Yeshiva University, New York City, Doctoral Program Conference, 7 May.

Sievers, Burkard. 1994. *Work, Death, and Life Itself: Essays on Management and Organization*. New York and Berlin: Walter de Gruyter.

Spiro, Melford. 1979. "Whatever Happened to the Id?" *American Anthropologist* 81(1): 5–13.

Stein, Howard F. 1974. "Envy and the Evil Eye Among Slovak-Americans: An Exploration into the Psychological Ontogeny of Belief and Ritual," *Ethos* 2(1), Spring: 15–46.

———. 1985. "Psychological Complementarity in Soviet-American Relations," *Political Psychology* 6(2): 249–261.

———. 1986. "Social Role and Unconscious Complementarity," *Journal of Psychoanalytic Anthropology* 9(3), Summer: 235–268.

———. 1994. *Listening Deeply: An Approach to Understanding and Consulting in Organizational Culture*. Boulder, CO: Westview Press.

———. 1996. *Prairie Voices: Process Anthropology in Family Medicine*. Westport, CT: Bergin and Garvey.

———. 1997. *Evocations*. Pittsburgh: Dorrance Publishing Company.

———. 1998a. *Euphemism, Spin, and the Crisis in Organizational Life*. Westport, CT: Quorum Books.

———. 1998b. "Organizational Euphemism and the Cultural Mystification of Evil," *Administrative Theory and Praxis* 20(3), September: 346–357.

———. 2000. *Learning Pieces*. Foreword by Dr. Warren Lee Holleman. Pittsburgh: Dorrance.

Stern, Donnel B. 1997. *Unformulated Experience: From Dissociation to Imagination in Psychoanalysis*. Mahwah, NJ: Analytic Press.

Stoller, Paul. 1989. *The Taste of Ethnographic Things: The Senses in Anthropology*. Philadelphia: University of Pennsylvania Press.

———. 1997. *Sensuous Scholarship*. Philadelphia: University of Pennsylvania Press.

Streeck-Fischer, Annette. 1999. "Naziskins in Germany: How Traumatization Deals with the Past," *Mind and Human Interaction* 10(2), Fall: 84–97, special issue on Hypernationalism and Xenophobia.

Suarez-Orozco, Marcelo M. 1990. "Speaking of the Unspeakable: Toward a Psychosocial Understanding of Responses to Terror," *Ethos* 18(3), September: 353–383.

Tansey, Michael J., and Walter F. Burke. 1989. *Understanding Countertransference: From Projective Identification to Empathy*. Hillsdale, NJ: Analytic Press.

Taussig, Michael. 1980. *The Devil and Commodity Fetishism in South America*. Chapel Hill: University of North Carolina Press.

Uchitelle, Louis, and N. R. Kleinfield. 1996. "On the Battlefields of Business, Millions of Casualties, The Downsizing of America: First of eleven articles," *New York Times* 145(50355), 3 March. Section A, pp. 1, 26–29.

Wallace, Anthony F. C. 1961. *Culture and Personality*. New York: Random House.

Winnicott, Donald W. 1958. *Collected Papers: Through Paediatrics to Psycho-Analysis*. New York: Basic Books.

———. 1965. *The Maturational Processes and the Facilitating Environment*. New York: International Universities Press.

Zinner, John and Roger L. Shapiro. 1972. "Projective Identification as a Mode of Perception and Behavior in Families of Adolescents," *International Journal of Psycho-Analysis* 53: 523–529.

3

Downsizing, Managed Care, and the Potlatching of the Workplace: A Study in Cultural Brutality and Its Mystification

Logic and sermons never convince,
The damp of the night drives deeper into my soul.
—Walt Whitman

INTRODUCTION

It does not require an anthropologist to say that, in workplace organizations as in much of the rest of life, things are not what they seem. Yet I shall be arguing precisely this point about many of the governing beliefs and practices about business. "Spin" is all, and there is no gyroscope to all the spinning. Darkness has become light, and light, darkness. The subject of this chapter is learning to see in the dark—that is, learning to see into culturally, organizationally, enforced darkness. The widespread slogan, "Nothing personal, just business," is at once deception and self-deception. Human life is of a single piece: even business is a deeply personal enterprise.

At a more abstract level, this chapter studies the psychological linkage between individual, workplace (group), culture, and history. It explores organizational change as a "window" on catastrophic change in larger social units such as ethnic group or nation. It examines the (1) general cultural forces in the United States through (2) the psychodynamics of downsizing and managed care, via (3) the process of projective identification.

Substantively, then, this chapter studies downsizing, managed care, and the potlatching of American society. That is, it attempts to understand our own cultural self-destructiveness. Potlatching, which originated among Native American groups on the northwest coast of Washington and British Columbia, can be understood to consist of the systematic destruction of a group's own "property" in order to humiliate a rival or competitor, and thereby to win the struggle for status. I use the image metaphorically with respect to workplace competition in American—and globalized—society. It builds on a longitudinal study of a hospital downsizing (Allcorn, Baum, Diamond, and Stein 1996), and on an exploration of the language of euphemism in the corporate construction of reality (Stein 1998a, 1998b) in the United States. It inquires into the shared delusion of cultural normality, one created, enforced, and perpetuated by the dialectic of projective and introjective identification. It interprets economic explanation as obligatory mystification of brutality.

Methodologically, it inquires into how one "knows" culture psychodynamically. It emphasizes the role of *countertransference* as the central organizing principle of all human knowing. Its net ranges from anthropology and astronomy, to organizational psychology and consulting, to zoology. The knower is part of the knowing, part of what is known and what must remain unknown. The knower is the best and worst and ultimately only instrument of knowing (La Barre 1972). This chapter thus continues the argument that method and substance are thereby inextricably linked.

In this chapter I will (1) explore how the general culture enacts projective identification (as is specifically manifest in downsizing and managed care), and (2) through two case examples, describe how culture analysts and critics can use their own countertransference to detect, understand, and intervene in organizational juggernauts. Downsizing and managed care will illustrate this process. With organizational data, I will show how projective identification "works" culturally, for both subject and target.

I argue that downsizing and managed care are only partly (at most) the result of independent economic exigencies, and are largely driven by anxieties, wishes, fantasies, and defenses that come to be codified and enforced in rationalist-economic ideology and social policy. I hope to make more transparent the often-opaque process of cultural mobilization and the language summoned in its service (e.g., survival, sacrifice, productivity, necessity, profit, greed). Finally, as an alternative to demonization of others, I address issues of engaging those who implement downsizing and managed care policy. In all these matters, the disciplined subjectivity of the cultural observer-interpreter will be shown to be a crucial—and the ultimate—tool of understanding (Devereux 1967).

COUNTERTRANSFERENCE AND CULTURAL KNOWING

At the epistemological level, at least, the common dichotomy between "natural" or "real" or "hard" and "social" or "soft" science is spurious. All knowledge is personal knowledge. *What* we know about anything is *how* we know it. The instrument of knowing is part of the knowledge. Self is part of method, is part of theory, is part of intervention. Methodology is an abstraction from the ability or inability to learn from experience (if I may borrow from W. R. Bion). Organizational learning and consulting are no different. The question everywhere is what we do with what and who we are—whether we have access to that often-troubling data or cannot bear the anxiety such access would visit upon us (Devereux 1967; Boyer 1993, 1999).

Since the outset of my professional life, I have explored the unconscious as well as the conscious significance of group affiliation or identity. In the late 1960s, I began my career as a medical anthropologist with a focus on understanding the effect of patients' *ethnicity* (often termed "nationality") on physician-patient relationships and on the course of clinical work. In the succeeding thirty years, my interest in *group* contributions to clinical dyads and their work has expanded to include workplace organizations and their cultures, ranging from professional disciplines (family medicine, occupational medicine, psychiatry, internal medicine) to institutional units (departments, hospitals, clinics).

Today, managed care, downsizing, RIFing (Reduction in Force), rightsizing, reengineering, restructuring, deskilling, outsourcing, flattening, reinventing, and autonomous functional teams are all as much "group" presences in the physician's crowded examination room as is the patient's Germanness, Polishness, Hispanicness, or African American-ness. Moreover, these terms or concepts are part of the wider national, even international, imagination that have burst the bounds of organizational units in the United States. Together, they constitute an *ideology* of what organizational life—and, by extension, human life, human meaning—is about. In them the social researcher and consultant have an abundant wealth of material for use in countertransference.

In this chapter, as with the previous one, I explore my own "subjective" experience—organization-related studies and poetry—in order to reach more "objective" insights about hatred, violence, and the dark side of workplace organizations. This chapter is part of a personal and professional journey toward seeing—feeling—what is "there" but is not supposed to be seen (Bollas's "unthought known," 1989). It draws on my experience as an employee and participant observer in workplace organizations, and as consultant to them.

The ultimate discourse (subject, topic) of this chapter, though, is not workplace organizations or mass society, but knowledge—knowing, not-knowing, resistance to knowing, and coming to know (Bion 1990; French and Simpson 1999). It is about what the poet John Keats described as cultivating the "negative capability": "when a man is capable of being in uncertainties, mysteries, doubts, without any irritable reaching after fact and reason" (1817/1974: 705). It is about what can and cannot be known, what may and may not be known, and what must and must not be known. It is ontology wrapped in epistemology, with psychoanalysis as Ariadne's thread through the labyrinth of wrappings. Its discourse is the question or riddle of the enigmatic Sphinx (Lawrence 1997): What is man/woman? For himself or herself and others? And how is knowing of any kind bound up with these relations?

The subject of this chapter is "countertransference" because this chapter centers on the nexus in which knowledge, knowing, knower, and the relationship among knowers takes place. It is an effort to map thought—to be a cartographer of mental space (Young 1994; Stein 1987; Stein and Niederland 1989). Toward this end, I present two vignettes or "case" illustrations that link individual experience, workplace group, and the larger dynamics of culture history. The first is from an organizational consultation. The second is a fortuitous conversation at an academic medical conference. Following the two vignettes, I discuss several core themes of which the vignettes are exemplars.

In these vignettes—as throughout my research on downsizing, re-engineering, managed care, and similar corporate doctrines (ideologies)—much of the imagery and language Americans have used to describe their experiences is drawn from the Holocaust (Stein 1997, 1998a, 1998b; Allcorn, Baum, Diamond, and Stein 1996). I have become persuaded that the psychological "use" or invocation of the Holocaust is not an attempt to co-opt or preempt the suffering of the Jews and other groups under Nazi domination. Rather, it is a struggle to find a symbol peaceful enough to make sense of, and give voice to, one's current suffering. Attention to the phenomenology of the experience—that is, taking seriously the words and their affect—convinces me over and again that we are witnessing atrocity rather than exaggeration.

FIRST VIGNETTE: THE EMPTIED OFFICE AND CULTURALLY PERSECUTORY SPACE

The following narrative comes from an early 1990s' consultation with a woman whom I shall call Betty, the Chief Financial Officer of a large computer software company. The narrative is assembled from notes I made during and after the consultation. It is slightly fictionalized to preserve the confidentiality of the person and the place. If one can "quantify" suffering, I would say that the client's story line was as difficult for me to hear as it was for her to speak. I had to fight my own wish to flee, my own derealization ("This kind of thing does not happen even when it does."). My countertransference told me about the speaker's cata-strophic, unassimilatable experience via my inner experience of her (Dev-ereux 1967).

The strangest thing happened last Monday, Howard. I was off sick Friday. I came in to work on Monday morning and the office next to me was cleared out. Desk, chair, computer, a couple of file cab-inets and book cases, wastebasket. And that's it. Empty. I still can't believe it, and it's already Friday. It's like there's a big hole in this place. I knew the guy ten years. He was one of our number crunch-ers. A quiet guy, just did his work. It seemed like he was always here, always working. He is a computer whiz anyone in the unit could go to for a computer glitch. We aren't—maybe I should say "weren't" since he's gone—weren't exactly friends, but we worked together a lot on projects. He was kind of part of the furniture.

It's so eerie, Howard. I'm numb over it. I keep going next door to look in his office expecting to see him. Maybe I'm imagining that he's gone, and he's not. But the place is so empty. I've heard of this kind of thing happening other places when people get RIFed. Here today, gone tomorrow. But I've not heard of this here. It's like he disappeared. Like he never was here. I'm not being sentimental about him.

He and I didn't have something going—if you're thinking that. I just can't believe they'd do it—and the way they did it. I asked around the firm, and everybody gave the same story. Because it wasn't just him. It happened all over the place, Howard. About five hundred people RIFed in one day.

At 9:00 A.M, Friday, security guards showed up all over the plant at the offices and workstations of people who were going to be fired. They escorted them to the big auditorium over in the cor-porate conference center. They didn't even tell them why they had to go, except that it was an important announcement. After they walked them in, they left and locked the doors behind them.

The way I heard it secondhand, the CEO then went in after every-body was there, delivered a little speech on how the company had to downsize radically in order to survive and be competitive. He told them not to take it personally, and thanked them for their service to the company.

The security police escorted them back to where they worked, helped them clear out their belongings, then took them down to administration to hand over all their keys and receive their last paycheck. The police walked them to their cars, and that's the last they saw of this place. They weren't to come back. Gone. Just like that. I suppose they couldn't be trusted not to sabotage the computers, or to steal equipment. I don't even want to think about the way it happened. It's like a roundup, Howard.

I asked around, and nobody knows where he went. No forwarding address or telephone number. It's weird. Like he just disappeared. You wonder if you're next. You try not to think of it. Work harder, maybe they'll keep you. It's ridiculous, because you know it's not true. But, Howard, you've got to believe that you're valuable to them.

This first vignette exemplifies many key themes in the psychodynamics of downsizing and its organizational cognate forms. The introjection of devastation, identification with the aggressor, and survivor guilt are common. The indigestible process—represented by the dramatic event—haunts the organization. For downsizers and downsized alike, persons become dehumanized into nonpersons in order for downsizing even to be thinkable. Close coworkers, colleagues, even friends, become labeled as "dead meat" or "excess fat" to be trimmed and cut off. (In Britain, the term "redundant" is widely used to refer to these employees.) Distancing from others implements and affirms one's inner splits. Via splitting and projective identification, the "bad" is expelled, evacuated to the outside in order to preserve the survival of the "good," the vulnerable inside of the organization. The ideology attempts to heal, to seal over the persecutory emptiness felt both intrapsychically and organizationally. Efforts are made to fill the haunting desolation. The vicious circle of psychopathology operates organizationally and culturally, as well as individually. Attempts to fend off annihilation anxiety only make it more real and menacing. My interviewee in the first vignette, Betty, was troubled because she experienced conflict. She did not fend off inner conflict through enactment in the outer world.

SECOND VIGNETTE: FROM PROJECTIVE IDENTIFICATION AND DISSOCIATION TO CULTURAL INSIGHT

In this next section, I describe a second event that became for me a kind of "seed crystal" in a supersaturated solution of "data." It was an intercultural, interdisciplinary moment. It provided the opportunity for the method of countertransference-based learning to take place in me with frightful clarity. To use a different metaphor, it was a moment of understanding that condensed—as in dream-work—many strands in my life and work.

I shall briefly set the stage for the vignette. The specific occasion was a seminar/workshop I conducted with nurses and nursing students in

1998. An invited speaker at a conference of nurses, I had just concluded a three-hour seminar/workshop on current social calamities such as managed care, downsizing, restructuring, reengineering, deskilling, and culture. I had argued for situating economic or business explanations within cultural ones (e.g., Allcorn et al. 1996; Bertman 1998; Lotto 1998), rather than placing medical economics as the "driving force" of all healthcare culture. I depicted the cultural destructiveness and self-destructiveness in these official business strategies. I explored the contrast between the official economic ideology of "the bottom line," and the commonplace experience of these catastrophic changes in the language of the Holocaust. One of my chief goals in the talk was to help prepare these practitioners for a "market" world in which holism was devalued. Many of the nurses, themselves veteran practitioners, told stories during the conference that corroborated my own observations, interview data, and material from workplace consultations.

The conference organizer, who had invited me to make the presentation, had known me for several years. A nurse-educator, she is a senior academic healthcare professional and administrator. Over several consecutive years, she had generously invited me to speak at nursing conferences that she had planned. The interdisciplinary facet of our relationship is that, despite the fact that we both are anthropologically trained, she is also a nurse (that is, a trained and licensed clinician) and I am not. Further, most of my clinical work is with physicians. She was familiar with a number of my publications. Prior to the conference, she had assigned to the participants the chapter on managed care in my recently published book, *Euphemism, Spin, and the Crisis in Organizational Life* (1998a). She had also read the book. Throughout my presentation, she seemed unusually quiet. Afterwards, when everyone else had left, she came to the front of the room, where we proceeded to talk for about a half-hour. Time stood still, as in a tomb.

Even before she spoke her first words, something about the situation felt eerie, ominous. She seemed sullen, somber, at a loss for words, as if she were transfixed, in a trance. She looked as if she were moving and speaking in slow motion. I felt as if I were an iron filing in the presence of a strong magnetic field. I felt overpowered, menaced. I felt in danger, that I had to resist—but resist what? (I must add the obvious point that this narrative is reconstructed after the event. If many details are changed or lost and some distorted, I believe that the intersubjective atmosphere is accurately evoked.)

She sat down in a chair in the front of the auditorium perhaps six feet away from me. She was behind a large table. For a while it seemed as if she were staring at me, saying nothing. She began to speak, as if doubting the fact that she was talking to me: "If I didn't know you and hadn't seen you at these conferences for years, I wouldn't think you were the same person who had written that book. It didn't sound like you. I've read articles and books by you before, such as your book on Oklahoma culture, and they sounded like you. But this . . . [silence]." She left long silences between each sentence, between phrases. I felt alternately curious and alarmed. I paid deliberate attention to the content of her words. She continued: "I found the book overwhelming, overpowering, pessimistic, hopeless," she said with heavy pauses between each word. "I found the comparisons of managed care and the Holocaust overdrawn. I'm not Jewish, but the Holocaust is the most horrible event in human history. Downsizing causes terrible suffering, but it is nothing like the Holocaust, which is without comparison. I just couldn't see how you could think that way."

I felt dazed, as if I had just been struck. She might be right, I told myself—and probably was. I was trying very hard to think of our conversation, and of her words, as a kind of collegial feedback, intellectual sparring, even as literary criticism. I remember haltingly saying that I'd like to think about her comparison about how I sounded in earlier writings and in this book, that in this book I was not making *comparisons* between downsizing and the Holocaust but quoting many workers and managers and executives who used Holocaust language and images to depict their experiences of downsizing. It required great effort for me to speak at all, as if she were exerting some colossal force on me. As I listened to her content, and considered it seriously, I started to pay attention to what happened to me, how I felt, as she spoke. Something else was going on, and I did not have words for it. More than being right or wrong about a book felt to be at stake. I observed her and myself to discover other answers.

Often between utterances, she just sat there, frozen, looking at me. I felt like an alien, foreign object, to her, and to the room. I felt myself physically distancing myself from the book I had written. I assured her that it was not my last book, that I am not symbiotically fused with my writing, that I enjoy thinking aloud at conferences. Words, words. As she spoke, as we spoke, as we sat there, I felt increasingly dissociative. Suddenly I knew what it felt like to dissociate. I could feel it was happening to me in a very "normal" academic discussion. In the vernacular, I felt as if I were going "out of my mind," "crazy," "*Verrückt.*" I could feel myself separating, one part pushing another out of it. Part of "me" was becoming "not-me," some entirely "other" entity. I felt like screaming, like running, but I was frozen there. I could not move. I could feel two distinct selves begin to take shape: one of them, the person who wrote the book and who my colleague did not like; the second, the person who was having the conversation with her, and who wanted her to like him and to invite him back to the conference. Slowly, my interior response to her changed from unformulated (unformulatable) to formulated experience, from dissociation to integration and differentiation, from the sense of physical dread to a reclaimed imagination (Stern 1997). I felt that I had regained myself again. This was my countertransference in the raw, unprocessed, ready to be used for organizational understanding.

I realize here as I write that I am vacillating between "third person" and "first person." I felt like I had to distance myself from the book, if not repudiate it altogether, if I were to regain her favor. I started to feel that another person, a second Howard Stein, had written that awful book. The experience of distinct, multiple conscious selves, often-termed "multiple personality(-ies)," became phenomenologically plausible to me. It became unbearably frightening. Splitting and dissociation, my becoming a distinct "not-me" (something else, somebody else) were the price of admission to shared humanity with her.

Some part of me, I am grateful, was able to observe and take note of this bizarre process, and gradually gained the upper hand. I (or do I call that part "he"?) became ethnographer and analyst of my own intersubjective dance with my colleague. I watched myself; I watched her. After a long silence, she qualified herself by saying: "There is a lot of good analysis in the book, and we agree on most things you said in the book. But I just cannot understand how you could make so much of the Holocaust symbolism. How could you think *that* way?" We were at an impasse. (I was not about to argue that *I* had not imposed Holocaust imagery on people who were describing their attempt to come to terms with the horrors of downsizing and managed care, but rather that the images were *theirs*.) She sat there—again—staring at me. I "saw" and "heard" echoes of my mother in her, and in the current interaction: how could I be *her* son, and still think or act *that* way? In this reverie, I recognized foreignness to myself in myself. If I felt alien, I wondered what my colleague had alienated from herself? I did not try to defend myself, to explain myself. We sat there, wordlessly. She stared at me. It felt like many minutes went by. As we sat there, I felt like a condemned man who had committed an inconceivable, unforgivable crime. I simply let it unfold, and continued to listen and to observe. I wanted to give her (and us) more room.

As if out of the air, she began to speak, now softly and pensively, her words more connected than before. "Of all professions," she began, "I don't understand why *nurses* don't resist the downsizing and deskilling [that is, the firing of traditional nurses, and their substitution by workers trained exclusively for narrowly focused tasks] of our own ranks. Managed care has hit us hard. Don't we know our own worth? Why don't we speak up for ourselves? Hospital executives who replace us say all we do is 'hand hold' with patients, and who needs all this training and pay just to do that? Why don't we fight back and tell them that we design discharge plans, individualize treatment, and we're often the only ones to know the patient in the hospital and in the home? We just sit back and let it happen to us, let them do it to us without protest. It's terrible to watch. Why don't we put up resistance? It's so sad and disheartening."

Interestingly, in the last part of my presentation, I had called for a conscious resistance to this onslaught against caring. This resistance, I said, begins with an acknowledgment of what is really taking place. It begins when one can break with the secrecy and deception perpetuated by the language of downsizing, reengineering, and managed care—a language one might have already made one's own (internalized).

The eeriness (the unreality) I had felt earlier in the conversation now began to dissipate. My prior impressions were now further validated by verbal and non-verbal material. I felt more whole, less psychotic; my feelings were, in turn, intersubjective cues to her state of integration as well. She began to experience and articulate in herself those feelings of identity confusion and annihilation that she had fended off by doubting me. Her very language in describing the state of nursing was steeped in symbolism of the Holocaust—a language she had questioned and impugned in my work. The very images of passivity, pessimism, and destruction, to which she had objected "in me," she now uttered with her own voice. They were now part of her identity rather than protectively (and projectively) dissociated from it. "How could *you* believe . . . ?" became "How could *I* believe . . . ?" Her protest, in essence, that "Maybe we are *not* Jews" masked an unconscious identification that "Maybe we *are*, in fact, Jews." Disagreement over my book had protected her from making the identification conscious. Agreement would feel unbearable. Much, if not all, of the intellectual disagreement between us served to protect her from feelings of sadness, despair, and helplessness.

For the moment at least, instead of feeling myself invaded and coming apart, I could sense her struggle with her identity confusion. And for the moment, I ceased to be the enemy, as she encountered her own disappointment and despair.

CULTURAL UNDERSTANDING VIA COUNTERTRANSFERENCE TO PROJECTIVE IDENTIFICATION

I want to turn the discussion here back to my colleague's and my own emotional state, because it offered a wealth of "cultural" materials. Our disturbance is part of our data. How the interaction *felt* was part of the interaction itself; it was part of the content (the "data") of the discussion. As she spoke, I felt increasingly "crazy," out of my mind, as if something spatial were occurring to me. I was being forced out of my own skin. I felt as if she were trying to force or press something out of me and into me. The conversation felt like a violent invasion. She unconsciously embodied the very thing she consciously disembodied in her verbal attack on me. What at one level she repudiated, at another level she illustrated. I felt that the conversation between us was some kind of enactment, a repetition, which preceded my understanding (Freud 1920; Hirsch 1996).

If what I was saying in my published, ethnographic accounts could not possibly be true, then what was happening to her, in her fusion of her personal fate and her fate as a nurse (if not the fate of nursing "itself"), could not be happening. To validate herself (to protect herself from persecutory anxiety), she had to discredit me. There was a deep stake in her disagreement with me. In fighting me, she was fighting her own self-realizations. I believe that instead of experiencing an internal (intrapsychic) conflict, she was experiencing a conflict between us (termed "object relations conflict"), expressed in the serious doubt she had about me and about my current book. Under the emotional circumstances of the discussion, I could not rely on her to validate or clarify what she was saying. I could only go on feelings and body sensations that overwhelmed me (Bion 1959).

Let me try to put this process into something of a formula: She could not notice herself; she could notice herself only via me, inside me, as flawed attributes of me. She could notice only me. She could inspect only me. Her knowledge and critique were projective. She was talking about herself (and, by extension, her cultural attachments) in the (projective) guise of talking about me. The question is why? We make others bear (or at least enlist them to support) what we cannot ourselves bear.

I decided to study this strange cultural (interprofessional) exchange, to make it understandable, via my countertransference. I attended not only to the words, but also to the tone and to the harrowing, hollow silences. I did not interpret. (If I had wished to do so, the attempt would have been heard as persecutory. Besides, we were not in a therapeutic relationship, but colleagues discussing a "text" and a subject. So what would have been my grounds to interpret?) I did not flee. I listened to myself, to my reverie. Everything I was hearing, seeing, and feeling from her pressed me to mistrust myself; from somewhere inside, I summoned the strength to tell myself that I must trust myself.

I could smell and taste destruction, hers as well as mine. The "frame" of the context was an academic medical conference, not therapy, and even in therapy the moment would not have been right. I was the "good enough" target of paranoid-schizoid thinking that she utilized in the service of projective identification. I sensed a split between the intellectual or cognitive and the emotional. The subject was catastrophe and the aversion of catastrophe in the guise of academic discourse. I felt terrified as she spoke. I struggled to hold onto our intersubjective reality, to keep listening to her, to learn what this conversation was about, and not to defend my book, its ostensible subject—but, in fact, its *metaphor*.

I would characterize this conversation as a bizarre, frightening interaction, but one that is not unusual for me in "field" situations or in the workplace (which has come to be one of my ongoing field situations). Such an interaction as this teaches me about the nature and function of culture, and of the place the elusive concept of "selfhood" plays in social life. In the initial part of the conversation, to preserve the relationship and my good graces with her, I felt that I had to question or invalidate, if not annihilate, my "real self" (Winnicott 1965) and substitute for it a "false self" that was compliant, conciliatory, and made in her image. She-in-me, as an object-representation, became fused with my self-representation, and substituted for my real (and other) self-representation. I could feel the processes of splitting, dissociation, and introjective identification taking place inside me; I could, in parallel fashion, feel the splitting and projective identification taking place in her. Both were unbearably violent experiences.

Let me approach this material from the viewpoint of countertransference. If I did not become a literal "multiple personality," the dissociation still took and takes an enormous toll. My colleague wished to "disappear" (if I may make it into a transitive verb) a disturbing part of herself in me, by doubting if not displacing that part of me. I felt as if she were taking an axe and shovel and hewing a part of me out, casting it aside, then filling me up with her substance. During our conversation, it felt like a death struggle to keep alive, to keep the right to stay alive as myself. I felt a split occur in me between my "good" or valuable self and my "bad" or devalued self, but I was confused as to which was which. She reversed my inner values, and I had to struggle with myself to keep them. The victory was hard-won and is only recent. It has only lately become a tool for understanding.

Over the years, such identity assaults have occurred to me for "wrong-thinking" in the workplace. As they happen, I feel myself capitulate. I mistrust myself, even install others' version of me inside of me as a replacement for the self I have banished. Over time, after these assaults continue to occur, I disappear, or it feels as if I have nearly disappeared. Peter Gay describes his experiences as a German Jew in the early years of Nazi Germany: "After three or four years of trying to stand erect in the whirlwind of hate and contempt, the most resilient among us were exhausted by the effort of keeping our defenses intact" (1998: 31). The same words describe my response to the assault on my work and integrity. If "only" symbolically, I fulfill that odious wish of Hans Frank,

Governor General of Poland under the Nazis: "My only wish of the Jews is that they should disappear." I now try to understand the wish to disappear and the need to make others disappear—as my colleague unconsciously did in the innocent conference interaction I have just described.

The question becomes: What would my colleague *lose* were she to permit Holocaust images (and their associated catastrophic feelings) to enter into the present rather than be relegated exclusively to the past? Why must that specific past not be invoked? The answer, I believe, is that she would be faced with overwhelming fantasies and feelings of utter vulnerability, helplessness, desolation, and annihilation in the here and now. The present circumstances would feel *that* bad. Her emotional logic of denial amounts to saying: Even though our current situation is bad (evil), it is not *that* bad (evil). Her later words affirm what she earlier denied.

To summarize the second vignette: in this unexpected interdisciplinary "field situation" in American biomedical culture, I learned much about the process and experience of culture. The teaching tool was projective identification; the learning process was its metabolization. To invalidate herself and sustain her invalidation, my colleague had to invalidate me, to see my ideas as false and persecutory. I came precariously close to identifying permanently with (introjecting) her projections as true for me rather than as a temporary means to insight about her. That is, I came close to accepting as a (conscious) statement about me what in fact was a (unconscious) statement about her. What she could not bear about me turned out to be what she could not bear about herself and the situation of nursing in the United States.

More abstractly, this second case study of projective identification shows, at least in part, how culture "works," how and why it is learned, and why it is so difficult to relinquish—in ourselves and in others as we each "use" each other projectively as containers. It shows further how individual, cultural, and historical change are psychodynamically linked. Paradoxical in its destructiveness, projective identification can function as a principle of social integration, structure, and mobilization.

For both the projecting subject and the target, projective identification serves as a principle of subject formation, deformation, intrusion, and transformation—at the individual, dyadic, and group levels. For the cultural analyst or critic, one can examine one's own emotional states induced by projective identification as a means of understanding the emotional needs of the other who is doing the projecting.

PROJECTIVE IDENTIFICATION, LANGUAGE, AND THE
SOCIAL DESTRUCTION OF MEANING

Although the two organizational narratives I have presented are individual and distinct, they can also be read as exemplars of a cultural *class* or genre of accounts. They are thematically representative and culturally typical. Their typicality commands, I believe, the conclusion that the widely used interpretive framework called "the social construction of reality" be substantially supplemented by one that I term *the social destruction of meaning and the social production of meaninglessness*. Here, "social" is coercive, intrusive, mandatory. Its work rests upon the deadly dance of projective and introjective identification.

What Theodore Schwartz (1973) has termed a "paranoid ethos" abounds in the contemporary culture of the United States and increases internationally with economic globalization, liberalization, privatization, and the elevation of shareholder value to the highest good (Sievers 1997). In this, and in subsequent "discussion" sections of the chapter, I wish to focus on the cultural ramifications of the two vignettes—specifically, the paranoid ethos that pervades downsizing and managed care. This focus should help link unconscious forces, sentiment, ideology, and institutional form.

In a recent study of the problem of knowing in workplace organizations, Lawrence makes a distinction between two types of thinking: "thinking-to-be-in-touch-with reality . . . as R+," and "thinking-not-to-be-in-touch-with reality . . . as -R (1997: 9). The latter comes into being through what W. R. Bion (1970: 92) called "catastrophic change"—that is, change that induces deep regression to persecutory, psychotic anxiety (Klein 1946; an argument similar to Devereux 1955). "-R" comes into being to avoid the disorganizing experience of psychotic anxiety. Lawrence's argument helps us to understand how and why the creation of meaninglessness occurs:

The process of evasion begins from a hatred of reality both internal and external. This is because reality is construed and felt as being a "catastrophic chaos of utter unpredictability" (Rayner 1995: 159) and to entertain this experientially would threaten to burst asunder the psychic limits between what is safely understood to be finite and the infinite. There is a hatred of the capacity to think so any mental processes that would facilitate the attainment of R+ have to be denied. Emotionally this arises from the anxiety that if R+ was to be engaged[,] the resultant experience of reality would be so overpowering that it would be persecuting. It is felt that it would overwhelm and even annihilate the thinker who dares to see reality in all its complexity. *So it has to be destroyed or, more accurately, the human desire to make meaning has not just to be denied but sadistically obliterated. Meaning is to be expunged by concretisation and the evacuation of symbolism.* Reality is simplified. (1997: 10; emphasis added)

Inside and outside realities blur and confound one another. Social reality and internal representation intensify and mirror one another. Social space becomes persecutory space, heavily rationalized by the doctrine of "good business" based on the "bottom line." The world of work becomes a schizoid landscape replete with inanimate, exploitable, disposable things. The workplace becomes devoid of people. Symbolically, we have unleashed the "clean" neutron bomb upon ourselves—that, at least, is my fantasy of this deathscape. It is the task of the observer and consultant's countertransference to recognize and contain the terror in the client's transference. The work of the consultation begins at this place and often returns to it. It is a question of feeling that which is unbearable, but which is no less real.

In *secular* guise (economics), the linked processes of downsizing, managed care, reengineering, restructuring, etc., are *sacred* in motive: the apocalyptic wish, promise, vision, and power to cleanse and purify the organization. The apocalyptic vision is of death and rebirth: rebirth through violent, sacrificial death. The workplace organization is experienced and viewed as a biological, organic body, its members merged with the body they constitute—an idealized maternal-infant symbiotic fantasy (Koenigsberg 1975). Workplace apocalypse is a means toward "reinventing" (a common word, meaning revitalizing) the symbolically dead, killed-off workplace.

The popular work of Michael Hammer (Hammer 1990; Hammer and Champy 1993) on radically "reengineering" organizations exemplifies the presence of apocalyptic fantasy and deed in the manifestly rational workplace. The subtitle of one paper is "Don't automate, obliterate" (1990). Corporate apocalypse—a "new heaven, new earth," on earth—is the final and only *end*; people are merely *means* to achieving that end. The only acceptable "whole" object (in the psychoanalytic sense) is the idealized, anthropomorphized organization. People are experienced and treated as part-objects, as mere mechanical functions and extensions of ambition.

The semantic web of downsizing, RIFing, reengineering, restructuring, outsourcing, deskilling, and managed care are *the language of gesture and wish conducted and couched in the language of euphemistic words.* The words disguise the deed they help to implement. The words are a great lie about what the deed is in fact doing: namely, unfathomable sacrificial destruction in the name of essential business. Business is a code word for brutality, but the code must not be broken.

In corporate break rooms and hallways, other—contradictory—words leak out to tell the tale of dread behind the warrior sham of official spreadsheets. Ours is a world split into a language of metaphorical Nazis and Jews, Nazis and Slavs, Nazis and Gypsies, the transporters and the transported, the movers and the moved. It is a world of steep and rapid fall from triumphant executioner to executed sacrifice. Lack of emotional safety and imminent vulnerability are its hallmarks.

In this feverish marketplace, all people—of whatever rank or status—are ultimately disposable. It is a world in which thousands of people have been actually escorted and herded into gigantic auditoriums, locked in by the security police, notified that they are all to be fired today for the health and survival of the company, and informed that they have until the end of the workday to gather their belongings, turn in all their keys, and be escorted to their motor vehicles. They are not to be trusted: yesterday's loyalists are tomorrow's saboteurs (see Allcorn et al. 1996 for a review of relevant literature; also, this volume, chapter 1).

The workplace is a world of endless lists and selections for continued employment or unemployment, of waiting in queues for assignment to the same or a different job, of uncertainty over whether one's permanent job will be redefined as temporary. It is a world of closed silos, fat ones, tall ones, and a world of fast-moving, densely packed trains. It is a world of executives' admonitions to get on the train with them, lest one be left standing at the station, or worse.

The economics-laden language of downsizing, reengineering, and managed care is saturated with Holocaust images and emotions: gigantic death chambers; sadistic Doctors Mengele, directing the naked to the left or to the right; the clattering suffocation of trains, the transport of the socially dead to the place of biological death-making. The work of ominous symbolism assumes the dress of mere business. Here, as in the earlier vignettes, *the evidence for the Holocaust metaphor lies in the action that carries the seed of its plausibility.* (This notion is based on an insight I owe to Henry Ebel, 16 May 1999.) It is my countertransference that leads me (and others) *from experience of action to its symbolization.* By listening via my own unconscious, I can comprehend and hold on to others' projection of Holocaust imagery and experience on contemporary workplace cataclysm. My countertransference is essential to hearing and validating their transference to the workplace and to me.

This tool of countertransference is one that others can fruitfully use as well. The data are abundant. It is a matter of allowing oneself to see and hear—to feel—their presence. I permit myself here a single example. Following a presentation I had made to a medical humanities series at Duke University in late May 1999, Professor Peter Petschauer, a noted psychohistorian who had been a participant, related to me a word association that he had just tried out on himself. It was one he used in order to independently test my account of downsizing, restructuring, and managed care in the United States. He began by saying that the sounds "f" and "p" frequently mutate into one another in language. The psychologically and culturally telling sequence of his association was: "RIF," "RIP," "Rest in Peace," "rip," "ripping." In his word association lay the images of death and destruction that are at the core of corporate American euphemisms.

Professor Petschauer then told me of a moving conversation he had had with a member of the audience immediately after my presentation, while participants were standing around and visiting. A woman who was a current faculty member at the medical center said to him: "I keep reading the [news]paper about the news in Kosovo, the killing of Albanians, the NATO bombing in Yugoslavia." In her next sentence, she said tearfully to him, "They're [administration] thinking about eliminating my department at the Center." Emotionally, the distant was part of the near—she used the distant to help herself comprehend what was happening to her.

In summary, through our countertransference, we can recognize the experiential validity of people's emotion-laden word associations that link organizational "eliminations" in the American workplace, the Holocaust, current ethnic cleansing—by Serbs of Muslims in Bosnia, and by Serbs of Albanians in Kosovo—and other social forms of vast human destructiveness. The emotional response to the *action* is the key to the truthfulness in the *metaphor* that attempts to comprehend the action.

HOLDING ON TO THE FORCES OF PROJECTIVE IDENTIFICATION IN ONESELF TO UNDERSTAND CULTURAL UNREALITY

What does a student and critic of culture and society, or an organizational consultant, "do" with narratives such as the two vignettes above? *Listen.* In organizational consultations such as the above situation, the first requirement for observer and consultant is to bear the unbearable, to bear witness with the speaker, to serve as a "holding environment" for the experience and to validate it. "It happened. This really happened," is the consultant and observer's Kantian and Freudian imperative in the face of atrocity. The psychodynamically informed observer and consultant's fundamental role is to affirm the inner experience that business-as-usual is not always "just business." It is to use one's own countertransference to affirm the psychic reality of the client. It is to integrate rather than to dis-integrate, to realize rather than to de-realize, to bring into rather than chase from memory. It is to claim one's own authorship of even the most terrible-to-imagine feeling and fantasy. As student, theorist, and consultant, one can validate in others only what one can "own" in oneself.

Permit me here to introduce a comparison of events that at one level are entirely different, but that at another level might be seen as functionally and psychodynamically equivalent. In *The Drowned and the Saved*, Primo Levi (1988) describes a particularly ghoulish scene at Auschwitz, based on an account by Miklos Nyiszli, a Hungarian physician and survivor of the last Special Squad (1988: 54–55). In between gassings, Nazi SS members and Jewish inmates who were members of the SK (*Sonderkommando*, or Special Squads) would engage in soccer games, complete with side-betting and drinks. The ultimate destinies of the two groups were, of course, opposite. Members of the squads, the "crematorium ravens" (1988: 55), were nonetheless Jews and would suffer their Jewish destiny to be killed. In Primo Levi's words, in veterans of the squad, the SS

> recognized to some extent colleagues, by now as inhuman as themselves, hitched to the same cart, bound together by the foul link of imposed complicity. So, Nyiszli tells how during a "work" pause he attended a soccer game between the SS and the SK (*Sonderkommando*), that is to say, between a group representing the SS on guard at the crematorium and a group representing the Special Squad. Other men of the SS and the rest of the squad are present at the game; they take sides, bet, applaud, urge the players on as if, rather than at the gates of hell, the game were taking place on the village green. (1988: 54–55)

Although we in the United States and in the increasingly globalized economy do not have death camps, we have symbolic parallels. We have an increasingly American cultural way of creating fugitives and playing out death wishes by bottom-line thinking. CEOs and other upper management say of expendable workers the equivalent of what Hans Frank, Nazi Governor General of Poland, had said of the Jews. The wish for another's disappearance is a death wish, irrespective of how it is officially implemented.

The above scenario transposes in spirit, in symbolism, to these corporate North American shores. At the national holidays of Thanksgiving and Christmas, workplace organizations put on lavish festivals of food and drink, and even gifts, for employees. Sometimes, the event is catered. Sometimes, corporate or hospital executives will even perform "role reversal" with subordinates on this occasion. They will be the ones—this one time—to serve rather than to be served. In this instance, the "main dish" to be served is turkey or ham, given to a procession of hundreds if not thousands of employees who wait in line. The CEO, CFO, chairman, or other high-level manager will often make a brief holiday speech, wishing everyone well and infusing them with the upbeat spirit of the season. There might even be prizes or gifts.

After the New Year and in the months ahead, these same executives might summarily fire hundreds, even thousands, of these same employees. The style of summary firing with no warning is prevalent. Those who are not fired during a specific "RIFing" (an acronym further euphemizing the euphemism "Reduction in Force") are typically "restructured" and "reengineered" in their jobs, and await the next wave of RIFings. Managers and workers alike are expected to do "more with less" and be productive, efficient, loyal, and upbeat while their morale is assaulted by dread of the future and guilt from being a "survivor." Anything but the generosity of "The Christmas Spirit" prevails. The parallel I suggest between these two American scenarios and soccer on the greens of Auschwitz is not hyperbole. Americans are simply put out on the streets to fend for themselves, to disappear to who-cares-where.

The widespread wish that unwanted peoples *disappear* further links the "ethnic cleansings" of recent years (Rwanda, Bosnia, Kosovo) with their equivalent *corporate cleansings* through downsizings, RIFs, and the like. Both these forms create mass *refugee* problems, and are by-products of the wish to secure boundaries or borders, and thereby organismic-like survival, via *expulsion of unwanted parts*. Those who remain behind, though, are by no means free.

PROJECTIVE IDENTIFICATION AND *DE FACTO* CAPTIVITY IN THE AMERICAN WORKPLACE

The linkage of paid work and social worth has created an increasingly large cadre of vulnerable people in the United States. Without "work," one has nothing, no present and no future. Moreover, according to the cultural ideology, without "work," one is entitled to nothing—and even with "work," one is entitled to as little as possible. Managed health care is one of the key doctrinal and institutional forms that projective identification now assumes and fuels.

Psychiatrist Harold Bursztajn describes many contemporary workers and patients as constituting a *"de facto* captive population," tied by dependency on employment, often unable to choose a health plan or physician (1997a, 1997b, 1998; Bursztajn and Brodsky 1997; Bursztajn, Gutheil, and Brodsky 1998; Bursztajn and Sobel 1997). Bursztajn urges that the ethical standards of the 1947 Nuremberg Code be adopted to protect patients and workers placed in such highly vulnerable, *de facto* captive circumstances. Specifically, he draws attention to the need to protect patients-cum-workers through their voluntary, informed consent in health care (1998: 985).

Patients-cum-workers become *de facto* economic prisoners. For all practical purposes, workers have little or no choice within the social experiment of downsizing, restructuring, managed care, outsourcing, deskilling, and the like: "Just when the doctor-patient relationship had been moving toward a greater degree of shared responsibility, managed care has disturbed this evolution from paternalism to mutuality by circumscribing the decision-making authority of both parties" (Bursztajn and Brodsky 1997: 4, quoted with permission). In their division of labor, managed care organizations and employers have been given "authority without responsibility," while physicians have been assigned "responsibility without authority" (1997: 4; Bursztajn 1998).

> At a time when many employers offer only one health care benefit package, many patients are de facto captive. . . . 50 years after the promulgation of the Nuremberg Code, . . . [it remains unaddressed as to whether] informed consent as a process is applicable to innovative, experimental managed care programs that are now doing "more with less." . . . [Further, physician] profiles [in managed care organizations] often penalize physicians for hospitalizing patients, or even for requesting approval to hospitalize patients when such approval is subsequently denied. There thus exist de facto physician gag clauses, which not only substantially control clinical judgment and practice but also compromise meaningful informed consent as a process. (quoted with permission, Bursztajn 1998: 985)

What becomes of the physician's historic fiduciary (that is, moral) responsibility, patient advocacy, and the sheer trust required for one person to place himself or herself in another's care under the dependency- and regression-inducing conditions of sickness (Katz 1984, 1996)? Patients-cum-workers become *de facto* economic prisoners. Principle #9 of the 1947 Nuremberg Code stipulated a person's right to withdraw from or terminate participation in an experiment, that is, to escape (Shuster 1997). How might such a stipulation be now understood under the current experimental employment conditions? For all practical purposes, millions of people as workers have little or no choice within the social experiment of downsizing, restructuring, managed care, and the like. One may speak of "wage serfdom," where people (who often call themselves "survivors" of RIFings and restructurings) stay and hold on, or leave for the likely promise of tenuous employment and downward mobility.

To be sure, they are "free" to leave. But, given such punitive social realities as "preexisting [medical] conditions, financial limitations," hectic workplace lives, and "simply being overwhelmed by barriers of time, effort, or understanding" (Bursztajn and Brodsky 1997), what does this "freedom" to leave mean? Many employers, managers, insurance companies, and physicians' offices alike are only too happy to be rid of people who suffer in any form—workers who are anything but perfectly tuned producers. "My only wish of the Jews is that they should disappear." The *freedom to disappear* into the street and the night is evidently what many American administrators and clinicians have in mind as well. Bursztajn, Gutheil, and Brodsky, writing of the triage model in managed care psychiatry, observe, "Today there is cause for concern that the labeling of people as dead (or its equivalent) will leave them fit only for discard" (1998: 34).

PROJECTIVE IDENTIFICATION, DEATH ANXIETY, AND THE PROBLEM OF EVIL IN THE WORKPLACE

Death anxiety abounds in the United States. Americans occupy themselves with trying to divest themselves of it and to deposit the anxiety into others who come to embody death. Death anxiety is best visible in the manic defenses and rationalizations that fend it off. For instance, we feverishly try to forestall fantasized death through greater productivity and quicker profit. The disposal of those people who are not maximally productive is part of a ritual sacrifice to keep the corporate body alive, at least for a time. One can see business as not only about "pure" business, but also about death, the dread of death, the imminence of death, and "putting" one's own anxiety into another. Everyone becomes an embattled island in the tall, vertically and horizontally integrated bureaucratic "silos" of work.

Money is the currency that mediates life and death. The accumulation of money, together with access to money, make the difference between life and death, between livelihood and decay. Money is used as the medium through which some persons or groups exert the power of life and death over others: the medium through which some may temporarily prove that they are alive by *sacrificing* others (Henry Ebel, personal communication, 10 January 1999). The workplace is a cultural site in which that power is exercised. The exercise of that power is part of a culture-wide ritual to secure life magically through death. We literally try to purchase temporary life (and organizational revitalization) through perpetual death.

At least in some respects, popular culture in the United States is ahead of scholarship in this realization. The popularity of cartoonist Scott Adams' "Dilbert" newspaper cartoons, books, and now television program is one measure (Stein 1998a; 1998b). Consider also an item from the popular culture of the United States: a widely syndicated "Rubes" cartoon by Leigh Rubin in the 21 February 1999 newspaper, *The Sunday Oklahoman*. It depicts a scantily clad, smiling tribal shaman holding his victim by the loincloth at the end of a stick at the summit of a steep volcano.

The shaman says: "On behalf of myself and the rest of the tribe, I'd like to thank you for appeasing the volcano god and ensuring us another year of good health." The victim looks bulge-eyed over the edge of the precipice. The caption at the bottom of the cartoon reads: "How certain tribes pay their annual health insurance premium." One is reminded how primitive managed care, downsizing, and reengineering are at their motivational core (at their implicit, in contrast with their explicit, order; Bohm 1980).

What does this chapter contribute to theory—psychoanalytic, organizational, cultural, historical? To say that this chapter has focused on the *phenomenology* or experience of massive organizational change merely begs and postpones the central issue that theory is only as valid as the experience upon which it is based: the observer or consultant's as well as the analysand or client's experience. It is, I believe, easy to recognize, for instance, Thomas Ogden's "autistic-contiguous position" in the struggle over organizational shape and texture; Melanie Klein's "paranoid-schizoid position" and Donald Winnicott's "persecutory space" in the massive anxiety and mistrust; Sigmund Freud's "counter-oedipal" destruction of workplace offspring; and Donald Meltzer's concept of the suffocating "anal claustrum" (1992).

But all these, as partial explanations, can handily serve as defenses against the monumental anxiety and chaos the experiences unleash. Even to say, psychohistorically, that the hatred of and within organizations is a displacement of and acting out of early childhood familial trauma and ambivalences (deMause 1982), while true, can also distract us from the real destruction that takes place at the symbolic level in the workplace.

We require, I believe, both-and rather than either-or theories. I do not claim that the evil done in organizations in the name of business is beyond comprehension, just as I do not believe that the Holocaust is beyond comprehension (Adams and Balfour 1998). But comprehension requires the full intelligence of the heart. Anything less is a turning away from the disorganizing experience of psychotic anxiety—and from the possibility of recovery from trauma and its inner elaborations. We require the fullness of the experience behind the abstraction of theories. To encompass the problem of evil in workplaces, and in the cultures of vast social units, we must know what evil feels like, and how it works (Alford 1990; 1997). That is, we must develop the capacity to sense the triumphant joy over someone else that, for the moment, divests and diverts the terror from oneself.

To demystify "the office," "the workplace," the starting place is to allow the ordinary, the expectable, to become strange, even surprising. "The office" is often bizarre *in the guise of* the ordinary: its deceptiveness lies in the appearance, the dissimulation, of ordinariness. One may speak of "the everyday atrocities of the 'workplace,' where the most primitive human motivations are played out by people wearing shirts and ties" (Henry Ebel, personal communication, 22 March 1999). "The office," in fact, "is usually a very weird place, in which symbolic murder and mutilation are daily events. 'Downsizing' and the Nazi 'special handling' are euphemisms that cry out to be placed in the same folder" (ibid.). Sometimes what we (mis-)take for the ordinary deserves to be regarded as extraordinary. Then, perhaps, we might be open to regarding it as a problem instead of as a—if not the only—solution.

CONCLUSIONS: COUNTERTRANSFERENCE AS GROUNDING IN CULTURAL COMPREHENSION

In this chapter, I have attempted to link person, workplace organization, culture, and history via the use of countertransference in organizational (and wider cultural) study and consultation. I hope to have contributed to the understanding of the phenomenology and psychodynamics of the contemporary American workplace, where persecutory anxiety is heightened if not chronic, where threat, dread, and loss are part of the organizational landscape, and where the imagery of death abounds. Later chapters will offer more examples of this process. I have argued that the concept of countertransference is at the center of organizational and cultural understanding precisely because it constitutes the methodological and theoretical core of *all* human comprehension. I have relied upon my own countertransference to grasp the psychology that largely drives downsizing and managed care.

In the process of exploring my own countertransference (to the data, as data), I have, I believe, used my own creative processes not to replace more conventional data-gathering approaches, but to supplement them. Starting from originally accepting the classical position of countertransference-as-*distortion*, I have come also to trust countertransference-as-*grounding*. We need room for both, and to know how—with one another's loving guidance—to tell the difference.

One of the pillars of Judaism and Christianity alike is the commandment, "Thou shalt love the Lord thy God with all thy heart, all thy soul, and all thy might (strength)" (Deuteronomy 6:5). As a Jew, I first learned it from my father at about the time I began to learn to speak. Little did I imagine fifty-some years ago how completely the admonition would also apply to knowledge and to the process of knowing. Far from being a narrow skill, it is part of an attitude of being in one's capacity as critical cultural researcher, as consultant, and perhaps as citizen. This attitude underlies the "totalistic" understanding and use of countertransference.

Today, in our social science and psychoanalytic discourses, we would speak in the language of "disciplined subjectivity," of "reflexivity," of carefully examined "countertransference." But it is still a matter of knowing—of comprehending—with all one's heart, with all one's soul, and with all one's might. Our study of organizations and our efforts to assist them deserve the same devotion. Perhaps we can serve the rebirth of authentic hope in workplaces if we first have the courage of facing the dread we now find rampant (Mitchell 1993). Any effort at social enlightenment and criticism must begin by standing still long enough to see and feel and bear the overpowering darkness. A starting place is the experience of the darkness that is, and again is not entirely, our own.

The next chapter enters that organizational darkness through the partly biographical study of an individual executive's workplace odyssey. It shows how deeply personal and idiomatic the Holocaust metaphor can come to be in American workplaces.

REFERENCES

Adams, Guy B., and Danny L. Balfour. 1998. *Unmasking Administrative Evil*. Thousand Oaks, CA: Sage.

Adams, Scott. 1996. *The DILBERT Principle: A Cubicle's-Eye View of Bosses, Meetings, Management Fads and Other Workplace Afflictions*. New York: HarperBusiness (HarperCollins).

Alford, C. Fred. 1990. "The Organization of Evil," *Political Psychology* 11(1): 5–380.

———. 1997. "The Political Psychology of Evil," *Political Psychology* 18(1): 1–17.

Allcorn, Seth, Howell S. Baum, Michael A. Diamond, and Howard F. Stein. 1996. *The HUMAN Cost of a Management Failure: Organizational Downsizing at General Hospital*. Westport, CT: Quorum Books.

Armstrong, David. 1998. "Introduction," W. Gordon Lawrence, ed., in *Social Dreaming at Work*. London: Karnak. Pp. xvii-xxi.

Bertman, Stephen. 1998. *Hyperculture: The Human Cost of Speed*. New York: Praeger.

Bion, W. R. 1959. *Experiences in Groups*. New York: Ballantine.

———. 1970. *Attention and Interpretation*. London: Tavistock.

———. 1990. *Brazilian Lectures*. London: Karnac Books.

Bohm, David. 1980. *Wholeness and the Implicate Order*. London: Routledge and Kegan Paul.

Bollas, Christopher. 1989. *In the Shadow of the Object: Psychoanalysis of the Unthought Known*. New York: Columbia University Press.

Boyer, L. Bryce. 1993. "Countertransference: Brief History and Clinical Issues," in L. B. Boyer and P. L. Giovacchini, eds., *Master Clinicians on Treating Regressed Patients*. Volume 2. Northvale, NJ: Jason Aronson. Pp. 1–24.

———. 1999. *Countertransference and Regression*. Northvale, NJ: Jason Aronson.

———. 1997. "Medical Historical Perspectives Regarding Managed Care and Medical Necessity: True and False." Chairman of Symposium on Ethical Issues in Managed Health Care. American Psychiatric Association Annual Meeting, San Diego, CA, 19 May.

———. 1997. "Medical Necessity, Managed Health Care Denial of Benefits, and the Nuremberg Code." Panel: "Medical Ethics: Who Gets the Care?" Moderator: Professor Uwe E. Reinhardt, Ph.D., Princeton University 250th Anniversary Symposium, Princeton, NJ. 29 May.

Bursztajn, Harold J. 1998. Review of *Managing Care, Not Dollars: The Continuum of Mental Health Services* (Robert K. Schreter, Steven S. Sharfstein, and Carol A. Schreter. Washington, DC: American Psychiatric Press, 1997). *American Journal of Psychiatry* 155(7): 985.

Bursztajn, Harold J. and Archie Brodsky. 1997. "The De Facto Captive Patient: Clinical and Ethical Strategies for Restoring Choice under Managed Care." Unpublished ms. (cited and quoted with permission of senior author).

Bursztajn H. J., T. G. Gutheil, and A. Brodsky. 1998. "Ethics and the Triage Model in Managed Care Hospital Psychiatry," *Psychiatric Times* 15(9): 33–38.

Bursztajn H. J., and R. Sobel. 1997. "Accountability without Health Care Data Banks," *Health Affairs* 17(6): 252–253.

deMause, Lloyd. 1982. *Foundations of Psychohistory*. New York: Creative Roots.

Devereux, George. 1955. "Charismatic Leadership and Crisis," in Gézà Róheim, ed., *Psychoanalysis and the Social Sciences*. New York: International Universities Press. Pp. 145–157.

———. 1967. *From Anxiety to Method in the Behavioral Sciences*. The Hague: Mouton.

Ebel, Henry. 10 January 1999. Personal communication, quoted with permission.

———. 22 March 1999. Personal communication, quoted with permission.

———. 16 May 1999. Personal communication, quoted with permission.

French, Robert, and Peter Simpson. 1999. "Our Best Work Happens When We Don't Know What We're Doing." The International Society for the Psychoanalytic Study of Organizations, 1999 Symposium, Toronto, Canada. 26 June.

Freud, Sigmund. 1920. "Beyond the Pleasure Principle," *The Standard Edition of the Complete Psychological Works of Sigmund Freud*. Volume 18. London: Hogarth Press, 1955. Pp. 7–64.

Gay, Peter. 1998. "My German Question," *The American Scholar* 67(4): 25–49.

Hammer, Michael. 1990. "Reengineering Work: Don't Automate, Obliterate," *Harvard Business Review* 68(4): 104–113.

Hammer, Michael, and James Champy. 1993. *Reengineering the Corporation: A Manifesto for Business Revolution*. New York: HarperBusiness.

Hirsch, I. 1996. "Observing Participation, Mutual Enactment, and the New Classical Models," *Contemporary Psychoanalysis* 33(2): 359–383.

Katz, Jay. 1984. *The Silent World of Doctor and Patient*. New York: Free Press.

———. 1996. "The Nuremberg Code and the Nuremberg Trial: A Reappraisal," *Journal of the American Medical Association* 276: 1662–1666.

Keats, John. 1974. "Letter to George and Thomas Keats, December 1817," in *The Norton Anthology of English Literature*. Volume 2, third edition New York: Norton. Pp. 704–706.

Klein, Melanie. 1946. "Notes on Some Schizoid Mechanisms," *International Journal of Psycho-Analysis* 27: 99–110.

Koenigsberg, Richard A. 1975. *Hitler's Ideology: A Study in Psychoanalytic Sociology*. New York: Library of Social Science.

La Barre, Weston. 1972. *The Ghost Dance: The Origins of Religion*. New York: Dell.

Lawrence, W. Gordon. 1997. "Centering of the Sphinx for the Psychoanalytic

Study of Organizations." 1997 Symposium, International Society for the Psychoanalytic Study of Organizations, Philadelphia.

———, ed. 1998. *Social Dreaming at Work*. London: Karnac Books.

———. 1998. "Prologue," in *Social Dreaming at Work*. London: Karnac Books. Pp. 1–8.

———. 1998. W. Gordon Lawrence, Marc Maltz, and E. Martin Walker. "Social Dreaming at Work." (concluding chapter), in *Social Dreaming at Work*. London: Karnac Books. Pp. 169–181.

Levi, Primo. 1988. *The Drowned and the Saved*. New York: Summit Books.

Lotto, David. 1998. "The Corporate Takeover of the Soul: The Current State of the American Health Care System," *Journal of Psychohistory* 26(2): 603–609.

Meltzer, Donald. 1992. *The Claustrum*. Perthshire, Scotland: Clunie Press.

Mitchell, Stephen A. 1993. *Hope and Dread in Psychoanalysis*. New York: Basic Books.

Ogden, Thomas. 1989. *The Primitive Edge of Experience*. Northvale, NJ: Jason Aronson.

Rayner, Eric. 1995. *Unconscious Logic*. London: Routledge.

Rosenfeld, H. A. 1947. "Analysis of a Schizophrenic State with Depersonalization," *International Journal of Psycho-Analysis* 28: 130–139.

Schwartz, Theodore. 1973. "Cult and Context: The Paranoid Ethos in Melanesia," *Ethos* 1(2): 153–174.

Shore, Karen. 1997. "Don't Let Them Take Your Mind and Spirit: On Being Called a 'Provider.' " American Psychological Association, Acceptance Speech, Distinguished Psychologist of the Year.

Shuster, E. 1997. "Nuremberg Code," reprinted in "Fifty Years Later: The Significance of the Nuremberg Code," *New England Journal of Medicine* 337: 1436–1440.

Sievers, Burkard. 1997. "Psychotic Organization as a Metaphoric Frame for the Study of Organizational and International Dynamics." Unpublished ms., originally titled "Cacophony and Organizational Psychosis." Keynote Address to the Conference, "Uncertainty, Knowledge and Skill," Limburg University/Keele University, Hasselt (Belgium), 6–8 November.

Stein, Howard F. 1987. *Developmental Time, Cultural Space*. Norman: University of Oklahoma Press.

———. 1994. *The Dream of Culture*. New York: Psyche Press.

———. 1996. *Prairie Voices*. Westport, CT: Bergin and Garvey.

———. 1997. "Death Imagery and the Experience of Organizational Downsizing: Or, Is Your Name on 'Schindler's List'?" *Administration and Society* 29(2), May: 222–247.

———. 1998a. *Euphemism, Spin, and the Crisis in Organizational Life*. Foreword by Seth Allcorn. Westport, CT: Quorum Books.

———. 1998b. "Organizational Euphemism and the Cultural Mystifcation of Evil," *Administrative Theory and Praxis* 20(3): 346–357.

———. 1999. "Countertransference and Understanding Workplace Cataclysm: Intersubjective Knowing and Cultural Knowledge in Interdisciplinary Applied Anthropology," *High Plains Applied Anthropologist* 19(1): 10–20.

Stein, Howard F., and William G. Niederland, eds. 1989. *Maps From the Mind: Studies in Psychogeography*. Norman: University of Oklahoma Press.

Whitman, Walt. 1992. *The Essential Whitman*. Selected by Galway Kinnell. New York: Galahad Books.
Winnicott, Donald W. 1965. *The Maturational Processes and the Facilitating Environment*. New York: International Universities Press.
———. *Playing and Reality*. London: Tavistock.
Young, Robert. 1994. *Mental Space*. London: Process Press.

4

The Holocaust as Trope for Managed Social Change

INTRODUCTION

As I write and make presentations on the onslaught of change in the American—and increasingly globalized—workplace, I am repeatedly asked, usually with doubt if not a note of censure in the questioner's voice: "How can things really be *that* bad so as to justify comparison with the Holocaust?" In different words, the person is asking: "How can the organizational darkness you are directing us to see be so desolate, so irredeemably bleak?" It does not seem to matter to my interlocutor (or interrogator) that I was not the one to choose the symbol. What occurs feels akin to "Shoot the messenger" (or reporter). The "message" is too jarring to be metabolized.

This chapter explores some shared psychological meanings of Holocaust imagery (Levi 1988) by people experiencing downsizing, reengineering, restructuring, managed care, and other forms of "managed" social change in the United States. I present a brief case example to illustrate how the evidence for the Holocaust metaphor lies in the action that carries the seed of its emotional plausibility. The vignette takes us, I believe, close to the heart of a person's experience that leads to the "choice" of the image: in this case, both of the Jew as victim, and of the Nazi as destroyer. If generalizations in interpretation or abstractions in theory are to ring true, they must be firmly grounded in life. The story, not the theory, must first persuade. Only fidelity to the data can advance theory and method, and honor the reality of the subject we are studying.

It is my countertransference that leads me (and others) from experience of action to its symbolization, that is, to the conscious recognition that even this is "like" the Holocaust. By listening via my own unconscious, I can comprehend and hold on to others' projection of Holocaust imagery and language onto contemporary American workplace cataclysm.

Since the end of World War II and the revelation of the Nazi war of extermination (Dawidowicz 1975), the word *Holocaust* has been adopted by many different groups, under varied circumstances, to designate the nature of their suffering (Beisel 1999). The English word *Holocaust* itself comes from the Hebrew word, *olah*, a sacrifice to God in the form of a *completely* burnt offering. An *olah* is a specific kind of sacrifice in which none of the animal is kept for human consumption, but is offered up in flames and smoke to God. Whatever else atrocities, genocides, and other horrors are called by those who undergo them, they are often characterized as a Holocaust. At least one common structural denominator is the concentration of power that makes institutional terror possible.

While participating in my own workplace organization, in my frequent role as speaker or presenter at national conferences, and in my capacity as organizational consultant (interviewer, participant observer), I have often heard downsizing, reengineering, restructuring, and managed care described in the idiom of the Holocaust. What is one to make of the cultural borrowing of this highly charged image? What is its psychodynamic significance? What, exactly, does it embody and condense? How does this use correspond to, or differ with, the use of the Holocaust by other groups? As a Jew, how do I listen to these narratives and not discount them as flights of hyperbole?

In this chapter I shall present an extended example of this use and suggest some interpretations. I attempt to answer the question: Exactly what kind of trope is the Holocaust in workplace organization thinking?

THE HOLOCAUST AS METAPHOR FOR EVIL

In *The Holocaust and the Crisis of Human Behavior*, George Kren and Leon Rappoport ask: "Why does the Holocaust not fade away?" (1994: 3). They reply:

> . . . insofar as the Holocaust is seen in general moral terms, it stands out as the ultimate expression of the human capacity for organized evil and has come to serve as the standard to which all lesser or proximate evils are compared. Accordingly, over the past decades any substantial threat to the existence or basic rights of an oppressed population or minority group has triggered appeals to the Holocaust. (1994: 4)

The Holocaust can be used "as a reminder of past evil, and . . . as an explanation (or analogy) of present events" (Gary Holmes, personal communication, 1 October 1999). Among those who commit atrocities, it is commonly invoked to diminish personal responsibility for action, if not to exonerate oneself, and to rationalize for oneself a victim ideology ("I was just following orders").

A widespread group psychological use of the Holocaust is to turn suffering from an absolute, lonely experience, into a comparative, relative experience. One encounters statements such as: "We suffered (a) as much as you did; (b) more than you did." Such comparative positions serve what Franco Fornari (1966) called "the paranoid elaboration of mourning," substituting vigilance and anger for vulnerability and grief. It is a salve for loss through continued fighting.

David Beisel (1999), by contrast, argues that

> what we are witnessing with the appearance of widespread competitive victimhood is not merely multicultural copycat-ism, but something truly profound, even revolutionary, in the history of childhood. . . . [E]ven if improvements are merely only a couple of decades old, the new victimhood may be telling us that the sons and daughters of a new generation, by identifying with the Jewish victims of Nazi persecution and expressing themselves through competitive victimhood, are not only ready to express the silent suffering of their parents, but are preparing themselves to weep their own impacted tears. (1999: 92)

Given the rancor of demands for entitlement in the choice of victim-identity, I wonder whether even this psychological advance is not sabotaged by the regressive withdrawal of empathy from others not of one's ethnic, national, or corporate kind.

By contrast with this widespread narcissistic-defensive usage, I find that many Americans evoke Holocaust images (e.g., Nazis, SS police, Jews, Gypsies, Slavs, trains, Dr. Josef Mengele, selection for life or death, gas chambers, labor camps, large scale executions, euphemisms, secrecy, rumors, disappearance) as an idiom by which to comprehend the extent, depth, and kind of suffering they have experienced in the workplace since the early 1980s. The "symbol choice" directs us—if we can bear to hear it—to the speaker's catastrophic experience and to the psychohistoric dynamics of work-group representation or group fantasy. When individuals, families, workplace organizations, and ethnic-national groups suffer catastrophe, they search for metaphors that—affectively and cognitively—attempt to answer the question: What is this experience like? (Ogden 1997). The effort at "likening" becomes an intermediate area between consciousness and unconsciousness. It becomes a way of containing and of holding on to the horrific experience.

Because I wish here primarily to immerse the reader in the phenomenology of business-as-Holocaust, I refer the reader to a growing literature by psychologists, psychiatrists, physicians, and scholars of contemporary managed social change (Allcorn, Baum, Diamond, and Stein 1996; Barondess 1998; Li 1996; Lotto 1998; Stein 1998; Warner 1996).

A POIGNANT LETTER FROM A COLLEAGUE

In late September 1999, I received a letter from a senior Jewish academic and teacher in an American biomedical setting, a person I have known for fifteen years. Her poignancy and remarkable candor take us to the heart of my subject matter: *the Holocaust as trope for what passes officially for American corporate "business as usual."* My colleague had read my book, *Euphemism, Spin, and the Crisis in Organizational Life.* In the summer of 1999, I had sent her a manuscript for a plenary I would present at the Society for Psychological Anthropology in Albuquerque on 22 September 1999. It was titled "From Countertransference to Social Theory: A Study of Holocaust Thinking in American Business Dress" (now, slightly modified, as chapter two in this book). With only a few minor adaptations to assure confidentiality, I quote her letter in its entirety, and with her permission.

> I read your paper "A Study in Holocaust Thinking. . . ." It was tremendously powerful—shocking really. Simply the juxtaposition of the two language categories of the title—holocaust and American business—is profoundly troubling. The article raised deeply personal issues for me. This is what I must share with you at the moment.
>
> As you may recall, I spent two years (1992–1994) as acting chair of my department of internal medicine, a challenging, demanding, and ultimately extremely painful and soul-crushing time for me. When I relinquished that position, I spent the next year on sabbatical, attempting to become a prototypical National Institute of Medicine hard science researcher—and shortly thereafter underwent a series of health crises, including the near loss of the sight in one eye (wonder why!). In any event, I never really allowed myself to process the administrative experience or to reflect on why it had caused me such anguish. Reading your article, I was overcome by feelings of guilt and shame, as I realized how—on a small scale— I came to approximate the aggressors you portrayed.
>
> Although I always tried to act with integrity, I think looking back that I was frequently co-opted by the dominant bottom-line cor-

porate thinking that you describe so well. For example, I personally fired two colleagues whom I had known and worked closely with for over ten years, simply because they could no longer prove their "utility" to the system. I am convinced now, with hindsight, that their terminations were only symbolic in nature, did nothing substantial to assuage our budget problems, and were primarily sacrificial acts to appease forces both within and without the department. The more I read of your analysis, the more I realized just how guilty I was of the sins you cite—the euphemized language, the personification and subsequent glorification of the institutional organism, the denial of the still small voice within, the sense of having "disappeared" good human beings, who in a day became obliterated from our world. There are other examples as well.

I guess I am sharing all this because I believe I am basically a good human being who has always identified more with the oppressed than with the oppressor (and indeed as a social scientist and non-M.D., as you well know, have always been more oppressee than oppressor). Yet how easily power corrupted me and created a damning shift in perspective. I began to dream the collective dream, and it wasn't that hard. Clearly I paid a price—I attribute my subsequent health problems at least in part to the internalizing and somaticizing of tremendous levels of anxiety and distress—but on a conscious level I thought I was just exhibiting necessary toughness, showing I could be "one of the boys."

The striking thing in what you write is that to NOT dream the dream, play the game, you almost have to be crazy—and very brave, to trust your inner experience in the face of overwhelming disconfirming messages from the outside world. But on balance, it is better to be crazy than cruel. I had the opportunity to become a nazi—a little baby nazi to be sure, but there it was—and I seized it eagerly. Eventually, as your article points out, I was eaten in turn, when I was no longer useful to the survival of the machine. I don't wonder at all how the holocaust could have happened.

Well, my friend, I hope these thoughts are not too depressing. Although I admit to being temporarily devastated as these unlooked-for insights worked their way up from my unconscious, on balance I learned a great deal. For example, I think my subsequent physical recovery and professional fulfillment are both direct results of my having had the wisdom to voluntarily renounce the chair position (which out of pragmatism more than anything else, the dean had asked me to accept on a permanent basis) and relearn the skill of listening to my own heart. That inward turning is also what eventually moved me away from hard research toward the medical humanities, and I can honestly say I have recovered my soul in the process.

So while I have had to face that good people, including myself, can do bad things, I have also discovered that *teshuvah* (Hebrew, for repentance) and redemption both are possible. Good lessons for the new year. And I have to thank your article for helping me to bring all of this into such clear focus. I thank you for your plain speaking, your courage, and your unwillingness to deny and distance from some very brutal truths. If this be insanity, then we need more of it.

I really owe you (and your article) a great debt for articulating things that I knew but chose not to know. I have actually been thinking about writing something about that whole experience, but up until now it still seemed too close, too personal, and maybe too much like sour grapes. Also too inchoate. Perhaps your wonderful article will help provide me with a framework. Anyway, I'll see.

DISCUSSION

This single example, a personal letter, can be read as a cultural or historical exemplar or distillation that articulates what many people say. For countless others it serves as the "unthought known" (Bollas 1989). My colleague makes the implicit explicit, the unconscious conscious. She describes part of the journey to unconsciousness and back to consciousness. Her letter reveals hard-won insights into herself, into processes widely shared in contemporary American culture—and the personal cost of unconscious identification with the aggressor. It is reminiscent of Robert J. Lifton's [1979] studies of "psychic numbing" and "doubling" (similar to Melanie Klein's [1946] "splitting" and "projective identification"), and of Donald Winnicott's [1965] distinction between the "false self" and the "real self."

In part at least, my friend and colleague's experience seems to be, among other things, the lure of power and acceptance—to be "one of the boys"—which was the bribe-of-the-conscience for a while, until her body (her health) talked back. Had she become a "victim" to her wish to belong and to have real power? The ambition to be "one of the boys" condenses gender, status, and social mobility aspirations, to name but three. The three-decade-old feminist revolution notwithstanding, she felt compelled to become a symbolic male in order to succeed—and in the process betrayed herself. Then, too, it is as if she had to become a Nazi (= male, assertive) in order to escape the fate of being a Jew (= female, historically feminized, passive).

As I read and reread her letter, I remembered seeing her at medical conferences, impeccably attired in formal business suits and carrying a fashionable attaché case—different from her previous more relaxed comportment. I remembered her manner to be respectful and pleasant, but certainly more distant from the earlier years of our intense friendship.

The letter shows how, in the juncture between personal life history and organizational (cultural) history, the true self is (here, temporarily) cast aside and recovered. It shows how Holocaust thinking, imagery, and acting can be engaged in within "normal" American health care, university, corporate, and government settings—how behavior that at first seems disturbing and repugnant (not-me) becomes recognizable (me: as in "I did that"; "I was that"). Her letter is about secrecy from others and secrecy even from oneself; and about breaking the spell and bondage of that secrecy. Finally, the letter is an intersubjective document, an interpersonal space, in which she trusts to see herself and to be seen. It is about personal insight and the kind of emotional setting in which such insight may emerge and be integrated.

CONCLUSIONS

This chapter has described and interpreted the symbolic linkage between modern large-scale American business organizational style and the Holocaust. A personal narrative was used to illustrate with painful concreteness how American workplace experience comes to be represented in the idiom of Nazi atrocity. I have argued that the Holocaust can be used psychologically as a trope for the experience of massive forms of "managed" social change in the workplace, forms that go by such terms as downsizing, RIFing, surplusing, separating, outsourcing, reengineering, restructuring, and managed health care.

Via a single personal document, I have offered data that help us to understand how the Holocaust comes to be a compelling internal representation and external expression within the world of American business. The individual case study brings cultural metaphor into the realm of personal choice, meaning, experience, and life history. It helps to ground abstractions in real lives. Although it is, in a narrow sense, only an "N of 1," it is an exemplar of widely felt, but less articulated sentiment. In the process of exploring one executive's professional journey, I hope to have contributed to a deeper understanding of organizational darkness in countless ordinary workplaces. The next chapter will continue this exploration, only in the language of far more psychologically "ordinary" workplace catastrophes.

REFERENCES

Allcorn, Seth, Howell S. Baum, Michael A. Diamond, and Howard F. Stein. 1996. *The HUMAN Cost of a Management Failure: Organizational Downsizing at General Hospital.* Westport, CT: Quorum Books.

Barondess, Jeremiah H. 1998. "Care of the Medical Ethos: Reflections on Social Darwinism, Racial Hygiene, and the Holocaust," *Annals of Internal Medicine* 129: 891–898.

Beisel, David R. 1999. "Reflections on Competitive Victimhood," *Clio's Psyche* 6(3), December: 89–92.

Bollas, Christopher. 1989. *In the Shadow of the Object: Psychoanalysis of the Unthought Known*. New York: Columbia University Press.

Dawidowicz, Lucy. 1975. *The War Against the Jews, 1933–1945*. New York: Holt, Rinehart, and Winston.

Fornari, Franco. 1966. *The Psychoanalysis of War*. New York: Anchor/Doubleday, 1975.

Holmes, Gary. Personal communication, 1 October 1999.

Klein, Melanie. 1946. "Some Notes on Schizoid Mechanisms," *International Journal of Psycho-Analysis* 27: 99–110.

Kren, George and Leon Rappoport. 1994. *The Holocaust and the Crisis of Human Behavior*. New York: Holmes & Meier.

Levi, Primo. 1988. *The Drowned and the Saved*. New York: Summit Books.

Li, James T. C. 1996. "The Physician-Patient Relationship: Covenant or Contract?" *Mayo Clinic Proceedings* 71: 917–918.

Lifton, Robert Jay. 1979. *The Broken Connection: On Death and the Continuity of Life*. New York: Simon and Schuster.

Lotto, David J. 1998. "The Corporate Takeover of the Soul: The Current State of the American Health Care System," *Journal of Psychohistory* 26(2), Fall: 603–609.

Ogden, Thomas. 1997. "Reverie and Metaphor: Some Thoughts on How I Work as a Psychoanalyst," *International Journal of Psycho-Analysis* 78: 719–732.

Stein, Howard F. 1998. *Euphemism, Spin, and the Crisis in Organizational Life*. Westport, CT: Quorum Books.

Warner, Ernest. 1996. "Ethics and Morality vs. Managed Care," *Journal of the Oklahoma State Medical Association* 89 (August): 275–279.

Winnicott, Donald W. 1965. *The Maturational Processes and the Facilitating Environment*. New York: International Universities Press.

5

Ordinary Brutality at Work

Brutalization of work and worker—of person and of production—assumes many forms that do not necessarily or automatically conjure images of the Holocaust. One may reply that inside their worlds, Nazism, Stalinism, Maoism were all quite "ordinary." Perhaps one day we shall view our own era with horror as well. For now, the "ordinary" violence in the workplace this chapter explores is of a "symbolic" rather than brutally physical kind.

This chapter explores several examples of ordinary brutality at work via five vignettes taken from my experience as worker, teacher, and consultant. Although I offer some interpretation, here I primarily try to let people speak for themselves. Voicelessness is, for certain, a casualty of the insistence that "nothing personal" is taking place, that everything is "business as usual." To give, to have, and to receive voice are special gifts.

"NATIONALISM" AND "XENOPHOBIA" AT THE WORKPLACE ORGANIZATIONAL LEVEL

Over the past decade and a half, I have come to focus on understanding cultural processes within workplace organizations in the United States: for example, hospitals, clinical departments, corporations, industries, government, educational institutions, and private and public administration (1994, 1997, 1998a, 1998b). I have discovered that *much of the emotional life of organizations not only "resembles" that of the nations and*

*ethnic groups of which they are an institutional part, but it is in fact identical
in a different form and social unit* (Stein 1999). This is true both in relatively
stable times and in the current era of convulsing social change (downsizing, RIFing, reengineering, restructuring, outsourcing, deskilling,
managed care, corporate mergers and takeovers).

My inference comes from various settings. In addition to observing the
workplace cultures where I am employed (health sciences center), I have
often served as formal and informal organizational consultant. These
roles have offered me the opportunity for intensive, comparative fieldwork. For several years in the mid-1990s, I was invited by the CEO to
serve as longitudinal internal consultant to the downsizing of The University Hospitals in Oklahoma City, a role which gave me firsthand insight into the emotional as well as structural processes involved in a
major social form of our time. At the same time, I was involved in coau-
thoring a study of another hospital downsizing (Allcorn, Baum, Diamond, and Stein 1996), which allowed me to compare the group
psychology at two vastly different sites.

The first two vignettes or illustrations are taken from fieldwork and
consultations I have done in *workplace organizations* in the United States
during the past decade. Some of it is from participant observation, while
some derives from formal consultations, internal and external. The material is compiled from field notes, slightly fictionalized to disguise organization and speaker. The two vignettes will attest to the presence in
corporate workplaces of core psychodynamic and cultural processes
found in *ethnonationalist* movements and groups. "Nationalist" sentiment, ideology, and action can be enacted in a "corporate" idiom and
can take a "corporate" form.

Vignette I: The Jew in Their Midst

The following example illustrates the operation of patently "national-
istic" thinking in ordinary workplaces, businesses, and institutions. It
entails a conflict between a unit director and a researcher working in his
unit in a large research and development institute. The supervisor is a
brilliant, ambitious academic medical researcher who is building his own
institute and wide regional network. The language of their conflict points
to the presence of unconscious issues fueling the strife. In the employee's
narrative, the supervisor constantly degrades his worker, often humiliating him in private. Although the employee's ostensible job description
was to serve as an applied sociologist on R&D projects, the supervisor
forbade him even to use the concepts of "culture" or "society" in his
work because "nobody will understand you." The colleague-employee
was widely published in the supervisor's field, but the supervisor often
said to him:

You've published a lot, but very few people in the field can understand what you're saying. . . . You keep asking for respect, but
you don't deserve any. You've received numerous national awards
for your work, but they are given by the wrong organizations.
Don't you understand that they don't count around here?

Oddly, many of the ideas the employee proposed and championed,
and which the supervisor publicly ridiculed or harshly condemned, the
supervisor later adopted as his own in projects, grant applications, and
publications. When the employee would try to inquire about this mys-
terious appearance, the supervisor would insist that the ideas were his
own, or had come from an entirely different source. He separated, dissociated himself from his colleague's/coworker's influence. Identification
was mostly unconscious; dis-identification, repudiation, was vigilantly
conscious.

On one occasion, the supervisor temporarily softened and confided in
the employee:

Maybe I envy you a little. I've always wanted to be a field and
stream biologist, not a hard-driving researcher and administrator
responsible for the production of a large group of people. I look at
you and I see what I'd like to be: here's a guy who does what he
likes and doesn't listen to anyone. I sure would like to have the job
description where I could devote 50% of my time to writing and
publishing.

For a moment, the supervisor allowed himself to identify consciously
with his worker. Quickly, admiration returned to envy. The colleague
came again to embody what Erikson (1968) spoke of as the "negative
identity," that is, the condensed image of all one rejects about oneself
and one's internal representations. On a later occasion, while the employee was driving the supervisor to an affiliate R&D site, the supervisor
engaged in lecturing the employee as to the nature of his colleague's
problem. He was diagnosing his worker's problem, and offering him
help:

What is it with you Jews? You act just like the other Jews I've
known. I've never been able to understand why you act as if you're
so special. Look at the history of the Weimar Republic before Hitler
came into power. Jews were overrepresented in government, in the
arts, in science, in medicine, in the media, in everything. They were
in control of the whole country. Can't you understand why Ger-
mans wanted to get rid of them, to get their own country back?
It seems to me like the Jews bring persecutions upon themselves.

I know it's terrible to say—and I'll deny that this conversation ever took place if you say anything about it—but the Jews push their way into everything. What happened to them was horrible, but much of it owes to their own doing. It's the same here in America. Jews have infiltrated the government, the news media, the arts, science. They want to control everything.

And you're just like them. You act as if everyone is against you, and it is not true. You get surprised when we push back. I don't know how to get you to realize that I'm on your side. You just need to downplay your writing projects in the home office. You've got to realize that few R&D specialists anywhere can read and understand your papers. Your future here in the corporation depends on your ability to be less rigid and to trust me.

The protection the supervisor proffered was a protection racket. The employee had touched something raw in the supervisor. His employee had come to represent something sinister, a side of himself he had wished to be, but had repudiated. Hypernationalist (e.g., Nazi) stereotypes and xenophobia played a central role in the supervisor's perception, experience, and management of the workplace conflict. Its "transference" to the employee was a motivating force for the diatribe and harrassment.

Vignette 2: From Exodus to Liberation—Rectification of Names, American Style

In the following vignette, I am serving as consultant to the Union Textile Company, and am speaking with Jack, an upper-level unit manager. He is recounting the recent history of the company, one that entails massive, brutal, social change.

Howard, there's something terrible going on here in our textile company. Like an infection more and more people are coming down with. Except the infection's supposed to be the cure. It's eating away at us, even though everyone's going around like we're perfectly normal—even better than normal.

About ten months ago, seven middle managers all resigned within a month of each other. They had all worked together and the rest of us here knew them all. They helped us get through some rough times when a lot of the upper executives were flying all over the place making presentations and showing how great we were doing. Except they rarely were home, and when they came home they had their fingers in everything. That's what's behind the word "micromanage," having to control everything and everybody. It's like they take over your thoughts and invade your body. That's what it feels like. Well, the seven who up and left helped stabilize the place for nearly a decade. They hardly traveled anywhere. They were home-bodies. They helped us to get through a day, a week, a month. They weren't visionaries, just hard workers. They were the grunts who did the detailed stuff. But they got chewed up and spit out. Promises were made—Howard, I don't know the details—and were broken. So were the spirits of these seven.

For months after they left, many of us referred to it as "the exodus." It felt like it. We missed those guys. We felt that they abandoned us. We tried not to think about them, just bury ourselves in work. We were supposed to pretend that nothing happened, that everything was just business. We were supposed to suck it up and make up for their work while we trained their replacements. How do you train someone to become a Rolodex that's worth a billion dollars in contacts? The men and women who took their places aren't bad, they're just not the guys who became our friends. We don't know whether to try to leave or stay here.

It's gotten bad for us. But we're not supposed to feel that. It's supposed to be like everyday's Thanksgiving, when the CEO, the CFO, and the various vice presidents put on white coats and chefs' hats and serve all the employees in line. But it isn't. The other day at a managers' retreat, the CEO—he loves to give Sunday sermons—gave us a pep talk. He said, "You know, I'm tired of hearing people talk about what happened nearly a year ago as though it were a tragedy for the company. We call it The Exodus, The Leaving, The Bailout, The Jumping Ship. It's as though we think we're worse off since they left. That's a bunch of crap. That's a myth. We've *benefited* from their going. They weren't especially loyal and I don't remember them contributing much to the organization. We're not survivors of some calamity. This is a big opportunity for us."

(Still quoting his CEO, Jack speaks now in a frenzied, triumphant voice, as though a general, leading a charge) "I'll tell you: Some people call this an Exodus. From this day forth, we're going to call it The Liberation! Union Textiles is in for a great future. And everyone here is privileged to be a part of it!"

Howard, I'm ashamed to admit it, but I'm scared by talk like this. The people who left Union Textiles had faults, but they weren't garbage. We're a company, and this is getting to feel like a football rally or preparation for war. It's not the way everybody tries to make it look. It's ugly, Howard, and a lot of us are downright depressed. And when we're not depressed, we're downright scared. It's like we're a chapter from *Nineteen Eighty-Four. This is*

America, the United States, Howard! This kind of thing doesn't happen here.

This vignette vividly illustrates at the corporate (mid-scale group) level many of the psychological processes familiar in nationalist movements. Leadership, with the identification and intimidation of the group, advocates an ideology based on us/them, good/bad distinctions. A radically sunny, revitalizing vision of the group rests upon a radical disparagement of categories of group members, past or present. Shame and guilt are denied and reversed into manic pride, as if to say: "They didn't leave us; we are rid of them." What began nearly a year earlier as a *de facto* purge that drove a cadre of mid-managers to seek employment elsewhere, reappears now as an active, ideological purge to rid the current organization of feelings of badness. They are to be "disappeared" effaced from the memory of Union Textiles.

Much as with deposed imperial and national leaders, the presence of these corporate managers is to be reversed from glory to ignominy to symbolic annihilation. The leader, an ambitious CEO, capitalizes on his workers' dependency, anxiety, and wished-for grandiosity to identify uncritically with his own corporate plan and with his rewriting of group history. As with shamanic leadership (Devereux 1955; La Barre 1972), the vulnerability of the group and the destructive narcissism of the shaman are symbiotically made for each other.

An equally radical distinction is made between foreigners (bad people) and the real people (good people). Once familiar people become foreign, estranged, and are re-classified from human into nonhuman, from loyalists to menaces. Organizational xenophobia serves to shore up organizational hyper-groupism (the workplace equivalent of hypernationalism). "Inside" is purchased at the price or expense of "outside," an expulsion to the outside of those first dehumanized inside. Leaders enlist allies by distinguishing them from clear-cut enemies (Volkan 1988).

It is, I believe, our reluctance (resistance, in the psychoanalytic sense) to classify "merely" symbolic violence with actual violence that leads us to separate ideological Stalinism or Maoism with the "ordinary" psychological terrorism of many workplaces such as the above. Yet functionally, the managerial "house-cleaning" the CEO triumphantly declared is the same as bloody "ethnic cleansings" in the Balkans in the late 1990s. What, I must wonder, are the consequences for worker morale and productivity, and for subsequent generations of Americans, when what doesn't happen here, does happen here? When "there" becomes "here"?

ORGANIZATIONAL CATACLYSM AND MEMORY

In organizational disasters as in "natural" disasters and wars, their toll and putative "effect" are far from simple or entirely immediate. People "do" things with what they have experienced, bring narratives and meanings to them, and make sense of them long after. The "effect" plays insidious, unrecognized roles in shaping the future.

Vignette 3: "You're Making Too Much of Something"

The third vignette illustrates the toll taken on organizations, and their members, as they strive to "return to normal" after repeated downsizings, restructurings, and reengineerings. The course of the beginning of one consultation is emblematic for many I have experienced. Here, I am speaking with a man whom I shall call Jerry, a veteran manager in a large chemical manufacturing firm. We are in a preliminary role negotiation about the consultation his company seeks. Before committing himself, he had asked to see written copies of some of my earlier consulting work, and opened with some comments on it.

(Somewhat formal, businesslike) Howard, I want to talk with you about what a consultation with our chemical firm would entail. I've taken a look at the report to the petroleum company that you gave me. It gives me an idea of how you work, what you look for, and what some of the outcomes are. Overall, I like what I see and I think you can help us to achieve our goals.

(Slowly) There's one part, though, that I don't understand. In one section, where you're talking about how people experience downsizing, you go on and on, page after page, about how awful it is for everyone involved. It's like reading a wall of words or running into this wall. I get your point, but (hesitation) why do you need to go into it for so long? (Protestingly) I don't get it, Howard. Please understand, I'm not questioning that RIFing's difficult to live through. But it's like you wallow in it. Or you describe how the petrochemical employees wallow in it. We've got to get over it and get on with the work of the firm.

Hell, Howard, I've had *my* share here during the twelve years I've been in the division. And I didn't go whining about it. For several years, in addition to doing my regular job, it's as if I had a full-time second job trying to protect my employees and my whole unit from being wiped out. Some of the senior executives, and an earlier consulting firm, recommended dissolving our unit, RIFing several of the managers and employees, and merging the remaining ones with another division in the company.

(Jerry continues, more animated, louder, almost shouting) I can't begin to tell you how many hours, days, I spend on the phone, in meetings, firing memos, to try to protect my men. It's like we were in combat with our own! Day after day, I never knew what missile I'd have to dodge next and keep from blowing up here. It's like for three years I did nothing but justify our existence. Howard, I couldn't sleep. I put on thirty pounds. My home life went to hell—partly because I was hardly there, and when I was, I was worried sick about taking care of my people. How do you protect people when all the rules keep changing? I didn't know how to justify our existence. It's not as if we were making the company lose money. Nobody was more productive than our team. You could never anticipate what mattered to make a difference between life and death.

(Intensely, as if looking through me into the distance) And it was hard for me to face them every day. What was I going to tell them? And how could I help. Sometimes the only thing I could do was to wait with them, and listen. Sometimes they'd ask, but mostly they'd just keep quiet and work like a bunch of desperate beavers to build their dam. I could tell from their faces that they were preoccupied. They were sullen, just not themselves. And sometimes I went out of my way not to face them. I'd just get off the elevator and bolt into my office and bury myself in work. The ordeal lasted so long. It's like we all went on permanent alert status.

(Out of breath, exhausted, he catches himself, stops, briefly laughs, looks directly at me, and says slowly) Look at me, Howard! I'm doing the same thing I just accused you of. I'm going on and on about it. You must be bored stiff listening to all this. But this is the first time since the ordeal ended three years ago that I've had the chance to talk about it with anyone. We were too busy to think.

You can't imagine how horrible it was! And it lingers, even when you think you've forgotten about it. Somehow, you brought it all back. I didn't realize that it was still so raw. (He has a look of "recognition" about him; more relaxed, more at peace.)

Many people who have been downsized and RIFed, or who have struggled to protect their personnel—and with a sense of guilt of having to fire them—protect themselves by doing their jobs with a vengeance. Both consciously and unconsciously, they try not to remember what happened to them or what they did. The past becomes oppressive, and only the present counts. The attitude is often one of "suck it up and move on." When they are confronted by the past again, they often become uncomfortable, impatient, if not openly hostile. They are often imprisoned by unconscious guilt (including survivor guilt), shame, rage, and by what Shatan (1997) calls "impacted tears." They traumatize others, bind them to their own traumatic pasts to protect themselves against feeling their own shattered vulnerability.

In the above consulting scenario, Jerry the mid-level manager accused me of exaggerating the emotional experience of downsizing, only to realize as we spoke that he had made the accusation in order to fend off his own powerful, repressed feelings and their associated memories. His verbal explosion at me was a momentary acting out, that is, remembering in action, which was a prelude to his remembering in words and feelings.

His initial disagreement was an attempt at counteridentification, that is, to distance himself emotionally from me, from my experience, and from the report I had written. In a self-protective maneuver, he accuses me of "wallowing" in the material. He does this in order to fend off how volatile his own experience remains—if he will allow himself to think about and to feel it in the present. Wishing to disagree with me about the emotional intensity—and toll—that I had documented in my report, he ends up not only agreeing but, in his own way, "wallowing" in his suddenly unrepressed experience, despite his conscious intent.

CLEANSING THE ORGANIZATION: CHARISMATIC LEADERSHIP AND ORDINARY DEHUMANIZATION

The decade of the 1990s is known for vast slaughter of people in the name of "ethnic cleansing"—even as a "new world order" had been declared following the collapse of the Soviet Union and the end of the Cold War. From Rwanda to Bosnia and Kosovo, the "purification" of populations by eviction and murder became known worldwide through television and other media. Bloodless corporate cleansings have similarly occurred in those vast—little noted—population movements triggered by downsizing, reengineering, and managed health care.

Vignette 4: Why Is He Here?

The fourth vignette illustrates the ordinariness of workplace dehumanization and victimization under the guise of charismatic corporate leadership. It illustrates the process of management by intimidation. The leader rewrites history during the course of a management retreat. His tactics of isolation and splitting are dynamically similar to the ethnonationalist ethnic cleansing of "them" from "us." CEO George fosters group solidarity (based on dependency) through internal enemy-making.

The setting is a corporate executive retreat, perhaps forty middle managers in attendance. The speaker is George, the CEO of a division of a large multisite company. He is reconvening the retreat group after a morning coffee break. Sitting very straight and formal, he looks around to get everyone's attention, then speaks in a serious tone. (My notes here are approximate and evoke the intensity of the group process and not always the exact words used.)

(As if recapitulating) The executive retreat's going well so far. I hope you all had an enjoyable coffee break. Let's get back to work.

I have a concern (pause), one that's a harbinger of things to come. A few days ago, I was in an upper-management meeting with the CEO, the Vice President for Financial Affairs, the Vice President for Operations, and many other top executives of the home office. They started throwing questions at me I couldn't answer. I want to bring those concerns to you. They're looking at costs; they're looking at space utilization so that we can make it more profitable.

They asked me point blank why Irv's (a mid-level manager and internal consultant) here in the unit, even why he's here in the company at all. They think it's a poor fit. They can't see that Irv contributes anything. (Hearing a sound from across the room, looking up, hearing Irv say something, then continuing) . . . *Irv, let me finish.* Please don't interrupt until I've given the whole story. (Looking directly at Irv) I know that you've received many performance awards over the years, even some national recognition for your work. I know you didn't go out and buy those plaques yourself. But don't you see how hard this is for me? Look at the position you put me in.

(George continues, hearing Irv attempt to say soomething) What's that you're saying now, Irv? We've worked together here for ten years and, of all people, I should know what you do and why the company should keep you. Irv, you don't understand. Try to see it through my eyes. They put me on the spot. I wasn't expecting them to pin me down. And, to be honest, I haven't supervised your work directly for a long time. I just assumed you were doing your job.

(Angry now, on the attack) Don't make this any harder on me! The times are heartless. Profit's down, competition's cutthroat. Upper management is trying to keep the ship afloat. We're just trying to survive, Irv. We have to show that we deserve to work here. It's nothing personal, Irv. I decided to bring this issue back to our executive retreat because I didn't know how to answer them. Maybe you all can help me to explain what Irv is doing here.

(George addresses the group, looking around, while keeping composure, almost like a general addressing his troops) And it's not just Irv, ladies and gentlemen. It's thousands of employees and managers here like Irv. Upper management is in a mood to downsize a lot of us because they can't determine what many of us do for the company. After downsizing is reengineering and outsourcing some units. (More excitedly) I was at a loss to explain to them about Irv's situation. So I brought it back to our executive retreat here. (Complete silence from the group)

Here, the CEO George comes to feel powerless, even persecuted by employee Irv. The projection of hostility turns into sham innocence and denial. It is as if George, and the group, are held hostage, victimized by Irv, whom the leader is victimizing by humiliating him publicly, among other things. George creates the illusion that Irv's predicament is entirely outside the moral order inhabited by George and fellow upper management. He diminishes his own anxiety by casting his own fate with the organizational hierarchy, and he dissociates himself from his long history with Irv. Irv becomes group sacrifice.

FAMILY MEDICINE AS HISTORICAL MICROCOSM

Organizational theorists and consultants alike grapple with the issue of the *boundary* of the social unit they are trying to understand or to help. What happens when the boundary of the problem is coextensive with the boundary of the entire society? The recent history of corporations or professions can be approached as a historical microcosm of the society. The brutality "inside" is part of the brutality "outside." We pay attention to what "they" did to "us" in order not to notice (and to feel) what "we" do to "ourselves" (e.g., Russians focus on Hitler as demonic partially in order to "forget" atrocities under their own leader, Stalin). We engage in splitting and projection in order to preserve the sense of unambivalent goodness inside the group upon which we feel dependent for our very lives.

Vignette 5: From Counterculture to Brave New World

It is both paradoxical and ironic that my final, and extended, vignette on the dehumanization of worker and of work comes from family medicine. I wrote earlier in this book that things are not what they seem—and often "seeming" refers to official positions and doctrines. Things are supposed to "seem" certain ways, and yet often they are not. But one is not supposed to notice: respect, self-respect, job advancement, sense of belonging, and even employment itself, are bound up with failing to notice. I have served as a faculty member and clinical teacher in a family medicine department since 1978 and have functioned nationally in many of the profession's activities. Of all the biomedical specialties, family medicine has for three decades proclaimed its distinctiveness if not uniqueness in its humane, personalized attitude toward patients, illness, and treatment of disease. Yet there is often an immense disparity between espoused ideals and lived reality, between the mission statement embodied in plaques and the actual agendas carried out.

Family medicine is a discipline, practice mode, and organization that developed both out of, and in reaction to, the "general practice" philosophy and style that had prevailed during the era of specialization and before. Stephens (1987: 3) identifies the rise of family practice within the climate of social (not only medical) "reform that existed in the 1960's and early '70's before the current backlash of political and economic conservatism set in (Stephens 1976)." Family medicine began as a social movement simultaneously within biomedicine and American society.

> Without doubt family practice attracted a motley crowd of physicians and fellow-travellers whose claims were extravagant and utopian and whose politics were opportunistic; but it also symbolized a generation's passion for equity in medical care, its desire to open up the stern rigidities of medical education to a broader more humanistic curriculum and to decentralize the power of the medical schools (Stephens 1979). (1987: 3–4). . . .
>
> Now the focus of change in medicine is almost entirely on cost control, and corporate capitalism, abetted by a laissez-faire federal policy to promote competition in health care, is having a go at reorganizing the entire "health care delivery system." (1987: 4)

Numbering among most frequently cited "core values" of family medicine are continuity of care (or longitudinality), comprehensiveness of care, empathic care from a personal physician, care for the person as well as for the disease, care for the individual in the context of one's family, care for the medically underserved. In contrast to the public articulation and assertion of these as eternal verities, one can infer—as well as be told by those embittered by the disparity—a far different set of operant values. For instance, "Follow the money" (that is, who and what types of projects are well-funded) can be amplified to also read: (1) "Follow the *technology*" (who receives what level of high technology to function); (2) "Follow the *support staff*" (who receives what quality of medical and administrative staff to accomplish tasks, a measure of the social worth of the person and project); (3) "Follow the *status* and *advancement*" (who gets promoted, and how long it takes); and (4) "Follow the *symbols* and *awards*" (who receives what types of symbolic as well as financial recognition).

At a family medicine departmental faculty meeting a decade and a half ago, participants were discussing family medicine values, priorities, and decision-making in a rather philosophical vein. Someone introduced the notion of the "Golden Rule" as a guiding principle (which reads, "Do unto others as you would have others do unto you," a frequently invoked aphorism in the Judeo-Christian traditions). The chairman abruptly retorted: "Around here, we live by a different Golden Rule: 'He who has the gold, makes the rules.' " The conversation was over.

In the continuing struggles over funding, stature, space allocation, "turf," power, and other social desirables in biomedicine, those who advocate for greater health care access (equity) for indigent or "underserved" populations, for careful integration of the complexities of sickness and healing, and for careful attention to the personal, relational side of medicine, now (at the turn of the century) number fewer among physician and medical educator ranks and are far less socially acknowledged or "rewarded" for their contributions to their departments. A value-based social "selection" process is clearly at work. There are numerous interest groups and internal specializations within family medicine, a fragmentation that parallels and replicates the very institution of biomedicine and its American culture that the discipline of family medicine had initially sought to reform.

Since the mid-1980s, the time- and ostensibly cost-saving demands of managed care have placed even greater outer constraints on family physicians (as well as others in the so-called primary care disciplines). Among the first, and most superficially espoused values to be discarded are those that require time and intimacy and caring. Attentiveness to the lived nuances of human lives and their communities is quickly sacrificed for brief, supposedly efficient medical and related "mental health" interventions that rationalize ideological positions and professional claims, reducing anxiety and guilt. A physician friend calls it the "cattle drive principle." What Stephens writes of family medicine situates it firmly in the American ethos of succession and success.

> One of the consequences of utilizing social needs as the basis for definition of a specialty is that the needs change and the specialty must continually adapt to the new demands.... [Further,] the eagerness for legitimacy and excellence, as defined by the medical schools, may turn out to have been a fatal flaw in family practice, which wanted acceptance and approval at any cost. (1987: 16, 17)

In late 1999, a family physician friend was fired from an urban clinic which had long served homeless people. She was fired (from a volunteer job) because she had personally widened the definition of "homeless" beyond people who live literally in the streets of her city, to include people who live in shelters. She was told that compassion must take second place to following the rules. The administrator who fired her was a fellow family physician who is known to his patients as a decent man, a good doctor.

In a recent essay, Johanna Shapiro and David Kim (1999: 373) write that

> continuity is one of the key elements that constitute the construct of primary care (Franks, Clancy, and Nutting 1997; Rivo, Saultz, Wartman, and DeWitt 1994), and is foundational to the concept of a "personal doctor" (Taylor 1997). Family medicine is particularly concerned about continuity, and training programs worry that their

preparation of residents may be inadequate in this aspect (Tannenbaum 1998; Irby 1995; Steiner and Stoken 1995; Tannenbaum 1998).
Residents change clinic schedules, take vacations, get sick, travel to
"away" rotations, graduate. Patients cancel appointments, are late,
are too sick to keep their appointment with their doctor. (1999: 373)

Can the current ideological assertion of cultural continuity within family medicine, and loyalty to the value of continuity in patient care, be
made in the face of radical *enforced* discontinuity in corporate practice?
Medical insurance companies, for instance, routinely include and exclude
physicians from their rosters. Patients who have been seen and cared for
by a given physician for years, if not decades, are summarily notified
that their long-time physician is no longer included on their insurance
plan—or that he or she is "out-of-plan" and that coverage will be far
less. For their part, many physicians blame clinic and insurance administrators for an economic and interpersonal predicament they also welcome: less hassle, less obligation to patients, and greater income if they
play by the rules of "capitation" (not spending beyond a ceiling amount
per patient in the corporate population).

What do group "values" mean and feel like when many of the original
ideals they rest upon have been abandoned, discarded, repudiated in
action, and are only ceremonially evoked? These questions are a variation on the universal cultural theme of the relation between group ideals
and practiced reality, between the espoused and the deduced (Richards
1956), and even between competing ideals, only certain of which can (or
may) be articulated.

Although family medicine began historically in the mid-1960s as the
zealous offspring of the "counterculture" and appears at the turn of the
millennium as an eager, ambitious participant in the Brave New World,
those polarities have contended with each other within family medicine—and within family physicians and their associates—all along. What
is different and new is the open, unabashed appeal to "the bottom line"
to justify the increasingly open indifference to the brutalization and
abandonment of patient, family, physician, and organization alike. For
many within family medicine and its allied "primary care" disciplines
(pediatrics, general internal medicine, obstetrics/gynecology), many of
the original, supposedly "fundamental" beliefs and values of the discipline have been cast to the side of the road.

The pattern of family medicine *professional* succession in academic institutions parallels and recapitulates the historic pattern of *ethnic* succession of waves of immigrant groups: from despised outsider to vigilant
insider. "Us," having once been "them," now relish the making of others
as "them" to feel the pain "we" once felt.

CONCLUDING THOUGHTS: RECOGNIZING THE BARBARIANS— WHEN "THEY" ARE "US"

From corporate workplace to nation-state, group thought and action becomes all-consuming under circumstances of massive anxiety and collective regression. Even xenophobia does not suffice to protect and offer peace of mind, for the enemy is within. Frequent "cleansing" fails to assure renewal. From corporate to national, purges become endless. Full-time attention comes to be devoted to boundary delineation, protection, and maintenance. In nations and other social units as well, xenophobia is one form this vigilance and obsession takes. Self-protective destructiveness ultimately becomes self-destruction—in solutions ranging from urban gangs, to corporate consulting teams, to Hitler's final Wagnerian immolation of Germany.

A self-cleansing movement itself is not exempt from all-devouring, self-consuming xenophobia, as the Soviet purges of the mid-1930s, and the final days of the Third Reich attest. The enemy is never entirely outside. Corporatism and nationalism's splitting off of group self-love from hatred of the foreigner is a fragile defense: eventually, even loyalists are suspected of treason and treated as disloyal. Purification can never be complete; impurity surely lurks somewhere. Groupish destructiveness and self-destructiveness are two sides of the same "coin": the processes of enemy-making that is at groupishness's frightened core. One can never do enough downsizing and restructuring.

In his celebrated poem, "Expecting the Barbarians," Konstantinos Kabaphes (Cavafy)(1948) describes the dread and excitement within the city gates as the day of the barbarians' arrival approached. As the arrival of the barbarians seems imminent, the entire society mobilizes. When the menace fails to materialize, "unrest and confusion" ensue. The poem concludes with what is at once a lament and a bitter realization: namely, that the barbarians were needed as "a kind of solution."

Universally, much as we despise them, we also need our barbarians (who embody our disavowed barbarity); unconsciously, we are our barbarians. For group and individual alike, "the other" is essential for emotional stability and internal definition. Corporatism (from workplace to nation-state) and its xenophobias rest upon a degree of failure of differentiation between self- and object-representation.

The lesson of any study of group fanaticism and xenophobia for the problem of everyday group relations—from workplace institutions in mass society to nations—is that we can help to reduce "nationalist" fervor and dread in its myriad of guises only as we can come to accept the fact that the barbarian has always lived within our gates—and within that conflicted estate of ourselves. The foreigner we most despise is ourselves in another's guise.

A break in the vicious circle of suffering and repetition that fuels in-group fanaticism and its xenophobia is mourning (Mitscherlich and Mitscherlich 1975; Volkan 1988; Stein 1998a). In mourning, we finally confront where the barbarians have been all along. In place of a group self-image based on absolute goodness and innocence, we recognize and encompass our own barbarity.

The barbarians are our own inner and externalized darkness. They are "us" in the unconscious guise (representation) of "them." They are the uncertainty we mask by our arrogance and decisiveness. They are the organizational depressions behind the manic cuts and abrupt reorganizations. They are the metazoan death we all face behind the desperate attempt to make our organizations (projective organisms) "survive" and "win." They are the love we crave even as we renounce and fend it off in our daily callousness and depersonalized policies.

The darkness of hypernationalist sentiment and value in the workplace can begin to lift as we begin to contain, within our personal and corporate selves, those parts we had banished far beyond our gates. The containment, in turn, begins with the work of mourning.

At the 6 February, 2000, concluding plenary of the mid-winter conference of Division 13, American Psychological Association, Consultation to Corporations and Business, Harry Levinson emphasized that in modern organizations where people work closely together, it is difficult to tear organizations apart. In the face of reciprocal identifications and identification with the workplace, people are ripped up and out during massive downsizings and restructurings. "All change is loss, and all loss has to be mourned, or people sit on their rage." Levinson observed an increase in depression in workers under such circumstances: conscientious people feel they are not as good as they would like to be.

He then admonished the conference participants: "[When you consult,] teach executives that they are the chief mourners." It is the task for organizational leaders to help their employees surmount, not to deny, mourning. The same could be said for consultants—and for anyone of goodwill in the workplace. Mourning will diminish barbarity in the workplace—and in turn, the need to have "barbarians" to detest and banish.

In the following chapter, I explore these issues in the context of an extended case study.

REFERENCES

Allcorn, Seth, Howell S. Baum, Michael A. Diamond, and Howard F. Stein. 1996. *The HUMAN Cost of a Management Failure: Organizational Downsizing at General Hospital.* Westport, CT: Quorum Books.

Cavafy (Kabphes), Konstantinos. 1948. "Expecting the Barbarians," in *The Com-*

plete Poems of Cavafy. R. Dalven, trans. New York: Harcourt Brace Jovanovich.

Devereux, George. 1955. "Charismatic Leadership and Crisis," *Psychoanalysis and the Social Sciences* 4: 145–157.

Engel, George. 1977. "The Need for a New Medical Model: A Challenge for Biomedicine," *Science* 196(4286): 129–136.

Erikson, Erik H. 1968. *Identity: Youth and Crisis.* New York: Norton.

Franks, P., C. M. Clancy, and P. A. Nutting. 1997. "Defining Primary Care: Empirical Analysis of the National Ambulatory Medical Care Survey," *Medical Care* 35: 655–668.

Irby, D. M. 1995. "Teaching and Learning in Ambulatory Care Settings: A Themic Review of Literature," *Academic Medicine* 70: 898–931.

La Barre, Weston. 1972. *The Ghost Dance: The Origins of Religion.* New York: Dell.

Levinson, Harry. 1999. Concluding plenary of the Mid-Winter Conference of Division 13, American Psychological Association, Consultation to Corporations and Business, St. Petersburg, Florida.

Mitscherlich, Alexander, and Margarete Mitscherlich. 1975. *The Inability to Mourn: Principles of Collective Behavior.* New York: Grove Press.

Richards, A. 1956. *Chisungu.* London: Faber and Faber.

Rivo, M. L., J. W. Saultz, S. A. Wartman, and T. G. DeWitt. 1994. "Defining the Generalist Physician's Training," *Journal of the American Medical Association* 271: 1499–504.

Shapiro, Johanna R., and David Kim. 1999. "One Patient's Short, Short Story: Is There Time to Craft a Happy Ending?" *Families, Systems and Health* 17(3): 373–377.

Shatan, Chaim. 1997. "Living in a Split Time Zone: Trauma and Therapy of Vietnam Combat Survivors," *Mind and Human Interaction* 8(4), Winter: 204–222.

Stein, Howard F. 1994. *Listening Deeply.* Boulder, CO: Westview Press.

———. 1997. "Death Imagery and the Experience of Organizational Downsizing: Or, Is Your Name on Schindler's List?" *Administration and Society* 29(2): 222–247.

———. 1998a. *Euphemism, Spin, and the Crisis in Organizational Life.* Westport, CT: Quorum Books.

———. 1998b. "Organizational Euphemism and the Cultural Mystification of Evil," *Administrative Theory and Praxis* 20(3): 346–357.

———. 1999. "Downsizing, Managed Care, and the Potlatching of America: A Study in Cultural Brutality and Its Mystification," *Journal for the Psychoanalysis of Culture and Society* 4(2), Fall: 209–227.

Steiner, E. and J. M. Stoken. 1995. "Overcoming Barriers to Generalism in Medicine: The Residents' Perspective," *Academic Medicine* 70 (1Supp): S89–94.

Stephens, G. Gayle. 1976. "Reform in the U.S.: Its Impact on Medicine and Education for Family Practice," *Journal of Family Practice* 3: 507–512.

———. 1979. "Family Medicine as Counter-Culture," *Family Medicine Teacher* 11(5): 14–18.

———. 1987. "Developmental Assessment of Family Practice: An Insider's View," in William J. Doherty, Charles E. Christianson, and Marvin B. Suss-

man, ed., *Family Medicine: The Maturing of a Discipline*. New York: Haworth
    Press. Pp. 1–21.
Tannenbaum, D. W. 1998. "New 'Horizontal' Curriculum in Family Medicine
    Residency," *Canadian Family Physician* 44: 1669–75.
Taylor, M. D. 1997. "Compassion: Its Neglect and Importance," *British Journal of
    General Practice* 47: 521–3.
Volkan, Vamik D. 1988. *The Need to Have Enemies and Allies*. Northvale, NJ: Jason
    Aronson.

6

"How Long Can We Circle the Wagons?":
A Study in the Sense of Doom at Work

INTRODUCTION

In the previous chapter, I considered ordinary brutality at work through several brief vignettes. In this chapter, I continue that exploration, but here I describe an extended case example of my work with a medical corporation I shall call MCA (Managed Care Affiliates, a pseudonym). I inquire into the significance that the organization played in participants' lives, and the consequences to their morale and functioning with the constant threat of closure. It is a study of growing organizational darkness, of how its members dealt with an increasing sense of doom, and of how a consultant worked with them.

This is the story of several years in the history of Managed Care Affiliates (MCA), one of several subdivisions of a large medical corporation. During this period I served as internal consultant within and between several branches and headquarters. MCA is in the business of providing services in many venues of "patient care": clinical and preventive; hospital (inpatient) and clinic (outpatient); geriatric, family, adolescent and pediatric medicine; wellness programs for the healthy; rehabilitation programs; and screening, referral, and consultation. At corporate headquarters, major programs, together with funding, are devoted to projections of future health trends, efforts to capture the market, development of health policy statements, design of medical practices based on cost containment and increased profit, and development and implementation of clinical decision trees based upon probabilistic analysis.

THE BOTTOM LINE OF ORGANIZATIONAL CHANGE

The Board of Directors of the main office recommended, and the share-holders overwhelmingly approved, the hiring of a new corporate CEO in the early 1980s, a time during which a new national consensus over costcontainment, corporate competitiveness, and governmental deregulation was congealing. It was a time when corporate medicine became explicitly profit-oriented and less avowedly service-oriented. Harry R. Kormos (1984) has labeled the era as the "industrialization of medicine." The new CEO, in tune with this emergent spirit, was seen by the Board of Directors who hired him as a "visionary" with a "grand vision of the future," a person who "flew high above everyone's heads, in the clouds, looking for megatrends of the future to capture the medical market." He had been chosen among the applicants because he showed the most promise of expanding the company into greater profit, visibility, stature, and power in corporate medicine. From the outset, he invested corporate money and personnel time heavily in a proliferation and succession of building plans and models, and architectural drafts, and in high technology acquisition involving multiple computer systems. Many of these had disappointing and costly results.

Soon after the installation of the new CEO and his staff, proposals, policies, and practices all reflected a new set of dichotomies or polarities. Among them was the corporate center versus the periphery (subsidiary companies); urban (or metropolitan) versus rural (where subsidiaries were mostly located); income generation and cost containment versus service; medicine as product line versus medicine as skill and service that in turn generates a livelihood; the new executives and managers versus the old ones ("young blood" versus "old blood"); centralized authority versus local autonomy; and high technology versus personal medicine. In his talks and reports, the CEO favored certain recurrent metaphors or images of medicine: "the automated physician" (emphasis on high technology-mediated, depersonalized care), medical practice as a "product line" and the physician as a "product line manager"; patient care as "managed care" given by "producers" of health care to "consumers" of health care; and "the bottom line" as "cost containment" through "managed care systems." Within these perspectives, the rural subsidiary organization, MCA, was devalued, despite the fact it continued to be a reliably high-income generator utilizing the old ways of a family service-oriented, moderately low tech, and hands-on approach to patient care.

A large turnover of junior executives and mid-level managers occurred with the installation of the new CEO. This turnover was quickly justified by a polarization of images. The old-timers were viewed as inadequate if not bad, while those brought in by the new CEO were admired as fresh and new. By contrast, MCA continued to be run by the "old guard."

When many of the "new blood" at corporate headquarters began to leave as well, this was further rationalized in terms of their having been poor "team players." For several years, many members of the corporation did their utmost to sustain their idealization of their "visionary" leader, upon whom they had become increasingly dependent. After several years, however, many began to realize that his aggrandizement was purchased at their expense.

After the transition in leadership at corporate headquarters, numerous small events set the stage for an atmosphere of doom within MCA. Representatives of the subsidiaries were often overlooked for notification of scheduling for such various corporation-wide meetings as marketing sessions, strategic planning, and the development of philosophy, policy, and goals. Ideas from MCA members were rarely solicited about decisions affecting their company's internal functioning. Spontaneous visits to MCA by home office executives, and telephone calls from them, diminished markedly. Those few personnel from the home office who regularly consulted with, gave seminars at, or did trouble-shooting for MCA found that executives in the home office consistently "forgot" to credit this time spent. They tended to define 100% time only in terms of that spent at the home office. In short, MCA personnel felt they had gradually become the target of "death wishes" on the part of the larger corporation. They felt that they were often treated as if MCA did not exist—save when its money was needed to bail out the home office's cash-flow problems.

Over the most recent years, MCA has seen an outflow and depletion of virtually all of those precious commodities necessary for its survival. Through the gradual centralization of decision-making and financial management, a sense of local autonomy about MCA's activities and about its fate has atrophied and been virtually lost. All important medical, administrative, and financial information about the organization has been computerized for management from the main office. Promotions in rank or replacement of vacant positions became notably rarer and slower at the MCA office than at the main office. Rewards for job performance were likewise far less frequent from the home office for MCA employees. On one occasion when the CEO, COO, and CFO discovered a major cash-flow problem in the home office accounting department, they "solved" their financial problem and embarrassment by peremptorily demanding a quarter of a million dollars that MCA executives had put in a "rainy day fund." This virtually depleted MCA's ability to protect its own operations, personnel, and future in the event of a downturn in the local or regional economy.

Some years ago, not only did the CEO from the home office forget to bring plaques for an award ceremony to MCA, but some months later, on a visit to MCA, the COO (Chief Operating Officer) likewise forgot to bring the awards plaques for presentation. MCA has consistently been asked to make layoffs, cutbacks, and to endure hardships that the main office has not sustained for itself. The chronic experience of unequal sacrifices has made MCA suspect that the home office was growing and thriving at the expense of the affiliate.

Reputation has likewise suffered at MCA, both in the eyes of local and regional supporters and vendors and in the eyes of the main office. In most recent years, local businesses, health agencies, and the local medical community who have long supported MCA enthusiastically have begun to wonder about whether MCA will survive. They wonder whether the main office is truly behind its local affiliate and have begun to question whether the main office would honor MCA's commitments. With local confidence in MCA's future undermined, many businesses and health agencies have adopted a "wait and see" attitude. Similarly, fewer managers have applied to train at MCA. Prospective applicants have heard "via the grapevine" that MCA might not be long lived and that the main office has been in keen competition with MCA. With the decline in prestige, the *credibility* of MCA has begun to decline both in the local organizational community and within the applicant pool on which MCA relies for its record of success and excellence.

MCA personnel experienced this progression of events as keenly felt, unrelenting, death wishes from and abandonment by the home office. MCA's initial persistent response was the even more unrelenting pursuit of excellence and success, to prove to themselves and to others they were indeed doing their job unsurpassed by any. Yet, as D. Wilfred Abse writes, "The very thought of having to justify one's existence is already expressive of a doubt about the right to be in the world" (1988: 90). The CEO of MCA said to me with exasperation a few years ago, "We do the job we're supposed to do, and we're punished rather than rewarded for our accomplishments. What do they want of us?" The simple, frightening—and intolerable—answer, one that could only be voiced in gesture rather than in word was: disappearance. During this period, the central office did not effectively act to deny or disprove this growing conviction. Both the main office and MCA acted as if extinction were the central agenda, to which MCA responded (for the most part) by striving to demonstrate all the more its quality if not indispensability. Yet, MCA could not perceive and accept that even "doing better" could not prevent their dissolution.

Over the years, a recurrent phrase used at MCA has been the frontier image of "circling the [Conestoga] wagons," a turning inward to protect the internal integrity of the organization. Feeling as if their very existence were under prolonged siege, members wondered how long the "encircled wagons" could survive. Moreover, the anger, resentment, rage, and sense of chaos they felt dare not be directed externally—to the main office or to vendors in the local community upon whom they also depended. Instead, they redirected these sentiments internally in the form of organizational infighting, schisms between sectors of the organization (care-giving, laboratory, business-administrative, public relations-marketing), increased incidence of MCA personnel illness and accidents, and widespread demoralization.

Over the last several years, I noticed from seminars and workshops, and from individual supervision of trainees and consultation with managers, that they were much less interested in and capable of devoting sustained attention on problem patients or problem families. During ordinary clinical seminars and workshops, and in informal hallway conversations, I began to notice—or to think I was noticing—the emergence of new patterns. Using such techniques or tools as participant observation, open-ended interviews, and naturalistic observation, I conducted fieldwork while doing my job. I began to keep detailed notes, both to document and make sense of the "pattern" I thought I was discerning, and to provide additional observational data to test and revise earlier impressions.

I gradually concluded, and corroborated from work throughout MCA, that preoccupation with apprehension of doom and with "survival" made all but the most routine clinical and educational activities lower priority than in previous years. This took place with some of the same managers and staff who once had been ardently devoted to psychosocial and community issues. From cues such as demoralization, greater infighting, and diminished empathy toward patients, I began to pay greater attention to and inquire into (both in the subsidiaries and in the home office) the reality of the threat and fantasies associated with their growing sense of fatalism.

Ironically, in this corporation's history, MCA has been consistently regarded by the home office and by other admiring and envious subsidiaries as the "flagship" of the institution. MCA has been envied as the most consistently productive, successful, and enjoyable worksite within the corporate system. Since its inception fifteen years ago, its virtue has been its vice. Envy-based disparagement by other components of the organization have eaten away at MCA. MCA's successes became the home office's and other branches' failures. Everything that MCA does well "makes" the others look bad. At one home office executive meeting, at which manager recruitment was discussed, an executive told the following story about how he thought MCA succeeded in its recruitment. "They send one of their cute secretaries to take him [a management candidate] to a drive-in and give him a good time [the implication being that of sexual favors]. That's why they get them and we sometimes lose out."

It is unlikely there has ever been an official written edict or explicit decision by headquarters to close MCA. Rather, members of MCA, and myself as well, have inferred and frequently reconfirmed this conclusion through the home office upper-management's acts of omission and commission, through its euphemisms, metaphors, and other turns of speech, and by its acts of mystification. Not-so-benign neglect has long characterized much of the home office's practice toward MCA. Personnel invoke anthropomorphized images of "depression" and "failure to thrive" to describe the prevailing mood at MCA. Over a year ago, the headquarters published a lavish brochure describing and marketing all facets of their company. It omitted any mention of the MCA subsidiary, even though at a managers' meeting I had urged planners to include MCA in the public relations brochure. The two most common responses I received from executives and managers at headquarters was "we didn't have room" and "we forgot."

Furthermore, at corporation-wide workshops and managers' meetings (at which I am usually the only quasi-MCA spokesman present), I often have reminded the group of MCA's existence when input from, or "strategic planning" for, the entire corporate "family" (as many members call it) has been the ostensible agenda. Several mid-level managers and junior executives have approached me after meetings and said, some with chagrin and embarrassment, "You know, it's easy to forget the MCA even exists, they're so far away, and you never see any of them down here." "Forgetting" has been frequently tantamount to the wish that MCA should disappear. Action at corporate headquarters often has seemed commensurate with the conclusion that this wish has been activated.

In most recent months, various MCA members would stop me in the hallways and begin to tell me about serious or terminal illnesses or deaths in their families. Although over the years I have consulted and counseled many MCA members on a wide range of professional and personal subjects, never before was there such a groundswell of thoughts on death. Our conversations would often drift to the fate of MCA, suggesting to me that as real as these family events were, they also served as displacements for the dread of MCA's organizational dissolution (cf. Yalom 1970:115) and loss of friendship networks and MCA identity.

The metaphors of death at MCA served in turn as a living (or death-in-life) metaphor of the "working" relationship between MCA and its home office: what headquarters dissociated and projectively identified in its subsidiary, members of MCA actively felt. On a theoretical note, mechanisms of defense such as displacement, projection, projective identification, splitting, and isolation, familiar in individual psychology and family relations can be used to regulate group cohesiveness, identity, aggressive and sexual impulses, and "status anxiety" (De Vos 1966). Families, corporations, whole societies, and international relations can be, at least in part, governed by an affectively and fantasy-based division of labor (Stein 1986). Roles can be based on the complementarity of inducing and embodying "bad" if not catastrophic feelings, fantasies, and wishes (Devereux 1980).

CONSULTANT AS LISTENER

In my roles both at the home office and the subsidiaries, I have strived to serve as an advocate for psychosocially-informed medical training and medical care, and as an advocate for group morale founded on reality acceptance and on a concern and respect for one another's welfare. I have attempted to help members of the subsidiary acknowledge perceptions and feelings they were dreading, while at the same time I attempted informally to document to the corporate executives at headquarters the consequences of actions and policies they would not openly acknowledge. My written documentation and privately spoken expressions of concern to executives at the home office were characteristically met with reassurances that their "flagship" affiliate continued to have their unwavering support—or with discounting, incredulous smiles. Still, I staunchly urged executives from the home office and MCA to make more frequent contact through visits, telephone, or letter. In sum, my advocacy was less for one "side" than it was for greater reality testing on the part of both.

My function at MCA became to listen, and insofar as it was possible for me to do so, to compare their stories with realities or official stories available to me from the home office, to help them to listen to each other with less condemnation and greater attentiveness and compassion, and through these, to help empower them to do whatever problem-solving and decision-making that was within their compass. In my rescue-fantasy, I had once wished to be able to "sound the alarm" or "blow the whistle" at the main office. However, neither alarm nor whistle were audible at top levels of the organization and even outside it. The fate of MCA, and of its members' mental and physical health, thus rested entirely upon themselves.

Our individual and group discussions gradually helped to decrease the infighting and to increase group morale and productivity. These discussions helped them to have the courage to look at reality as directly as they could bear. Labeling me as "the listener," then identifying with this *function* with which they had imbued me, they partly began to listen to each other. Their inner worlds became less fragmented, less ridden by persecutory anxiety. They were no longer on perpetual alert with each other.

SUBSEQUENT HISTORY

The dispirited leader of MCA did his best to rally from time to time. He always vocalized mottos such as "Onward and Upward," "Steadfast and Determined," "Bowed but Unbroken," "We'll Make It." However, his actions—largely inactions to take advantage of promised policy change at the home office, together with his increasing absences and emotional unavailability—expressed the opposite. Junior executives, managers, physicians, and medical and administrative staff of MCA alike frequently told me they thought their leader to be depressed, that they had to assume increasingly large numbers of his decision-making functions, which he had passively ceded to them.

Two veteran mid-level managers, one male and one female, joined forces and took charge as the company "father" and "mother" (their own terms) to absorb many leadership functions without ever embarrassing their titular head. The "pairing" of these two managers (Bion 1959) served less the fantasy of magical rebirth as it "kept the ship afloat" (their own and others' metaphor of what life in MCA felt like).

With demoralized leadership and group morale, the enemy was now as much within as without. Over a period of several years, during which the head of MCA had clearly and repeatedly announced his wish to retire and leave MCA in good hands, both the home office and local MCA junior executives did virtually nothing to secure a replacement and continuity of leadership. MCA was a captive of its collective sense of doom. I spoke on several occasions with senior executives of the home office, and I even wrote letters and memoranda to them as a subtle form of pressure ("documentation"), urging the central organization to assist in the transition, to make more frequent contact with MCA leadership, to show a greater interest in its future.

Yet even when home office executives made a site visit and created a momentary stir of enthusiasm and hope, MCA leadership could rarely sustain the enthusiasm to try to save their organization. They immediately mistrusted the sincerity and follow-through of their visitors, and fell back on the nostrum that the "handwriting [was] on the wall" long ago. Feeling tired, "burned out," helpless, and hopeless after having led his organization for a decade through almost eight successive years of corporate economic and political tumult, the CEO of MCA now discounted the sincerity of the head of the home office to provide any help he could to turn things around. Taking little initiative, and giving fewer "pep talks" to his workers than he once did, his refrain became "too little, too late." While not verbally giving up on MCA, and still wanting to have a successor take over "a ship in full sail," by his actions and inactions he hastened the very fate he feared. "If they really mean business, they should come up here and talk with us. You know the old saying, 'Don't tell me, show me.' I'm waiting for them to show me their intentions." He felt overwhelmingly discounted. His increasing passivity and fatalism unwittingly played precisely into the hands of those executives at the home office who had been passive-aggressively undermining all of MCA's functions.

At all levels of the organization, day-to-day work continued in perfunctory performance. Partly through identification with the depressed leader, many if not most members of MCA have given up on themselves as an organization. They have given up the sense of "we-ness" that is too painful to try to preserve if not reconstruct. If the demise of MCA becomes a fulfillment of the tacit wishes of the home office, it will be for many of MCA managers, trainees, and staff a self-fulfilling prophecy, one in which they have unwittingly colluded.

Over time, the group became more often resilient and rallying than regressed. Increasingly, MCA members verbalized to one another (as well as to me) and expressed their feelings about living with a foreshortened sense of time. These episodes of rallying attest to genuine creativity, productivity, and even intimacy rather than to a "manic denial" of reality. What could not be changed at least could be openly acknowledged. The taboo that had kept the dread shrouded in secrecy had been lifted. MCA managers, trainees, and staff began to talk openly about group-death, of the possible limits to, if not futility of, their still valiant efforts.

The inability to plan for longer than a several-month stretch, the style of short-term planning rather than the customary long-term planning, became more openly accepted. The idea that MCA could dissolve within six months or a year was still profoundly distressing to all its members. However, they now showed greater resolve and commitment to "give it their all" for as much time as there remained. Genuine sadness—rather than the frenetic activity to seal over the unspeakable dread—began to show. There was a sense among MCA employees that they had somehow managed to take at least part of their fate into their own hands, while also facing their common situation more realistically.

ORGANIZATIONAL ADAPTATION

Organizational effects of adaptation to the sense of doom in the above case example were numerous, pervasive, and have become indelible:

(1) increased infighting and factionalism;

(2) increased discrepancy between the group's self-expectation to perform at 100% efficiency and responsibility, and their inability to fulfill their expectations due to the absence of sufficient personnel and financial support;

(3) episodes of group despondency, apprehension, self-blame, helplessness-hopelessness, resignation, outrage;

(4) rallying periods of resolve, hope through the infusion of "new blood" (new junior executives, successful marketing, annual new groups of medical managerial trainees);

(5) constant "patching things up," as with trowel and plaster, while feeling pulled apart and falling apart (continuous negotiation with local

and regional subcontractors and vendors for new corporate markets and community support to shore up what has been lost from the main office);

(6) sense of abandonment, conviction that MCA is the victim of an outside plot, belief that annihilation is only a matter of time, that their fate is out of their hands, that the main office has no place for MCA in its future but is not telling them;

(7) decrease of reality testing and further regression;

(8) discreet search for outside jobs by apprehensive executives, managers, sales people, and staff, to "jump ship before it sinks";

(9) sense of impotence on the part of MCA leadership;

(10) merger of feared destruction with group self-destructive behavior by members of MCA; and finally

(11) proliferation of and vulnerability to rumors about firings, resignations, omens, together with a magical "watching for signs" in facial expressions and attitudes of MCA leaders and/or home office management personnel.

Many widespread dysphoric feelings within the corporate main office—aimlessness, leadership distant from the daily affairs of the members, lack of clear roles and expectations, demoralization due to unacknowledged contributions of members, fear of abandonment, and spasms of accountability for problems beyond any individual's control—were induced in the MCA affiliate office. The sense of integrity and safety in the home office was purchased in part by depositing the parallel sense of disorganization and danger in MCA—in fact, by provoking endangerment in MCA. Through MCA, the home office could divest itself of frightening, disorganizing feelings while "managing" them at a distance in a subsidiary that is at once a "part of" itself yet "apart from" it (Stein 1987).

Further, home office personnel experienced considerable ambiguity over their ideal professional identity, that is, regarding values of medical care-giving and training versus profit-making and hierarchy-maintaining roles. MCA became a Bion-type of "container" (1963) for devalued aspects of the home office, attributes which were nevertheless still touted as its official ideals. Home office executives and managers continued to espouse continuity of physician-patient relationships, consumer-oriented medical practice, "consumer-friendly" medical products, and contextually-based medical and business relationships rather than financially and technologically dictated corporate values (Stein and Hill 1988).

Over the years, the unconscious psychological foundation of MCA gradually shifted from what Wilfred R. Bion (1959) called the basic assumption of "dependency" to the basic assumption called "fight/flight." Interestingly, Bion's third basic assumption, called "pairing," only intermittently and briefly appears, as does the hope for new, young, permanent leadership. MCA culture lives mostly in the present, focusing on day-to-day operations and short-term planning. A more remote future is too dismal to imagine.

I could thus—and this is the fulcrum that "countertransference" plays in this consultation and study—use my own inner life (fantasies, feelings, memories) to help members of MCA tolerate, accept, and somewhat work through materials that were evoked by the chronic, menacing circumstances of their workplace. In short, I sought to place my "therapeutic regression"—those regressions that were genuinely helpful—at the service of MCA's grief work, reality acceptance, group morale, and task productivity (see Olinick 1969, for a discussion of the concept of "regression in the service of the other").

CONCLUSION

My work with MCA and its larger organizational system has taught me a great deal about how to listen to organizational groups, to allow meanings and feelings to emerge over time. It has also taught me a great deal about myself—unwelcomed and hidden parts of my own life that got shaken back into memory. It has taught me to trust how my own feelings and reactions provide crucial data about the organization, and how to respond to such reactions. Finally, it has taught me to take seriously the experience of organizational darkness, and to nourish simple human dignity under conditions that assault it daily.

Organizations and whole cultures do not die; only biological organisms do. Yet people identify with, become dependent on, become attached to, and even come to define themselves in terms of the organizations in which they work. When a place is threatened, the sense of place is also threatened. That "sense" is imbued with feelings of life and lifelessness, death and dying. Feelings of loss, and its associated anxiety, are as much aroused by symbolic objects (such as workplaces) as with real people. The feelings are often overwhelming—as if one's very life is threatened. The feelings within an organization are a part of that organization's reality and shape decision-making large and small.

This chapter has focused on *feelings* among organizational members as constituting part of the very workplace *structure*. In the following, and final, extended chapter, I discuss in considerable detail the process by which one organization—in fact, many interlocking organizations and their wider community—came to recognize their darkness and awakened from it. In this chapter I study how observer and consultant countertransference can serve as powerful, yet quietly effective tools of organizational and community healing and resiliency.

REFERENCES

Abse, D. Wilfred. 1988. "Kriegman's 'Nonentitlement' and Ibsen's *Rosmersholm*," in Vamik D. Volkan and T. C. Rodgers, eds., *Attitudes of Entitlement: The-*

oretical and Clinical Issues. Charlottesville: University Press of Virginia. Pp. 79–92.

Bion, W. R. 1959. *Experiences in Groups*. New York: Ballantine.

———. 1963. *Elements of Psycho-Analysis*. New York: Basic Books.

Devereux, George. 1980. *Basic Problems of Ethno-Psychiatry*. Chicago: University of Chicago Press.

De Vos, George A. 1966. "Toward a Cross-Cultural Psychology of Caste Behavior," in George De Vos and Hiroshi Wagatsuma, eds., *Japan's Invisible Race*. Berkeley: University of California Press. Pp. 377ff.

Kormos, Harry. 1984. "The Industrialization of Medicine," in Julio L. Ruffini, ed., *Advances in Medical Social Science*. Volume 2. New York: Gordon and Breach Science Publishers. Pp. 323–339.

Olinick, Samuel L. 1969. "On Empathy and Regression in the Service of the Other," *British Journal of Medical Psychology* 42: 41–49.

Stein, Howard F. 1986. "Social Role and Unconscious Complementarity," *Journal of Psychoanalytic Anthropology* 9(3): 235–268.

———. 1987. *Developmental Time, Cultural Space*. Norman: University of Oklahoma Press.

Stein, Howard F., and Robert F. Hill. 1988. "The Dogma of Technology," in L. B. Boyer and S. Grolnick, eds., *The Psychoanalytic Study of Society*. Volume 13. Hillsdale, NJ: The Analytic Press. Pp. 149–179.

Yalom, Irving. 1970. *Theory and Practice of Group Psychotherapy*. New York: Basic Books.

7

Rupture and Reconciliation: A Case Study

Are limbs, so dear-achieved, are sides,
Full-nerved, still warm, too hard to stir?
Was it for this the clay grew tall?
O what made fatuous sunbeams toil
To break earth's sleep at all?
—Wilfred Owen, "Futility"
[1963: 58 [1917]]

INTRODUCTION

How does one honestly conclude a book on organizational darkness? I say *honestly* because dishonesty is sorely tempting, consciously and unconsciously alike. We Americans—and increasingly, people worldwide—crave quick fixes, encouraging spins, instant enlightenment(s). We want to suffer no anxiety or loss of profit. A work-world steeped in brutality and brutalization requires first the acknowledgment of the breadth and depth of suffering. The first step is to de-normalize the officially, and obligatorily, normal.

This chapter consists of a case study in which organizational darkness came to light during a three-day consultation in the early 1990s. This chapter studies what can happen to dispel the self-blinding darkness in which many workplaces are engulfed. The study offers a process, not a magical formula. If there is organizational healing here, it is less because people claimed to have been hurt as it is because people acknowledged that they had hurt others out of fear of being hurt themselves. The consultation taught me as much as I contributed. It hints at what is possible for human beings in their workplaces. It suggests that there are human fundamentals neglected when we narrow ourselves to "bottom lines," and that people willingly and eagerly dispense with those bottom lines when deeper needs and values can be tapped.

The reader will find the core of what organizations, students of organizations, and organizational consultants find in the late twentieth and early twenty-first centuries: onslaught of change, mergers and takeovers, numerous losses, intense competitiveness, economic fears, withdrawal into one's own work-unit or "silo," mistrust of others, chronic rage and self-protectiveness, and sense of futurelessness. Although the consultation is not with a corporation in the strictest sense, it is in a broader sense a study of the interplay of many corporate entities locked in resentment, anxiety, and sullen silence. Although many cultural and structural details of the organizations will differ from those in the reader's repertory, I expect that many of the processes will be all too familiar. The question is how organizations release themselves from their self-inflicted imprisonment—how they bring themselves out of their darkness.

The case study, then, is first concretely about "itself" in its specificity and uniqueness—and second, it is a metaphor for how workplace shackles can be taken off. In the latter capacity, it is a kind of "answer" to the many "questions" posed in this book. In this chapter, then, I describe the unfolding of the consultation, the historic baseline of the organizations involved, and the intersubjective work that led to the lifting of organizational paralysis.

ORGANIZATIONAL CHANGE, LOSS, AND GRIEF: PRELIMINARY OBSERVATIONS

This case describes how the process of doing an organizational consultation—by serving on a "training team" as participant-observer and facilitator-trainer for an organizational group—offered an occasion for attaining greater understanding of the unconscious substratum of organizational culture. In this organizational consultation, I was invited to help solve a problem: specifically, to help organize and facilitate a several-day "retreat." In doing so I learned a great deal about how unresolved change, loss, and mourning can "freeze" work-groups culturally and condemn them to repeat the past in new guises. I was able to experience culture "turned inside-out," as it were, as the group dynamics allowed the emergence of what had been defended against. Latent became manifest.

For nearly two decades, I have conducted consultations with academic, medical, religious, ethnic, corporate, industrial, governmental, and other "organizations" (social institutions, often "workplaces," in which members are recruited from the larger society and then trained). During the course of these consultations, the triad of change-loss-grief repeatedly emerged as the central, hidden cultural theme (see also Deal 1985). From these experiences I have learned that a wide gamut of "presenting problems" can serve as repositories of what the Mitscherlichs called "the inability to mourn" (1975), and that workplace organizations (e.g., departments, companies, clinics) in Western society can be regulated by cultural psychodynamic processes identical with those we more customarily associate with historical if not ancient ethnic, national, and religious societies ("traditions") in their responses to social change and loss. Further, I describe how the "treatment" process, the facilitation of grief work, permitted the mental organization of that culture to be understood by participants and facilitators alike.

The case begins as an instance of applied organizational anthropology, and concludes as a contribution to a theory of workplace culture and beyond. It brings to the center of culture theory the place of change, loss, grief, and defenses against mourning in human experience. It explores the psychodynamics of adaptation to change and loss, specifically group defenses against mourning. I argue, supporting the work of Volkan (1988), Mitscherlich and Mitscherlich (1975), Rochlin (1973), and others, that aggression is often mobilized to shore up, to give cohesion to groups that have suffered loss. Narcissism-driven nativistic and revitalization responses to change can thus be seen as symptoms of an inability to mourn (La Barre 1972).

LANDING AND STARTING

The era was the early 1990s. From the air, it could have been any time in the past half-century's prairie quilt. The noisy twin propeller airplane flew at a few thousand feet above the North American Great Plains toward Midwest City, my destination. Below, ripened densely sown quarter-section (160-acre) fields of winter wheat, alfalfa, milo, corn, all arranged in endless parallel rows contained in orderly quarter-mile squares, stretched between horizons. This was a world organized by section lines, dirt roads, wire fences, grazing cattle, unruly prairie nature, and perpetual cycles of planting and harvesting. Recognizable by its isolated farmsteads, cylindrical grain silos, and occasional crossroads towns, this was the north-central European *Einzelhofsiedlung* (open-country settlement, see Arensberg 1955) transplanted and adapted to the North American frontier.

The Midwest City airport had no baggage claim area. The pilot removed the baggage from the plane, put it in the bed of a pickup, and drove the pickup around to the front of the airport for passengers to claim their bags on the way out. This serene and refreshingly informal world of the grain belt bore no resemblance to the unrelenting social change and strife in Midwest City I had learned about in several telephone conference calls. Nor was there any clear signpost saying "this school district is mired in grief." I was brought in as a "trainer" (a term whose connotations I loathe, but my title nonetheless) and "facilitator" to help "run" a retreat of a district's school principals, superintendent, assistant superintendents, and school board. I was invited to help solve a problem: specifically to help plan and facilitate a three-day retreat.

The focus of this chapter is less "problem-solving" than "problem-emergence." In our culture-wide zeal for quick, prescriptive fixes and short-term solutions, we seek premature closure and in turn often solve the wrong problems. This study, an object-relations fieldwork approach to organizational consultation and group facilitation, is ultimately about waiting, about giving time and making room, about timing and timeliness. It is part of the continuing dance of theory and experience in organizational study.

ACQUIRING A SENSE OF HISTORY

I had never before consulted with a city's school system, and thus had limited prior knowledge of its bureaucratic culture and organizational history. Moreover, administrators, superintendents, and board members had no prior contact with me or knowledge of my work. The training team's work in the retreat was founded on reading the considerable literature on the town, written by a team of ethnographers (one of whom was a member of the team) who had spent nearly a decade studying and writing about its farming culture, school system, industrialization, immigrant ethnic groups, residential patterns and conflicts, attempts to introduce bilingual education, health care system, mental health delivery, and so on. Over many previous years, I had talked extensively with consulting team members about their research findings and the process of ethnography in this complex town. To assure anonymity and confidentiality of group participants, I do not cite the published accounts of Midwest City. Nor do I identify group members except by pseudonym. I have shared an early version of this manuscript with five individuals, some on the training team and others on the ethnographic research team, and have incorporated their historical and cultural addenda.

My two more senior consultant colleagues wished to assemble a taut, three-day schedule of formal presentations, large and small group exercises, and the like, and then be totally open to whatever emerged from the group. Already, in long-distance conference calls, I could sense in their zeal to assemble an airtight curriculum a world falling apart, a need to demonstrate legitimacy, and a struggle to control uncertainty. I began collecting "field data" from our own anxious behavior as somehow informative about the Midwest City I had never seen.

For the first two days, the principals and superintendents met together as a group. On the third day, this group was joined by the city's school board. A long history of animosity and mistrust between the two groups existed, now exacerbated by, among other things, the recent failure of a school bond issue; the contentious resignation of a controversial superintendent; and the fact that at this retreat an already embattled school board would "enter" a group of administrators who had already spent two days together developing a sense of boundaries and identity. I visualized an emotional topography of the group and larger community, one in which a massive tortoise-like shell of hate, schisms, and myths of the community all protected the group from the sense of loss, grief, and vulnerability.

Even before I arrived, I had been told by phone and read in written reports key historical facts and events that constituted the experiential core of the retreat. Until 1980, Midwest City had been a largely English-, Scots Irish-, and German-American rural farming community of 18,000 people. As recently as 1950, an article in a school yearbook was in German. During the 1980s, population increased to 25,000 with the building and expansion of the food processing industry, itself founded on the heels of President Reagan-era decentralization and deregulation. Hispanics, Turks, Laotians, Cambodians, and Vietnamese numbered high in the new ethnic influx. Midwest City rapidly became a multiethnic, multioccupational community. A town once highly Methodist now has its Buddhist temple and Muslim mosque. Work at the food processing plants is dangerous, unpredictable, low-paying, subject to frequent shutdowns, and there is high worker turnover. In the public schools, there is considerable student turnover. Several retreat participants noted that the teacher turnover rate in Midwest City is the highest in the state. Over the past decade, the district has lost three superintendents. Added to the diversity is the fact that Midwest City has attracted teachers from forty-nine states of the United States. Devastation from a tornado in the late 1960s persists in townspeople's memories.

The onslaught of social change and cumulative real losses characterized the sense of place in Midwest City. Newcomer and old-timer alike felt out of place, dislocated. To that must be added a sense of physical, geographic isolation. Over my four days in Midwest City, many people volunteered how they perceived their town in relation to other state and Great Plains locations. Often they replied, at once defiantly and apologetically: "You can't get there from here!"

As soon as I arrived, the training team—consisting of members whom I will call Brad Swenton, an applied anthropologist familiar with the

Midwest City school system, Janet Brown, a professional trainer and nationally renowned organizational consultant, and I—went immediately into an all-afternoon and long evening planning session. Brad Swenton's wife broke the news that the son-in-law (Bob Kaiser) of one of the assistant superintendents (Walter Smith) had been brutally killed just the day before in a bizarre, still unexplained car accident in which he had smashed into a garbage truck in broad daylight. Bob Kaiser's death gave an almost unreal, immediate focus to a diffuse sense of apprehension and grief. To me, the death felt immediately uncanny.

Prior to the retreat's beginning, I sensed an air of mystery in the communication about the auto accident and the death of Bob Kaiser. The town's and principals' usually close personal, though informal, network for notifying people of important events had utterly failed. I sensed it was as if everyone were in a kind of daze, as if what usually would be talked about were suddenly taboo, or did not matter. Over the next three days, I came to see this numbing response as a metaphor and lightning rod for the overwhelming sense of trauma, loss, cumulative loss, and unfinished grief the school administrators and community had suffered. Whatever the dizzying array of official and ostensible agendas, I discerned from the outset the underlying issue to be the intertwining of personal, familial, school, and community grief. Our subject was grief work, resistances to it, and its ultimate breaking through in the group.

During the first two days of the retreat, I felt myself to be on utterly shaky ground, terrified by the chaos and rage and helplessness I sensed. I wondered what on earth I could do to help; I felt overwhelmed and inadequate for a task that became increasingly vague. I learned most of all not to drown my terror and ignorance in attempts at rigid control, withdrawal, and intellectualization. I tried instead to let that very terror be a precious guide—a difficult assignment. I gradually overcame my fear of being lost in the group's anger, confusion, sense of abandonment and betrayal, and numbness. I let go my fervent wish to find a safe, detached, high ground apart from the group's social earthquakes. By following the group, persevering with it emotionally, I learned from it how to respond next. My greatest countertransference intervention was an ability to wait, to listen, to endure not knowing, to hold on to what I was receiving, to absorb it, to feel it, to not know what next to feel or say—in short, to be led by the group. The most crucial data I collected were the group "in me," via projective identification.

The first two days of the retreat—with principals (administrators), the new interim superintendent, and an associate superintendent—were held in a large squarish classroom in one of the city's newer school buildings. The principals were seated in a large, wide-based "U"-shape facing toward the front of the classroom, where chalkboards and overhead/slide projector screens were located, and from where the trainers spoke.

The third day of the retreat shifted to the spacious ballroom of a local hotel. Before the trainers had even arrived, one or more board members or administrators had not only arranged the chairs in an enormous "U"—this time with long arms—but had put name cards in places designating where people should sit. Later, several people said privately to me that not only was the "U" a familiar arrangement in these types of meetings, but that "the people who mattered politically" were, here as in other settings, placed at the base of the "U," rather than along its arms. In a new setting, the retreat, the group recapitulated its own structure; indeed, school meetings had previously taken place at this hotel.

At the beginning of the retreat, many administrators expressed reservation, if not outright hostility, about getting together at all. Several raised questions of "Who had *wanted* it?", "*Whose* workshop is it?", "*Whose* training is this?", "Who *wants* it?", "*Whose idea* was the workshop?", "Why didn't they ask *us* principals what *we* thought about training?", "*Where* did the workshop come from?", and "*Who* was it *for?*" My fellow trainers and an assistant superintendent told me that for several weeks prior to the retreat, many principals had agreed to attend, but felt their participation was by command rather than by their own wish. Many said, "I don't know the purpose of the workshop," and that it was ostensibly "for our own good." One said, "We were told we were to have a retreat." Another said, resentfully, "We were told what we should want." Many raised questions of "ownership," of inclusion and exclusion, of boundaries. Mistrust was in the air long before it became, during the retreat, an obsessive theme. The "U"-shape served as a visual "container" and "holding environment" for all the early "bad" feelings (though it became part of the broad, inclusive foundation for the "good" ones that would later emerge).

Through listening intently during the first hours of the retreat, I learned that the fundamental social unit in this world of administrators was "my building." Each "building" was an emotional silo-like structure: its members were self-isolated, self-protective, self-sequestered in a constantly embattled state (Diamond and Stein 2000). Much of the first two days was devoted to developing a sense of "team" among the principals, in part to help overcome the fragmentation and competitiveness derived from the exclusive orientation to one's individual building. "My building" was not only a practical administrative unit, but a unit of identity, authority, boundaries, politics, and economy. Moreover, for much of the time the divisiveness, isolation, and competitiveness between administrators was not acknowledged, let alone discussed publicly: those subjects were taboo. During the retreat, this aggressiveness often came to be expressed through an inflated us/them dichotomy, between administrators as a group and the school board. In part, the board came to bear the burden of administrators' own disavowed hostility, suspiciousness, and mistrust among themselves.

Past school district superintendents, the fierce loyalties and rancor they inspired, and the town's inability to let go of that history, haunted the retreat. Let me briefly review the history. Dr. Gregory Hart had been a respected, even beloved, superintendent for sixteen years prior to 1980. Then came what many described as "the Frantz fiasco," a five-year period which ended when Dr. Paul Frantz was charged, tried, and imprisoned for embezzling the school district's money. His embarrassing era was followed by Dr. Jerry Rauschmann, who was brought in to be a kind of executive antidote to the humiliating, exploitative Frantz years. Instead, he took his mandate and became heavy-handed throughout the school district. He was seen as tyrannical, degrading, controlling, and intrusive. He would show up in classrooms unannounced, observe, and demand that teaching proceed as if he were not present. He was supported politically by a fiercely loyal faction of principals, who came to be known as "Jerry's Kids"—a phrase used frequently throughout the retreat.

Sometime during 1990 he was asked to leave because of the chaos he had sown in Midwest City. Many thought it was a crisis when he left, and felt abandoned and adrift. Others breathed a sigh of relief. Glenn Stuart had just been appointed the new interim superintendent. Although the history of superintendents is not the only trauma to visit Midwest City, the way it quickly became a taboo in conversation, yet exercised its pernicious influence, is a metaphor for how unrelenting social change had been dealt with in the school district.

METHODOLOGY AND THEORY: THE HOLDING ENVIRONMENT

Before I describe some of my specific consulting team roles at the retreat, and the group's emotional denouement on the third day, I wish to describe my approach to organizational consultation, one which might be labeled "object-relations oriented applied ethnographic fieldwork." What role can an organizational consultant (of whatever academic or professional field) play to facilitate grief work? What kind of help is helpful, and how does one go about helping? My reply about methodology rests upon some assumptions about human nature and about the nature of how we understand ourselves and others (La Barre 1978).

Throughout the Midwest City retreat and the planning sessions as well, my approach was to subordinate any *content* I might introduce to the intersubjective *relationship context* in which it was taking place. I tried to make sure that no information, interpretation, confrontation, or role-play would intrude upon and threaten the nurturant, safe environment we sought to create. I recognized that anything any of us—facilitator or not—might say to one another could be construed in terms of its relative truth value or in terms of the ebb and flow of our relationships with one another, or at some level both. Furthermore, since mistrust and suspiciousness had become endemic to Midwest City, anything anyone uttered at the retreat would be scrutinized for its ostensible if not hidden threat (Meissner 1978, 1988).

Everything I offered I tried to put in Midwest City idiom or context, to translate into its cultural idiom—one I learned mostly by being there. To help the group through the complexity of its conflicts—a cultural texture, the full weave of which it mostly did not even consciously know itself—I had to allow myself to absorb, to "contain" as a receptacle all the ambivalences, inner splits, and contradictions within the group. More than anything else, I wanted to help create a secure zone in which people could be heard and understood. To approach the keen competitiveness and hostility between various Midwest City organizational units, I showed overheads of regional geography and talked about unforgiving football rivalries, collegiate and professional. I jokingly referred euphemistically to "the state to the north" or "the state to the east" rather than naming the state, much as they referred to one another's schools, or to that other adversary, the school board.

Intersubjectivity was the foundation upon which I built my contribution to the retreat. What Ogden writes of the use of countertransference in psychotherapy is equally true of all ethnographic fieldwork, including applied:

> The analyst has no means of understanding the patient except through his or her own emotionally colored perceptions of and responses to the patient. Of these perceptions and responses, only a small proportion are conscious, and it is therefore imperative that the analyst learn to detect, read, and make use of his own shifting unconscious state as it unfolds in the analytic discourse. (1989: 16)

The organizational consultant learns about the individual or organization not only through naturalistic and participant observation, through open-ended as well as focused interviews, and through an examination of the "material" culture that ranges from documentary sources such as organizational charts, to the psychogeography (Stein 1987; Stein and Niederland 1989) of space-use in the workplace. He or she learns most importantly through the "intersubjective resonance of unconscious processes" (Ogden 1989: 17) between consultant and client. Devereux (1967) devoted an entire book to the study of the role of the observer's subjectivity as the most reliable instrument of ethnographic inquiry. We understand and help others by understanding ourselves, by having emotional as well as cognitive access to others' influence upon us (Hunt 1989). The intersubjectivity of the psychoanalytic situation (Modell 1984: 172) does not differ in kind from that of organizational consultation.

The foundation of all the advisory and strategic skills a consultant can provide is the effective bond between consultant and organization. Analyst and consultant alike should provide what Winnicott (1963) termed a "holding environment," symbolic heir to the actual mother's physical holding, her reassuring presence and countenance and reliability that served as "container" (Bion 1959) for the infant's physically experienced hopes and dreads.

"The analyst communicates to the patient an image of the person that the patient can become" (Modell 1984: 245). So does the anthropological organizational consultant to the client or system. In addition to the more commonly recognized "higher" intellectual functions performed by anthropological consultants for client organizations, a far more fundamental function—one I have learned from working with grieving institutions—is that of metaphorical "holding" via "the communication of genuine affects" (Modell 1984: 89). Winnicott writes that "the analyst is holding the patient, and this often takes the form of conveying in words at the appropriate moment something that shows that the analyst knows and understands the deepest anxiety that is being experienced, or that is waiting to be experienced" (1963: 240).

Modell makes the distinction between two types of symbolic actions of the holding environment: "where the setting itself, the area of relatedness, between the patient and the analyst" (1984: 4) is the locus of therapeutic action; and the "truth-giving function" of verbal interpretation to patients who are well differentiated from the therapist (1984: 4). Ogden (1989) emphasizes that even highly individuated people never outgrow the need to provide membrane- or envelope-like effective surfaces for themselves and for their relationships. We emotionally house each other. What we do is always contained within, and builds upon, that visceral housing. Describing the analytic process, Ogden writes that "psychological growth occurs not simply as a result of the modification of unconscious psychological contents; in addition, what changes is the experiential context (the nature of the containment of the psychological contents)" (1989: 26). We help others to experience unconscious content differently by generating "the experience of a sensory surface" (Ogden 1989: 33) via a therapeutic regression, through which a shared sense of "pattern, boundedness, shape, rhythm, texture, hardness, softness, warmth, coldness, and so on" (1989: 33) is created and defined.

Modell emphasizes that people for the most part do not literally regress in all functions to pre-symbolic bodily experience. Ogden more correctly emphasizes that, no matter how symbolic relationships become,—including clinical and consulting—the experiential bedrock on which they are founded remains a sensory "holding" environment in which people can learn to hold on to and internalize their best and their worst, because another in their presence has contained it first within him/herself. To make this process concrete, I draw upon a vignette of Ogden's, in which he describes having turned on a heater in his cold office, and his patient's response:

> I said, "It's cold in here," and got up to turn on the heater. She said, "It is," and seemed to calm down soon after that. She said that for reasons that she did not understand she had been extremely "touched" by my saying that it was cold and by turning the heater on: "It was such an ordinary thing to say and do." I believe that my putting the heater on acknowledged a shared experience of the growing coldness in the air and contributed to the *creation of a sensory surface between us* [italics added]. I was using my own feelings and sensations in a largely unconscious "ordinary way" (perhaps like "an ordinary devoted mother" [Winnicott 1949]) which felt to the patient as if I had physically touched her and held her together. The sensory surface mutually created in that way was the opposite of the experience of "coming apart at the seams"; it facilitated a mending of her psychological-sensory surface which felt as if it had been shredded in the course of the patient's interaction with her mother. (1989: 34)

Ogden continues that "this sensory 'holding' (Winnicott 1960) dimension of the analytic relationship and setting operated in conjunction with the binding power of symbolic interpretation" (1989: 34). For years I have conceptualized my work in organizational consultation in a similar way, and the formulations of Ogden (1989), Modell (1984), Searles (1965), Volkan (1987, 1988, 1991), Boyer (1983, 1989), Masterson (1985), and Kernberg (1975), among others, reveal the same dynamics. Their formulations describe from a psychodynamic perspective how I help organizations to grieve.

As consulting organizational anthropologist, I find myself offering a symbolic membrane around those with whom I work by listening deeply, for long periods of time. I make room, as it were, for their worlds within mine, before I say anything to them in the form of descriptions or interpretations of their local world. Within the safety of this envelope-like holding environment, I try to provide them a sense of being heard, being seen, being understood, being attended to, which often feels to me as if it is reciprocated by my and others in the group being enclosed in membranes they are offering in return. Feeling understood, each group member can tolerate his or her anxiety and understand him/herself better and can then extend the gift of empathy to others in the group. Within the mutually constructed safety net of the holding environment, grief that has been held so long in abeyance begins to be felt, and walls erected against it begin to topple.

Throughout the Midwest City retreat, I regarded the "setting itself," the "area of relatedness" between all participants, as the fundamental locus of "training" or "facilitation." I tried to act as if all my own contributions to the group were situated within the membrane of the "holding" function. In my organizational group work, when this effective knowledge is working best, I can sit back and fantasize that I am an outside observer who is securely enclosed within the group that functions on its own. I can infer that "client" persons and groups have identified with my auxiliary ego functions. They now listen more attentively to, and grieve more openly with, each other, unmediated by the consultant.

Before I describe my roles at the retreat, I wish to say a few words methodologically about the texture and semiotics of my relationships with organizational clients. For the most part, organizations requesting consultation or project management have not defined their problem as change/loss/grief. They will have invited me to assist them on some other, often compartmentalized issue, task, or project. Through the process of listening, asking questions, and spending time with personnel throughout the organization on their turf, I help them to reconstruct (Freud 1937) the role unspent grief plays in generating the masked story behind the espoused story. Ewing writes that

> what goes on overtly in social interactions may be at variance with covert processes that participants themselves (much less observing anthropologists) are not always aware of. Taking an absolutely interpretivist stance, in which the culturally particular formulations of informants are assumed to be the only data about interactions that are available to the observer, would make the elucidation of covert processes (and their overt consequences) epistemologically impossible. (1991a: 156)

Scott-Stevens similarly writes that

> the [organizational] consultant must be wary about taking at face value the client's descriptions of the issues at hand. The anthropologist/consultant should already be cognizant of the fact that few people are aware of the details involved in the working of their own culture or subculture. This phenomenon is as true of smaller subcultures, such as groups of people in corporations, as it is of larger societies. (1988: 11)

In organizational cultures the surface (manifest) picture often serves to protect people from intolerable (latent) feelings, fantasies, and impulses, such as are associated with loss and grief. Client organizations and individuals often do not want to know what they, at some unrecognized level, already know too well. This "not-knowing" is not some abstractly intellectual, purely cognitive, deficit. It is rather a protection from knowing because of what knowing would make us feel. An emotionally taxing, yet rewarding role for organizational anthropologists is that of serving as bridge—as cultural broker—between knowing and not-knowing among our clients. And here, as always, the most difficult bridge is within the rooms of our own inner houses.

My role becomes that of mediating between the known and the unknown, the knowable and unknowable. In organizational consultation or project management, I temporarily serve the dual function of real person and auxiliary ego, for the client or group. Through attentive listening, interpretation, gentle confrontation, and questioning for the purpose of gathering more information about the group, I achieve a degree of libidinal object constancy both with and for the group. I try to acknowledge the participants' disavowed real self (Masterson 1985) that has become submerged by defenses against anxiety (such as annihilation, abandonment, separation, castration). I pay special attention to the affective (that is, emotional, conscious, and unconscious) dimension of communication, not only to the words spoken. In being, insofar as possible, in an I-Thou relation (Buber 1958) with the group, I acknowledge its many contradictory levels of feeling—including renunciation of feeling—and serve as a refueling station for the real group self as it tries to emerge. This real self is, in my experience, often buried by the pain of loss and the grief that is being warded off.

When I serve as consultant, I openly speak about what often cannot and must not be avowed in the organizational culture. As relatively safe outsider, I make the first step: I try to be both direct and tactful. In so doing, I offer myself as a person with whom organizational members might identify, and then proceed independently with grief work. Stated differently, I first identify with, serve as a container for, the split off and dissociated grief they projectively identify with me. I then return, metabolized, the feelings and fantasies to them as empathy and interpretation. Such environmental acknowledgment is as essential for fostering self-identity and ego identity later in the life cycle as it is for establishing it in infancy (Erikson 1968; Masterson 1985: 56–57).

SUMMARY OF MY ROLES DURING THE RETREAT

My time for making official didactic presentations was small. My contribution was greater when I was officially off-stage, when I served as listener and participant observer, offering comments and interpretations, raising questions to the group about what I was hearing, seeing, and feeling. For instance, during another trainer's presentation, or during group discussion following a presentation, I might comment about the group process, wondering whether the level of cultural content being shown might not rest on deeper, more emotionally disturbing cultural materials.

As I prepared my three didactic presentations, I tried to provide an area of unthreatened play which administrators and board members could use to think and feel about their own groups and about Midwest City. I deliberately chose topics and examples temporarily safely distant—a kind of transitional "me" but "not me" that everyone could examine external to themselves, but could try on as facets of themselves—so that group members did not feel violated and defenseless. For the most part, I talked about Midwest City only indirectly. I used my own examples, and my early time with the group, to build a bridge with them, one that might eventually take the form of a quasi-therapeutic group alliance.

I made three twenty-minute presentations, two during the administrators' retreat, and one during the retreat with the board. The first, made to the school principals and superintendents, was on group identity and the sense of place ("psychogeography"; Stein 1987; Stein and Niederland 1989). I passed around the circle of participants a piece of the hated, recently torn down, Berlin Wall that a friend had given to me. There was a palpable sense of awe in the room as that cinder made its circuit. People did not pass it off like a "hot potato," but examined it, held it. I talked about the Berlin Wall not only politically, but psychologically, in terms of how people everywhere use various symbols to wall out others and erect protective barriers between parts or aspects of themselves. Several principals commented:

> How do we establish community in a school? There's so much turnover. It is not possible to get consensus in Midwest City. . . . We have a pervasive problem of trust, from teachers to building administrators to central administration. . . . We have this mentality of "win," but we win at somebody else's expense. That's the feeling. We need something in our district that we'd live and die for. We just don't know what the end is, what the mission is. . . . I vehemently oppose what the organization stands for. . . . How do you create a win-win situation for everyone? . . . How do we communicate and be a team? . . . We're going into our third meeting with the board. We don't need just a Band-Aid. We need to get well. . . . We're a chronically ill patient.

In my further use of maps, cartoons, and personal anecdotes, my paramount goal was to foster a sense of group-related "I-Thou" (Buber 1958), an atmosphere of mutual respect, mutual inquisitiveness, and a willingness to learn from, and be corrected by, each other. I wished in my initial presentation to set the stage for them to talk more openly about their local cultures.

The second presentation, made to the school principals and superintendents, was on organizational identity and organizational roles. I approached the topic of administrators' often competing, contradictory roles through the medium of role-playing with my collection of hats. I put them on, wore them while talking, took them off, then handed them to people in the group by first walking away from the "center" and "front" of the class more into "their" space. They passed the hats around, sometimes putting one hat on, then passing it along. I raised several questions to the group as I role-played: "What stories (if any) are people trying to tell about themselves, or to hide, through the hats they wear [e.g., identification]?"; "What stories and roles do we impose on others by 'reading' our own meanings and fantasies into their hats [e.g., projective identification, externalization]?"; "What hats do we keep putting on, when others have already removed them [e.g., introjection, obsessional character defense]?"

What hat or hats, I wondered aloud, will the new interim superintendent, Glenn Stuart, be saddled with? Dr. Paul Frantz's? Dr. Jerry Rauschmann's? What hat or hats does he want to wear? What hat or hats will he be allowed to wear? Several heads nodded in the group; I felt increasingly safe in raising "the dead" in our midst. I continued: "What hats do we unconsciously put on other people, delegating to them proxy roles to act out and represent idealized or devalued parts of ourselves?" I discussed several vignettes from my previous consultations on organizational leadership, succession, and group grieving. I walked, and talked, a fine line between trying to create a safe "holding environment" and introducing content which would increase anxiety in the group (cf. Modell 1984).

The third presentation, made to the joint group of administrators, school board, and superintendents, was on metaphors of organizational and community change and loss. I discussed varied examples of cultures and organizations whose members were unable to leave the past behind, because people felt aggrieved by what had happened in the past. I noted the emotional significance of adult events in relation to earlier, often repressed, childhood experiences. During the discussion, I commented on how physical the group's expression of issues of self-esteem and crisis had been; I wanted to draw attention to the emotional tone I had heard, not only the words. Several principals and board members attested to having experienced a time of "destruction and self-destruction. . . . If I don't trust you, I don't expect you to support me in a crisis. We need to be able to celebrate failure, to trust that you don't get ripped apart for making a bad decision."

I listened for feelings as well as words, then reflected, returned those feelings processed back into the group. I told them that, from what I had heard from and about them, I was overwhelmed by the participants' sense of abandonment, isolation, desolation, and sheer badness, as if it were impossible ever again to attain a sense of goodness in Midwest City. It felt to me as if they were "possessed" by a past from which they could not separate, a kind of persecutory anxiety of something that felt alien, now haunting them. They were expressing feelings of despondency, rather than only being polite or attacking one another. I kept persuading myself to persevere, to listen, to help them to keep listening to one another; I knew I must not be too impatient, to force a premature interpretation, closure, or "solution."

"How do organizations, communities, grieve?", I wondered aloud. I also wondered what impediments to grief work there were in the educational system in Midwest City. From what I had heard earlier in the retreat, and from studies such as that of the tragic history of National Socialism in Germany (e.g., Nedelmann 1986), I speculated that part of the inability to mourn, the avoidance of mourning, is expressed by blaming, hating, aggression, fighting—including outright warfare—scapegoating by projecting one's own inner chaos onto villains and victims. One way to avoid grief is to find someone (e.g., a leader) or some other group (e.g., a pariah) to embody and personify one's own evil, so that one can maintain the illusion and hope that what was lost can be restored (e.g., Fornari 1975). Ironically, under these circumstances, splitting feels like healing, though genuine healing is a process of integrating what has been split off and projected.

I said to the group that I had heard over the past three days numerous references to a feeling of "urgency" to do something, to have a plan of action or policy. I wondered whether, in addition to action being necessary to complete any task, the present sense of urgency to "do something" might not also be a response to grief: a kind of flight into relentless activity in order not to feel. What, then, would grief be? I suggested that it would involve reviewing history rather than banning its mention; reviewing events, feelings, images, telling and retelling the story over and again until it feels finished, worked through by being fully faced.

THE TRANSFIGURATION SCENE

Around two or three o'clock in the afternoon, as the group of principals and school board members were discussing the wish for "trust," communication problems, the fear of making "mistakes," and group defensiveness began to melt away. Suddenly, from the back of the room, the interim superintendent, Dr. Glenn Stuart, walked to the front. Politely, he stood to the side until Janet Brown, the senior trainer, finished a sentence. Then he said, "I realize I'm interrupting, but I'd like to do something with your permission. I'd like five people to come forward, and I want to charge you with something on behalf of the administrators and school board."

He then called five people by name. They walked to the front and faced him as the larger group watched, wondering what was going to happen. Shaking their hands, touching them on the shoulders, and patting their backs, as if in reassurance, he said to them, and to the larger convocation:

> I want publicly to make a promise to you that, as your new superintendent, I will do my very best to listen to you, to be clear and straight with you, and to do my best for Midwest City. In turn, I want to charge you with the responsibility of making known the school administrators' and board's needs as clearly and directly as possible, that you trust me to tell me things you think I'll disagree with as much as agree with. I want you to come up with a list of priorities for your schools and for education in our district. I realize that I'm an interim superintendent, but I want to assure you I'm going to work very hard for Midwest City, and I ask the same of you. Will you give me your support in our common goal?

They movingly assented and shook hands. He touched them on the shoulder and back, everyone returned to his or her place, and the group activity resumed with a brief comment from Janet.

Dr. Stuart had just conducted a spontaneous rite—complete with "laying on of hands"—within the retreat. The group process was beginning to transcend the past and to open a window toward a future that was not compelled to repeat the past. The facilitators' role reversal was itself now spontaneously reversed in the new superintendent's newfound authority. For the earlier part of this combined retreat, and for the prior administrative retreat, the three facilitators led and were the focus of much of the group process (e.g., through formal presentations and exercises). From this point board members, administrators, and superintendents increasingly began interacting with one another, only now occasionally mediated by one or more of the trainers. Stories and feelings underlying the school district impasse now began to emerge: for example, authority, legitimacy, abdication of personal responsibility, feelings of betrayal and of guilt, conflict over being passive versus active toward authority. The facilitators had served as "container" (Bion 1959) and "holding environment" (Winnicott 1965) for much of the group anguish over its members' history and feelings. Now, Midwest City participants came to be able safely and compassionately to "contain" one another in our presence.

Shortly thereafter, Henry Ramirez, a school board member, said: "The superintendent serves at the pleasure of the board. Most school board members are not educated in education [by comparison with principals, who usually come up through the ranks as teachers]. A board can rely so much on a superintendent that they can become a rubber stamp [referring to the board's feelings about their past history with superintendents]. We function not as a body, but as a receptacle for someone else, to stamp what they want. People were *abused* in this district. We're here today because people were *abused*."

There was utter silence in the group. The mood change was palpable. There was a hush of grace, of communion. Everyone's eyes were riveted on Henry Ramirez. The chief trainer, Janet Brown, acknowledged his courage to speak publicly. He continued, "A great deal of energy was spent on conflict [within the school board, between the board and principals] and on just surviving [*emphatic*]."

The new school superintendent, Glenn Stuart, said: "You and I can ask for trust, but it doesn't come automatically. You build trust by example. None of us lay out a plan to fail, to make mistakes. We can decide how long a person has to prove himself, but that's not the same thing as trusting or not trusting." Henry Ramirez continued, "I saw certain administrators and board members treated with favor. I treated them with disfavor [*strong*] out of anger. Ill feelings were fostered outside."

A principal or board member said, "Part of the problem of trust is that I treated my colleagues wrong. Dishonesty, being a hypocrite, giving different messages to different people, giving more money to some people, less to others, favors of leave. If this were a store, we'd be out of business, with mispriced goods, and a dirty store. Only a clean store attracts customers and thrives."

Henry Ramirez added, "I've mistreated other persons on the board. We can come out of this workshop as a real team and leave some of this history behind us." George Grund, a board member, said quietly: "Trust isn't something you can build in two years of serving on the board. I'm used to verbal agreements in my business. I don't need contracts. I'm not supposed to say this, but we should have different priorities in education. I have differences with other school board members on this point. We're here first for the kids, not for budgets or exam scores." Henry Ramirez continued, "Trust is unwritten. I disagree with George. I don't think it takes two years to build trust."

Barbara Jones, a board member, said: "Carl Shreck [a principal] and I go round and round on a lot of issues. But even so, you know the person cares about your well-being. The disagreement doesn't get in the way of that." Carl Shreck acknowledged her, "I've had good arguments with Barbara. We have deep philosophical disagreement [*said very slowly, deliberately*]. But I trust she's not out to get me." Nancy Wall, school board president, said: "Three years ago the superintendent asked board members to be in the schools 50% of the time. His intent is not questioned. In the schools, everyone started looking over their shoulder."

Carl Shreck said, his voice now cracking: "One of Jerry Rauschmann's expectations, that board members go into the schools and visit often, was part of the angry communication between Marla [a principal] and Henry [a board member] earlier. It has to do with *history [emphatic]*. We're seeing change through a suspicious eye. We're seeing change through the groups we were in." Henry Ramirez said, "Our perceptions on the board affect how we operate. There's a lot of diversity on the board. Some board members think we have problems, or if it ain't broke, don't fix it."

Janet asked the group, "Why are systems created? Who are they for? Hospitals aren't principally for patients, but for doctors and nurses. They're the system. Who is school for? Systems are created for the people in them." At that point, Janet had noticed that Lucille Brent, a school board member, was especially silent, looking rigid or perhaps angry, her head lowered to avoid eye contact. She asked Lucille Brent what she was feeling or thinking about. Up to this moment, for about the past half-hour, I had noted participants' voices were all breaking or cracking, as if they were on the verge of tears. They spoke very differently in tone from the more position-taking, angry, defensive, careful, guarded earlier tone in the group. Lucille Brent said quietly, "I'm the only board member left of those who hired Jerry [Rauschmann]. I felt very threatened and vulnerable during the election campaigns." She was now openly in tears, weeping as were many administrators and school board members, and myself, with group members making no effort to hide or deny their tears. Speaking very deliberately, and with astonishment, Janet affirmed her: "You're really old guard." Lucille Brent continued, struggling to get her words through the tears: "I have a real fear and I want not to be emotional [*said through her tears*]. I want to know what you think of me, and I don't." The group was quiet, serenely still, most people quietly crying in silence. It was a poignant moment.

After allowing several minutes of silence, Janet offered an example of her relationship with her own teenage daughter: "My teenage daughter didn't want me to make decisions for her. I'm not always right. I try my best. It's hard sometimes." Here, I think, Janet was identifying with Lucille Brent, saying that she, in relation to the schools and larger community, is put in a parental, externalized superego role, in which she must make choices. That she is making decisions for others might not be appreciated by them. She acknowledged Lucille's sense of isolation, of vulnerability, not only in the past, but now in the group.

Henry Ramirez said quietly, "I want to express my gratitude to Lucille for expressing her feelings. We on the board don't meet enough. We need to strive for boardsmanship [*emphatic*]." Janet talked then about "team building" on the board. Walter Smith was a principal and assistant superintendent, whose son-in-law, Bob Kaiser, had died prior to the retreat, with most of those present attending the funeral. He now spoke: "We're all responsible for what happened here the last four years. Not just Jerry Rauschmann or the board." Janet added, "People have been avoiding grieving and have a lot of pain."

William Schlager, a principal who had been gently teased because his face often became ruddy, giving away his feelings, said: "There are a lot of administrators sitting at the table who feel the same as Lucille. I don't expound on my feelings. I abuse my yard instead. I keep my feelings in. I'm proud of my German background. I'm glad that Lucille can express them [his feelings] for me."

At this point Janet suggested that the group take a fifteen-minute break. During the break, most people, in small groups or individually, wandered around the room and hallway in tears, continuing the catharsis and heartfelt confessions of ill feelings and resentments about themselves and others. After the break was over and the group reconvened, Janet talked about organizational "wellness" and how it can only be achieved by letting go of hurt. Lucille Brent and others in the group asked for feedback, and pleaded to have people not go back into cliques as before. The last one to enter the room, George Grund, wondered aloud whether he was welcome. "I like George!" Henry Ramirez said loudly, broadly smiling to him from his seat across the room. George Grund replied back: "I like you, too, Henry."

Nancy Wall said, "There's a danger of blaming Jerry Rauschmann rather than taking responsibility, too." Jim Unruh, a principal, said he wished he could have been in a meeting like this last year when forced school busing occurred in Midwest City. Carl Shreck—who had seemed to me an articulate and angry person—spoke, his cracking, angry, bitter, betrayal-filled voice finally giving way to flowing tears:

> We called ourselves "Jerry's Kids." There were people who were in, and people who were out. [*He struggled for words, speaking slowly, very different from the angry, machine gun-like diction that had characterized his speech at the school principals' retreat.*] Lots of people assumed that if you were in, you got treated better, that you had it easier. [*Now he is even more emphatic, talking even slower.*] If you were in, you didn't get certain things, contrary to belief. You wouldn't believe who he was hardest on. If you needed secretarial help [*he gave other examples, specific situations and needs*], you didn't get it. If

you were one of "Jerry's Kids" you didn't get things other people could expect to get.

I didn't speak to him the last two months [*bitter, enraged, tearful*]. I know I'm getting emotional. I couldn't forgive. I was obsessed with the anger and the hatred I felt toward him. I had gone through an identical experience not long before, in my personal life situation. Somebody had hurt me deeply and I couldn't let go of it. After I had fumed and held my grudge for months, a friend of mine said to me, "You need to forgive him." Only when I could forgive him, did I quit being obsessed with it and let it go.

The same happened with Jerry. I couldn't call him. I couldn't bring myself to do that. . . . I felt so angry, so humiliated, I couldn't bring myself to call him. One day, I was driving my car and I just said out loud to myself "I forgive him." I could feel the heavy weight lift from my shoulders. We need to forgive a lot of stuff and let it go so we can start.

My own notes here are incomplete. These moments in the group were also intensely emotional ones for me. Tears made it impossible for me to see the notepad through my glasses and to write. I was also preparing to leave the group, to return to the airport, and was dealing with feelings of love and loss, as I groped to gather up my materials. Deeply moved by what they had just heard, the group was silent for several minutes. It was a warm, connected silence. Nancy Wall later talked about how our "personal" and "professional" selves, or roles, are interrelated.

Looking at my watch, I reluctantly signaled to Janet that I needed to leave the group for the airport. The time and timing of my leaving could not have been worse. We "trainers" had not expected the session to be so intense, so "productive." It had continued far longer than we had anticipated, or "planned"! I also could not postpone my departure due to previously scheduled work hundreds of miles away.

It was a difficult farewell for us all, and I felt emotionally raw. The emotional closure I needed I would have to find for myself—this chapter is itself part of that work of mourning. As I left, I kept thinking of the recurrent image or metaphor of "Jerry's Kids." This must, I thought, refer not only to the faction around Jerry Rauschmann, the visionary leader and hated autocrat, but Jerry Lewis, the comedian, who champions the cause of children suffering from muscular dystrophy, children who are otherwise helpless, dependent victims in need of rescue by good parents. Behind the image of being favored (idealization) is the image of being abused (bitterness, outrage) by the administrative patriarch. This latter contrasted sharply with the earlier widespread metaphor of "Jerry's Kids" that referred to people who presumably had benefited from his favors. I wondered, too, whether part of the psychological plausibility of the "Jerry's Kids" metaphor might be attributable to administrators' identification with disabled children, thereby exonerating them of their own, largely disavowed, aggressive impulses and wishes. It is as if to say "there are no bad kids, only bad parents." The metaphor might also condense the image of the wished-for, protective, nurturant parent with that of the abusive, tormenting parent, with whom one has unconsciously identified.

UNDERSTANDING THE TRANSFORMATION

Massive, unrelenting changes had characterized the Midwest City school district for a decade. Factionalism and mistrust had come to serve, in part, as a coping response to all these changes. The group process of the three-day retreat suggests that the inability to mourn change and loss had led to cultural entrenchment, mummified in myths that rewrote the past. The retreat culminated in a painful but liberating grieving of many of the losses, and of the self-protective, but often destructive, narcissistic response to the changes. Only on the last day of the retreat did the principals' and board members' stylized politeness, anger, persecutory anxiety, mutual suspicion, and polarization begin to break down.

Vamik Volkan writes that

> when changes are not mourned, the inability to mourn and its psychological effects carry on from one generation to the next, like other grievances (Rogers 1979); children and grandchildren want to recreate aspects of what is lost, and of events pertaining to the loss in order to complete the mourning. This is potentially harmful, stimulating an unconscious thrust toward political action, a kind of persistent group compulsion toward mastering shared hurts. (1987: 925) (see also Pollock 1977)

The process of silencing, acting out, and sealing over group trauma occurs not only intergenerationally (as in traditional ethnic or national groups), but among members of organizations recruited from the larger society and socialized as adults (as in corporations and professional schools). What people are allowed to remember is inseparable from what they are induced and compelled (e.g., via projective identification) to forget. These are among the first lessons that are part of the informal, if not unconscious, "job description" in the negotiation of a social contract for new employees in an organization. In this way, the myth of the past is recreated and reaffirmed as part of the price of initiation to the organization. To be loyal, to become worthy of acceptance as "one of us," one must make others' beliefs and convictions about the past one's own as well. In this way, the defense against the hurt of loss and against mourning is transmitted to new "generations" of adult recruits (Mitscherlich and Mitscherlich 1975; Volkan 1991).

Veteran U.S. State Department diplomat Joseph Montville makes observations about the uses of psychoanalytic insights in international diplomacy that apply to the Midwest City retreat:

> . . . if the abstract losses one can identify in so many ethnic and sectarian political conflicts—for example, losses of territory, or self-respect—can be seen as . . . genuine, profoundly meaningful losses of a sense of permanent, predictable security, then the discovery of ways to complete political mourning is critical to the art of political conflict resolution. A people cannot "let go" of a lost abstraction of the ability to feel safe. And they should not have to "let go" of the hope for a secure future. (1989: 304–305)

How can so fundamental a sense of safety be conveyed and become an intersubjective foundation of group functioning? Montville gives numerous examples of the transforming quality of acts of contrition by former adversaries, specifically "the concept of accepting responsibility for one's flaws and asking forgiveness of those who have been hurt by one's hostile acts" (1989: 309). Participants in the Midwest City retreat could begin to "let go" of their harrowing past, could afford to be less haunted by it, and could accept responsibility for their acts and apologize for them, only when they first could feel safe (safely held) in one another's presence. The safety net of their own holding environment was the precondition for mourning to be possible.

What Leonard J. Friedman writes of Michael Balint's therapeutic approach characterizes the trainers' style during the retreat: "The essential aspect of psychoanalytic experience which Balint conveyed was the experimental mode of respectful participant observation. He used his psychoanalytic experience to foster in physicians the development of their skills in the professional use of human understanding, aware that a degree of personal growth was necessary in the process" (1971: 95). Therapy becomes less interpretation-centered (and hence, less therapist-focused) than anchored in the relationship itself. The late Simon Grolnick, for instance, wrote that "we understand each other by understanding ourselves, and vice versa. A reflection on the misunderstanding of 'the other' helps to bring about self-understanding (Winnicott maintained that we help our patient most in working out the effects of our mistakes on them.)" (1987: 138)

In an article on *acknowledgment* in psychotherapy, Rafael Moses (1990) writes of how apology for errors, by helping another person to feel understood, radically transforms conflict situations of escalating narcissism (e.g., as defense against shame) into empathy and compassion toward one's erstwhile enemy. Instead of unleashing fury that defends against vulnerability, acknowledgment diminishes or eliminates the need for retaliatory aggression in defense of the self. Describing Heinz Kohut's work on "failure of empathy" in psychoanalytic psychotherapy (Kohut 1971, 1972, 1977)—failures that lead to patients' feeling they suffer injustice at the hands of therapists—Moses continues with a moving account of openly acknowledging mistakes to the patient:

> [W]e have gained experience with saying: "I am sorry that I did thus and thus," or "I am sorry that I did not do thus and thus." When a psychotherapist or a psychoanalyst does say these words, the response is almost invariably an emotionally powerful one. The analysand is inordinately pleased. This all-knowing, all-powerful, parental figure has done—in this case—what parents so rarely do. (1990: 29)

In the Midwest City retreat there were several layers of parent/child transferences: between the facilitators, the school principals, and the school board (each side alternately embodying parental-authority-menacing and child-dependent-fearful roles); between the principals and the board; between individual administrators themselves; between board members themselves; between administrators or board members and past superintendents; and between the various professional educational groups and their town constituencies.

By late afternoon of the third day of the retreat, participants began acknowledging their own wrongdoing, mistakes in judgment they had made, and of having hurt others to diminish their own pain. They made heartfelt, tearful testimonies and apologies for acts of aggression toward all victims, not only between principals as a group and "the board" as a unit. The group's emotional tone signaled that members had relinquished their prior narcissistic shoring up of pride against shame. People were able to speak the unspeakable. Vulnerability became a strength; boundaries dissolved. We were all moved by the new feelings that had been evoked. It felt to me as if in the midst of so much anger and grief, people recovered the capacity to love again. Compassion, gentle humor, concern toward those whom they had injured, a keen sense of their own pain, revulsion at the evil deeds that had occurred, and love—all were exhumed and reclaimed by group members. At the same time, members arrived at the emotion-based insight that these tender sentiments had been masked, warded off until now, by protective rage, isolation, factionalism, splitting, and projection.

By the middle of the third day the retreat group emerged from its self-protective imprisonment in persecutory, paranoid-schizoid (Klein 1946)

"I-It" relationships, and courageously entered the realm of integrative, reparative "I-Thou" relationships. The inclusive sense of "we-ness" that was created and expanded in the combined group did not need an enemy to sustain itself. Group members no longer purchased their sense of identity, and of goodness, by finding or creating a group to embody their own evil. The process that unfolded did not have the defensive, trance-like, reality-distorting nature of Bion-type (Bion 1959) dependency, fight-flight, or pairing "basic assumption" groups; nor did it have the magical thinking that Anzieu (1984) characterizes as the unconscious, dream-like core of group process.

The retreat can be understood in the anthropological metaphor of Victor Turner's "ritual process" (1969). However, the rite must be construed as one that facilitated the *recovery of* (reconstruction, see Freud 1937), *and from, history*, rather than as ritual in the classical psychoanalytic sense of acting out history while concealing it (compromise formation). It was actively co-constructed as a holding environment by the trainers and by the group members. It was a sanctuary outside normal work space and time, one in which space and time could be playfully revisited, taken apart, and revised. Numerous role reversals characterized the retreat (leader/follower, teacher/student), facilitating a therapeutic regression, a working through of historical "stuckedness" and grievances, and the reemergence at the end of the retreat of hopefulness and creativity.

The retreat provided a Turnerian "liminal" experience that offered "anti-structure" to the ordinarily structured social world, a rite of passage (Van Gennep 1960) that is "betwixt-and-between" the familiar, but which did not return participants to the preexisting familiar. Instead, it transformed that reality itself. The structure of the retreat was, at least initially, disorienting, disruptive to the participants' usual ritual routines, spatial orientations, and social roles. Both intentionally and inadvertently we "trainers" separated administrators, superintendents, and school board from their ordinary world. These disruptions may have contributed to the therapeutic regression that permitted openness to new, raw emotional experiences, and to a cognitive-affective reorganization later on in the retreat; this process continued afterwards.

"How does performance relate to experience?" and "How does performance change experience?" asks Mary Douglas (1990: 252). What is it that makes for "an extraordinary time which draws out of the actors a power of reaction normally beyond their reach, providing an on-going structure for other experience?" (1990: 253). Further, what directs that power of reaction toward heightened sorrow, compassion, mercy, integration, joy, greater self-respect and respect for others, rather than revenge, rage, pride, perversion, and narcissism? My tentative answer is that we provided a holding environment that fostered a working through of massive social change, loss, and unfinished grief.

The retreat created an atmosphere in which all participants could become more differentiated, more integrated, more receptive to the synthetic function of the ego, more capable of holding on to ambivalence, more capable of responding to one another as fully human rather than as part-objects. Group members identified with and internalized the functions of the facilitators and became, in turn, healthier nurturing and clearer authority figures for one another. Relationships came to be less dominated by paranoid suspiciousness and intense ambivalence. The facilitators did not accomplish this alone. The retreat was cocreated by all participants. The facilitators provided a safe space for the group to expand its emotional capacity and sense of relatedness. The group also created an increasingly safe, nurturant space for its members, one in which forgiveness and reconciliation could occur, one in which both love and hate could coexist in the image people held of one another. Attack and withdrawal, despair and isolation, gave way to guilt and repair, to love and empathy.

As the end of the retreat neared I kept hearing with my third ear, from my unconscious (Reik 1948, 1953), the prelude and "Good Friday Spell" from Wagner's opera *Parsifal*. Its "diagnostic" message to me was that healing was taking place. In *Parsifal*, both the chalice and the spear are essential to the drama: love and aggression are reconciled through compassion. The spear that wounds is the very instrument that later heals. Psychodynamically, previously split instincts or wishes became more integrated. Repair had begun, rooted in compassion. I trusted my music's diagnostic aptness. The retreat had begun three days earlier on a note of "badness"—as if nothing anyone in Midwest City did could be good, as if the town itself were inherently flawed. It ended on a note of "goodness" that was not the emotionally polar (manic) opposite of badness (reaction formation or splitting), but rather one that acknowledged people as both good and evil.

If the price of ever-widening group affiliation, of inclusion and integration, is increased guilt, we can begin to understand how inner pain is fended off by outward-directed hostility, divisiveness, aloofness, resentment, vindictiveness, group fragmentation and factionalism—all fueled by chronic narcissistic rage. All this had long characterized Midwest City. More tender, loving feelings had not been given their due because of the paranoid-schizoid defense against the extent of change and the sense of loss in Midwest City (Klein 1946). Instead of grieving, people blamed others for their anguish. What Freud says in *Civilization and Its Discontents* has cogency for our time: "The fateful question for the human species seems to me to be whether and to what extent their cultural development will succeed in mastering the disturbance of their communal life by the human instinct of aggression and self-destruction" (1930: 92).

DISCUSSION

We must ask what world, what sense of history, we facilitators and the two retreat groups entered. I kept having the fantasy of an organizational or community "failure to thrive," my working metaphor for much of what I observed, heard, and felt. I sensed a group and its larger town reeling from a sense of embattlement and abandonment anxiety. The experience of accumulated trauma—social change from which there was no respite—had led to a profound lack of emotional object constancy, leading in turn to withdrawal, mutual mistrust, factionalism, narcissistic rage, persecutory anxiety, fear of anger and retaliation, a sense of helplessness and hopelessness—all of which were massively covered over by a frenzy of activity and a "win" attitude toward job functioning.

Oedipal-level conflict over sexual possession of the desired/forbidden parental object rests upon the foundation of pre-oedipal conflict. Former fathering- and mothering-figure superintendents (leaders) had been emotionally unreliable, betraying, exploitative, depriving, abandoning, punitive, and bullying. Members of the board and administrators had responded to the superintendents' abuse and abandonment, in the larger community historical context of change and loss, with greed, competition for scarce economic and emotional resources, and a fulminant "sibling rivalry." This was covered over by a social fiction of administrators versus school board (us/them), onto which much of the inner disorganization was displaced to manage enormous anxiety. In the retreat groups and in the larger city, fantasies of father-leader, the group-as-mother, and the group-as-family had failed to provide stability. In the wake of abandoning such fantasies nothing or no one could serve to contain feelings and wishes long enough for them to be sorted out and worked through. Virtually everyone I spoke with felt as if Midwest City were an inherently defective, "bad" place, that consensus was not possible, that one couldn't get anywhere from Midwest City. The sense of death was overwhelming, reified by the brutal car accident that preceded the retreat.

This deficient leadership, characterized by absent and punitive parent-leaders, and a history of decade-long massive community change, was the setting in which the retreat occurred. Given the long history of sacrifice (victimization) as a problem-solving mode in Midwest City, I wondered whether communal renewal was possible without making yet another person or group into a victim. It was into this context that the three facilitators came and worked as pre-oedipal nurturers and oedipal-level authority figures, transference objects who were nonjudgmental, who listened and helped group members feel heard, acknowledged, and understood. In so doing we facilitated differentiation and integration.

It would be easy to try to account for the success of the retreat by additively enumerating the presentations, exercises, and other specific activities, and concluding that it was the sum and sequence of these that worked. The heart of the matter would have been overlooked: the performance transcended performance itself. Anyone who has attended a musical performance emotionally knows the difference between lifeless, virtuosic correctness and the sublime. My tentative interpretation as to what made this "rite" effective comes from a passage by Leonard J. Friedman that summarizes Michael Balint's (1965) psychoanalytic technique, an approach that also characterized the facilitators' style in relation to the group:

> [His purpose was] to facilitate a new beginning in living for the patient in analysis, a state in which the patient could reexperience something like primary love, a setting in which he could take the unobtrusive but attentive analyst for granted in order to find himself in his own way. Balint saw that if this setting is not provided when needed and interpretations are offered as if the patient had an inner conflict in the classical [neurotic] sense, personal development is stunted in much the same way as it is in childhood when the child has to conform to preconceptions and needs of his parents which distort him. Such interpretations tend to be retained as foreign bodies, leading to identifications rather than mourning of the past followed by new development of the patient's freedom to love with primary intensity. Understanding love as he did, he could see hate as a reactive phenomenon, basically a fear response gone awry, a way of dealing with despondent dependence—not a primary instinct. (1971: 97)

The Midwest City school district had experienced a decade of intrusive, overwhelming change, and an onslaught of humiliation, against which citizens had massively defended themselves. A highly regimented, directive, manipulative, "packaged," "slick" training environment (in vogue in corporate management circles) would have inadvertently subjected the group to the very experiences from which members were reeling. The trainers' facilitative style was to give group members room to create more space to be themselves, internally and interpersonally; to let go of the false, compliant selves that sealed over their community-wide depression.

The Midwest City retreat suggests, as does Montville and others, that the human need for enemies can be mitigated through a mourning process (Montville 1989). In this way the past need not be denied and repeated. Perhaps one may say that, through the work of mourning a new form of wholeness becomes possible, one based on the greater synthesizing capacity of the ego, greater differentiation between self- and object-representation, and greater capacity for empathy and playfulness.

The culture history of Midwest City, and of the retreat, sheds additional light on the idea, proposed by Freud (1931), later amplified by Volkan (1988), Boyer (1986), Stein (1982, 1986), and others, that people need to have enemies. In the United States, for instance, with the resignation of President Mikhail Gorbachev and the demise of the Soviet Union, the U.S.'s long-standing adversary and "evil empire" not only disappeared, but was no longer available to serve as the U.S.'s "suitable target for externalizations" (Volkan 1988). Quickly Japan, Iraq, China, and others have temporarily assumed the representation of external national menace, while the homeless, people with HIV/AIDS, people on welfare, alcoholics, drug addicts, and others became targeted as "internal" American enemies. Stated more broadly, no sooner does one enemy collapse from internal factors or fall to defeat on the battlefield, than another is chosen to replace it and focus the terrible anxiety. This case study of Midwest City has suggested that massive culture change and accompanying loss of identity are defended against by the creation and shoring up of us/them dichotomies. It has also suggested how mourning can diminish this need for enemies by turning all combatants into "mere," vunerable mortals.

Grief and defenses against it can also help us better understand the perplexing dynamics of the experience of seeming cultural "wholeness" in organizations and nations. Ewing (1990) has rightfully criticized the view of the self as a singular, whole, autonomous elementary particle, and argues that, in contrast to the conscious experience of personal continuity, people occupy numerous contradictory states of consciousness according to social situation. I would extend her argument: individuals and entire groups purchase feelings of coherence, of cohesiveness, of wholeness, and of goodness inside, via institutionalized elaborations of splitting, projective identification, projection, dissociation, displacement, and other "outering" mental defensive processes. This comes to be ideologically formulated along absolute us/them lines, either in the form of external or internal enemies. What at the conscious experience of the self feels like wholeness (e.g., principals in "my building," or principals allied against school board) is in fact purchased at the price of dehumanizing both the adversary and the self. Both become depleted of more complete, conflictual humanity by virtue of what must be extruded from oneself and embodied in the other. Psychological "totalism" (E. H. Erikson 1968), together with its ideological form, totalitarianism, defend against fragmentation and grief. Here, hate is less an invariant, independent variable, so to speak, than an affect mobilized to prevent a sense of chaos, fragmentation, and psychotic anxiety.

We must qualify the claim "Man needs to hate" with something like "Man needs to hate in order that he or she not feel more disturbing emotions, fantasies, and wishes." At the school retreat and its antecedents, aggression was mobilized in behalf of the cohesion of the self and its projected, affiliated social unit in order that intra-group strife be averted, in order that people not make themselves vulnerable to loss again. Within the retreat's "holding environment," it became clear that the need for enemies is far from fixed, that the inability to mourn change and loss figures greatly in the very rigidity of that need.

During the first two days of the retreat the three trainers received massive amounts of information about change, loss, and resistance to mourning, through projective identification. At first I wanted to be rid of the horrible feelings induced in me. My initial gut feeling response was to attempt rigid control of the group, to withdraw emotionally if not to flee, and to intellectualize. These uncomfortable feelings were vital cues about the group's own defenses and history: it was making me feel as it felt, and likewise was making me feel like those parent-figures who had abused and betrayed group members. I then overcame my fear of being annihilated by the group's anger, rage, confusion, sense of abandonment, helplessness, and numbness (and by those feelings of my own which were induced in me). I relinquished my fervent wish to find a safe high ground apart from the group's social earthquakes. By listening attentively to the group, persevering with it emotionally, I learned how next to respond. I discovered that if I do not risk all by imagining and feeling everything the group is inducing in me, then I as facilitator cannot expect the group to risk anything for healing's sake.

On psychodynamic grounds one may question the long-term efficacy of shamanic transference or suggestion cures and rites. Was the retreat any different? From follow-up telephone conversations and letters with several participants, including the new superintendent, several months and then a year later, I am persuaded that a process of lasting repair based on insight and genuine working through of grief had begun. Between mid-1990 and mid-1991, massive building and remodeling projects were started in Midwest City; the school board publicized and succeeded in passing a several million dollar school bond issue; the transition from four retiring to four new school board members was smooth; a greater cooperative, even enthusiastic, spirit prevailed between board and administrators and superintendent, and among school administrators; and during this year, teacher turnover in the district decreased by half (from 22.4 percent to 11 percent). I hesitate to credit the trainers for these results or outcomes. The trainers and their techniques less caused something to happen, as allowed something to happen. The holding environment persisted long after the training team had departed and the retreat was over.

The mutative factor within that holding environment was, I believe, love. In *Experiences in Groups* Bion (1959) curiously and without precedent states that "the fight-flight group expresses a sense of incapacity for understanding and the love without which understanding cannot exist"

(1959: 146). According to Bion's typology, "fight-flight" is one of three unconscious "basic assumptions" that govern group behavior. In it, group members feel their very existence to be threatened: they mobilize to attack or flee. Bion's insight about the role of love bridges affect and intellect in groups. It gives additional depth to his later statement that "intellectual activity of a high order is possible in a group together with an awareness (and not an evasion) of the emotions of the basic-assumption groups" (1959: 160). Emotion and affect can be the enemy of high-order ego functioning work groups, or they can be their greatest ally (Sutherland 1990). I believe that it was love that at once allowed the school district's retreat to come to terms with its members' basic assumptions, and which liberated the group during and subsequent to the retreat.

Just as "basic assumptions" can undermine the "work" or "task" of the group, the emotions can also aid the work of the group. Similarly, to use a different pair of concepts, "expressive" activities in a culture can sabotage or enrich the "instrumental" activities. A group's instrumental task or "technical job has to come into the sphere of the ego's resources for mastering and using it" (Sutherland 1990: 134). Lanzetta and Roby similarly write that "the way the group 'utilizes' its resources and the procedures it employs for communicating essential information are as important as, if not more important than, 'knowledge' of the problem for determining its performance" (Lanzetta and Roby 1960: 146). The story of the Midwest City retreat shows how expressive activity initially sabotaged work, but ultimately rejuvenated it. A process more subtle than the often polarized concepts of groupishness versus individuality takes place. Group relatedness can itself foster either regressed de-individuation or distinctive identity. As Sutherland writes, the latter "has its own needs for group relatedness, namely, in groups in which his identity is affirmed and enriched by the extent of the ego's reality involvement in them" (1990: 135). The Midwest City retreat showed how, in a group setting, love could transform the "expressive" culture, and in turn enhance the group's "instrumental" tasks, its official reason for existing.

CONCLUSION: FROM CASE STUDY TO BROADER ORGANIZATIONAL UNDERSTANDING

This chapter has explored the hidden triad of change-loss-grief in the life of a Great Plains city. It has attempted to understand the "heart of darkness" in much of organizational life. The study began as no formal study at all, but as a piece of applied, practical social science in the form of consultation. It ended with a greater appreciation for the psychodynamic texture of any culture, including organizational culture.

According to the interpretation offered in this chapter, the facilitators' principal methodology in the school district retreat was the creation of a stable "holding environment" within which cultural (organizational) space could be created anew as a "facilitating environment" (Winnicott 1965). A crucial instrument of change in this transitional space was the countertransference of the facilitators. The new intersubjective space enabled a catharsis to take place and the beginning of a working through in the community to occur. The outcome of the group process illustrates the transforming power of love, perhaps in organizational cultures beyond the boundaries of Midwest City. The retreat was as affirming to the facilitators as it was to the administrators, school board, and superintendents for whom the retreat was designed.

If the retreat can be characterized by certain ingredients of its process—formal presentations, group exercises, the fostering of a "holding environment"—these cannot be packaged into a consultant's formula of lessons or protocols that can be directly extrapolated to other settings. What can be extrapolated to ethnographic fieldwork, to organizational consultation and other genres of applied anthropology, and to clinical psychoanalysis alike is the virtue of seeing all our work as taking place in Winnicottian "potential space" in which we less make things happen as we permit them room to emerge.

During the retreat—and perhaps in all fieldwork and psychoanalysis—the transformation that occurred was reciprocal. If what I did as participant observer and facilitator was helpful to the group, it was less something already and wholly within "me," as it was something of a numinous gift bestowed by the group's own projective identification. To a large degree, they gave me first what I needed to give them. As the retreat proceeded, I felt more of my own real self (in contrast with my conformistic false self) emerge and consolidate. I believe this was my countertransference response to the group's therapeutic strivings induced in me (Searles 1975).

After I had helped facilitate grieving in the retreat group and in its wider community, it was then my turn to mourn, for intimacies such as I had experienced as a consultant are gifts rarely so freely bestowed. The very writing of this chapter serves in part as a memorial to the event and its experience. I left not only affirmed in my approach to organizational consulting and in my comprehension of cultural processes, but—as Winnicott might say—with the sense that I was very much alive. And that, through mourning, whole cultures—even workplaces—can learn again to play. The internal, interpersonal, and cultural space this can create is unfathomable until one has experienced it for oneself.

This case study and chapter are "about" many different facets of organizational and cultural life. As in a dream, the case "condenses" many tributaries into a single immense stream. For example, this chapter is

about the emotional "geography" of affiliation: that is, when groups con-
strict, expel others, and when they expand, welcome, include others. It
is about the "psychogeography" (Stein and Niederland 1989; Stein 1987)
of human group boundaries, when they close down and when they open.
It explores the relationship between mental representation, affect, spatial
representation of the natural and social worlds, and intersubjective relationships within and between groups. It describes when transitional
space is persecutory, and when it is play. This chapter contributes to the
study of the mental representation of cultural space (Stein 1987; Stein
and Niederland 1989; Pollock 1991), specifically, the transformation of
intrusive, persecutory space into an area of play that Winnicott (1967)
called "potential space."

This chapter also expands ideas about the psychodynamics of interpersonal interactions (intersubjectivity) into more areas, for example, the
intersection between occupational organizations, town-or-community,
ethnic change, and national culture—all of these mediated by yet another
group, that of the "retreat" of school principals, administrators, and
school board. I describe and interpret how a chronically persecutory
space within and between these various discretely bounded social units
was transformed into an area of grieving and liberation, a potential space
that Winnicott (1967) would have called "play." In discussing the problems of achieving the establishment of a special mental space, a new one
culturally, within the group, I interweave other group members' transference and my own countertransference. Both of these provide crucial
information about the location and affective significance of participants'
cultural experiences in the retreat, and in their wider organizational relationship contexts. (This paragraph builds upon ideas expressed in a
letter from L. Bryce Boyer, 16 June 1991.)

Similarly, the case study sheds light on the complex relation between
"instrumental" and "expressive" facets of organizational culture: that is,
between reality and desire, between task and relationship, between work
and intimacy, between technique and symbol. In an earlier paper on the
symbolism of technology in Western society (Stein and Hill 1988), I discussed how technology, in addition to serving reality-adaptive functions,
could also be employed "expressively" for personal magico-religious
purposes. In this chapter, I show, quite differently, how the symbolic,
expressive side of culture can both subvert and improve task performance, how it can quietly revolutionize culture by giving people far
more internal and external space than they had imagined had been available to them.

In addition to being a case study, the chapter addresses perennial
questions in the human sciences. What is culture—including workplace
culture—for? Why do people make and join cultures? How does culture
cohere, perdure, change? If people are given to reify, to anthropomor-

phize their groups, what leads them to do so? If human culture is often maladaptive from the long-term view, why do people so commit themselves to their symbolic reality, such that to attempt to give it up brings about so profound a grief that mourning itself is renounced?

This chapter describes what I learned as a member of a three-person "training team" for a three-day retreat of a city's approximately twenty-six school principals and superintendents, and seven school board members. I was brought in and employed for four days to serve as a change agent to help the group get un-stuck. Employing a style of naturalistic and participant observation (Geertz 1983; Briggs 1991), the training team came to serve as a "container" (Bion 1959) and "holding environment" (Winnicott 1958) for the group. This leadership-therapeutic relationship and function allowed me to recognize the resistances and discover the conscious and unconscious fantasies, affects, wishes, and traumas underlying the manifest culture. I was able to help the group feel safe and trusted, so it could allow its unconscious to become collectively experienced consciously. Culture—what it is, what it means, what it feels like, what its functions are, its existence as a system of internal and externalized representations, how it is shared—is never so clear in outline both to the member and to the observer or consultant, than when as a symbolic object (Stein 1985) it is lost, or when it is under the imminent threat of loss. Grief, its denial through frenetic activity at work, and in revitalization, offers a clear outline of what is lost or could be lost.

Finally, this chapter gives further appreciation to the role of the facilitator or ethnographer's own experience, and to the healing, mutative power of love—even at "work." It affirms the centrality of the countertransference in acquiring, containing, processing, metabolizing, and returning data to the group. As Rosenfeld wrote of his work with schizophrenics (1952)—and clinicians such as Bion (1959), Boyer (1983, 1993), Devereux (1967) and others have amplified—: "Our countertransference is frequently the only guide" (1952: 126) to interpretation. Organizational data, like those from more traditional ethnographic and clinical settings, are often first gleaned, then later understood, by the facilitator's inner experience of the organization. The key is to realize that one is already gathering data when one feels most lost, most disorganized, even "crazy." Stated differently, the organizational consultant, like the fieldworker and psychoanalyst, is never *not* gathering data—even when one may feel distracted or overwhelmed by one's own feelings and fantasies. What seems at first extraneous turns out to be crucial affective knowledge (Boyer 1993, 1999): that one is already in the thrall of the group's projective identifications. The crucial issue for data gathering and interpretation alike is to realize that one's own feelings "in the field" are themselves authentic data, and not to discount them as extraneous intruders.

I have chosen to end my book with this study because it shows how "personal" ostensibly "impersonal" "business" practices, strategies, and philosophies are. It reveals the festering wound heavily crusted over by organizational and wider cultural defenses. It shows what is possible—and what prevents the possibility from being realized.

REFERENCES

Anzieu, Didier. 1984. *The Group and the Unconscious*, translated by Benjamin Kilborne. Boston: Routledge and Kegan Paul.

Arensberg, Conrad. 1955. "American Communities," *American Anthropologist* 57(6,1): 1143–1162.

Balint, Michael. 1965. *Primary Love and Psycho-Analytic Technique*. Second edition. New York: Liveright Publishing Company.

Bion, W. R. 1959. *Experiences in Groups*. New York: Ballantine.

Boyer, L. B. 1983. *The Regressed Patient*. New York: Jason Aronson.

———— 1986. "On Man's Need to Have Enemies: A Psychoanalytic Perspective," *Journal of Psychoanalytic Anthropology* 9(2): 101–120.

———— 1989. "Countertransference and Technique in Working with the Regressed Patient: Further Remarks," *International Journal of Psycho-Analysis* 70: 701–714.

———— 1993. "Introduction: Countertransference: Brief History and Clinical Issues with Respect to Regressed Patients," in L. B. Boyer and P. Giovacchini, eds., *Master Clinicians On Treating the Regressed Patient*. Volume 2. Northvale, NJ: Jason Aronson. Pp. 1–22.

Briggs, Jean L. 1991. "Mazes of Meaning: The Exploration of Individuality in Culture and of Culture Through Individual Constructs," in L. B. Boyer and R. M. Boyer, eds., *The Psychoanalytic Study of Society*, Volume 16. Hillsdale, NJ: The Analytic Press. Pp. 111–153.

Buber, Martin. 1958 (1925). *I and Thou*. Second edition, translated by Ronald Gregor Smith. New York: Charles Scribner's Sons.

Deal, Terrence E. 1985. "Cultural Change: Opportunity, Silent Killer, or Metamorphosis?" in *Gaining Control of the Corporate Culture*. R. H. Kilman, M. J. Saxton, and R. Serpa, eds. San Francisco: Jossey-Bass. Pp. 292–331.

Devereux, George. 1967. *From Anxiety to Method in the Behavioral Sciences*. The Hague, Netherlands: Mouton.

De Vos, George A. 1973. *Socialization for Achievement: Essays on the Cultural Psychology of the Japanese*. Berkeley: University of California Press.

———— 1975a. "The Dangers of Pure Theory in Social Anthropology," *ETHOS* 3(1): 77–91.

———— 1975b. "Affective Dissonance and Primary Socialization: Implications for a Theory of Incest Avoidance," *ETHOS* 3(2): 165–182.

Diamond, Michael A., and Howard F. Stein. 2000. "Silos of the Organizational Mind," unpublished manuscript.

Douglas, Mary. 1990. Book review of *The Anthropology of Experience*. Victor W. Turner and Edward M. Bruner, eds. (epilogue by Clifford Geertz). Urbana: University of Illinois Press, 1986. Reviewed in *American Anthropologist* 92: 252–254.

Erikson, Erik H. 1968. *Identity: Youth and Crisis*. New York: Norton.

Erikson, Kai T. 1976. "Loss of Community at Buffalo Creek," *American Journal of Psychiatry* 133(3): 302–305.

Ewing, Katherine P. 1990. "The Illusion of Wholeness: Culture, Self, and the Experience of Inconsistency," *ETHOS* 18: 251–278.

—— 1991a. "Can Psychoanalytic Theories Explain the Pakistani Woman? Intrapsychic Autonomy and Interpersonal Engagement in the Extended Family," *ETHOS* 19(2): 131–160.

—— 1991b. "Idiosyncracy and the Problem of Shared Understandings: The Case of a Pakistani Orphan," in L. B. Boyer and R. M. Boyer, eds., *The Psychoanalytic Study of Society*. Volume 16. Hillsdale, NJ: The Analytic Press. Pp. 215–247.

Fornari, Franco. 1975. *The Psychoanalysis of War*. Bloomington: Indiana University Press.

Freud, Sigmund. 1920 (1955). "Beyond the Pleasure Principle." in *The Standard Edition of the Complete Psychological Works of Sigmund Freud*. Volume 18. London: Hogarth Press. Pp. 7–64.

—— 1930 (1961). "Civilization and Its Discontents," in *The Standard Edition of the Complete Psychological Works of Sigmund Freud*. Second edition. Volume 21. London: Hogarth Press. Pp. 64–145.

—— 1937 (1964). "Constructions in Analysis," *The Standard Edition of the Complete Psychological Works of Sigmund Freud*. Volume 23. London: Hogarth Press. Pp. 255–269.

Friedman, Leonard J. 1971. "Michael Balint: In Memoriam," *Psychiatry in Medicine* 2: 95–97.

Geertz, Clifford. 1983. "From The Native's Point of View: On the Nature of Anthropological Understanding," in *Local Knowledge: Further Essays in Interpretive Anthropology*. New York: Basic Books. Pp. 55–70.

Grolnick, Simon. 1987. "Reflections on Psychoanalytic Subjectivity and Objectivity as Applied to Anthropology," *ETHOS* 15(1): 136–143.

Grotstein, James. 1981. *Splitting and Projective Identification*. New York: Jason Aronson.

Hunt, Jennifer C. 1989. *Psychoanalytic Aspects of Field Work*. Sage University Paper Series on Qualitative Research Methods. Newbury Park, CA: Sage, Volume 18.

Kernberg, Otto F. 1975. *Borderline Conditions and Pathological Narcissism*. New York: Jason Aronson.

Klein, Melanie. 1946. "Notes on Some Schizoid Mechanisms," *International Journal of Psychoanalysis* 27: 99–110.

Kohut, Heinz. 1971. *The Analysis of the Self*. New York: International Universities Press.

—— 1972. "Thoughts on Narcissism and Narcissistic Rage," *Psychoanalytic Study of the Child* 27: 360–400.

—— 1977. *The Restoration of the Self*. New York: International Universities Press.

La Barre, Weston. 1972 (1990). *The Ghost Dance: Origins of Religion*. Prospect Height, IL: Waveland Press.

—— 1978. "The Clinic and the Field," in George D. Spindler, ed., *The Making of Psychological Anthropology*. Berkeley and Los Angeles: University of California Press. Pp. 258–299.

Lanzetta, J. T., and T. B. Roby. 1960. "The Relationship Between Certain Group

Process Variables and Group Problem-Solving Efficiency," *Journal of Social Psychology* 52: 135–148.

Masterson, James F. 1985. *The Real Self*. New York: Brunner/Mazel.

Meissner, W. W. 1978. *The Paranoid Process*. New York: Jason Aronson.

—— 1988. "The Cult Phenomenon and the Paranoid Process," in L. Bryce Boyer and Simon A. Grolnick, eds., *The Psychoanalytic Study of Society*. Volume 12. Hillsdale, NJ: The Analytic Press. Pp. 69–95.

Mitscherlich, Alexander, and Margarete Mitscherlich. 1967 (1975). *The Inability to Mourn*. New York: Grove Press.

Modell, Arnold H. 1984. *Psychoanalysis in a New Context*. New York: International Universities Press.

Montville, Joseph V. 1989. "Psychoanalytic Enlightenment and the Greening of Diplomacy," *Journal of the American Psychoanalytic Association* 37(2): 297–318.

Moses, Rafael. 1990. "Acknowledgment: The Balm of Narcissistic Injuries," *Mind and Human Interaction* 2(2): 28–30.

Nedelmann, Carl. 1986. "A Psychoanalytical View of the Nuclear Threat from the Angle of the German Sense of Political Inferiority." *Psychoanalytic Inquiry* 6(2): 287–302.

Ogden, Thomas H. 1989. *The Primitive Edge of Experience*. Northvale, NJ: Jason Aronson.

Owen, Wilfred. 1963. *The Collected Poems of Wilfred Owen*. New York: New Directions. P. 58.

Pollock, George H. 1977. "The Mourning Process and Creative Organization," *Journal of the American Psychoanalytic Association* 25: 3–34.

—— 1991. Review of *Maps From the Mind: Readings in Psychogeography*. H. F. Stein and W. G. Niederland, eds. Norman: University of Oklahoma Press, 1989. Reviewed in *Psychoanalytic Books* 2(3): 437–440.

Rangell, Leo. 1976. "Discussion of the Buffalo Creek Disaster: The Course of Psychic Trauma," *American Journal of Psychiatry* 133(3): 313–316.

Reik, Theodor. 1948. *Listening with the Third Ear: The Inner Experience of a Psychoanalyst*. New York: Farrar, Straus.

—— 1953. *The Haunting Melody*. New York: Farrar, Straus, Young.

Rochlin, Gregory. 1973. *Man's Aggression: The Defense of the Self*. Boston: Gambit.

Rogers, Rita R. 1979. "Intergenerational Exchange: Transference of Attitudes Down the Generations," in J. Howells, ed., *Modern Perspectives in the Psychiatry of Infancy*. New York: Brunner/Mazel. Pp. 339–349.

Rosenfeld, Herbert A. 1952. "Notes on the Psycho-Analysis of the Superego Conflict of an Acute Schizophrenic Patient," *International Journal of Psycho-Analysis* 33: 111–131.

Scott-Stevens, Susan. 1988. "The Holistic Anthropologist: A Case Study of a Consultancy at a Western New Mexico Uranium Mine," *High Plains Applied Anthropologist* 8(1): 3–32.

Searles, Harold F. 1965. *Collected Papers on Schizophrenia and Related Subjects*. Madison, CT: International Universities Press.

——. 1975. "The Patient as Therapist to His Analyst," in Peter L. Giovacchini, ed., in collaboration with Alfred Flarsheim and L. Bryce Boyer, *Tactics and*

Techniques in Psychoanalytic Therapy, Volume 2. *Countertransference*. North-vale, NJ: Jason Aronson. Pp. 95–151.

Stein, Howard F. 1982. "Adversary Symbiosis and Complementary Group Dissociation: An Analysis of the U.S./U.S.S.R. Conflict," *International Journal of Inter-Cultural Relations* 6: 55–83.

——1985. "Culture Change, Symbolic Object Loss, and Restitutional Process," *Psychoanalysis and Contemporary Thought* 8(3):301–332.

—— 1986. "The Influence of Psycho-Geography upon the Conduct of International Relations: Clinical and Metapsychological Considerations," *Psychoanalytic Inquiry* 6(2): 193–322. Special issue on "Aggression and Its Alternatives in the Conduct of International Relations," special issue ed., John E. Mack.

—— 1987. *Developmental Time, Cultural Space*. Norman: University of Oklahoma Press.

Stein, Howard F., and Robert F. Hill. 1988. "The Dogma of Technology," in L. Bryce Boyer and Simon A. Grolnick, eds., *The Psychoanalytic Study of Society*. Volume 13. Hillsdale, NJ: Analytic Press. Pp. 149–179.

Stein, Howard F., and William G. Niederland, eds. 1989. *Maps from the Mind*. Norman: University of Oklahoma Press.

Sutherland, J. D. 1990. "Bion Revisited: Group Dynamics and Group Psycho-therapy," in E. Trist and H. Murray, eds., *The Social Engagement of Social Science: A Tavistock Anthology*. Philadelphia: University of Pennsylvania. Pp. 119–140.

Turner, Victor. 1969. *The Ritual Process: Structure and Anti-Structure*. Ithaca, NY: Cornell University Press.

Van Gennep, Arnold. 1908 (1960). *The Rites of Passage*. Chicago: University of Chicago Press.

Volkan, Vamik D. 1987. "Psychological Concepts Useful in the Building of Political Foundations between Nations," *Journal of the American Psychoanalytic Association* 35(4): 903–935.

—— 1988. *The Need to Have Enemies and Allies*. New York: Jason Aronson.

—— 1991. "On 'Chosen Trauma'," *Mind and Human Interaction* 3(1): 13.

Winnicott, Donald W. 1949. *The Child, the Family, and the Outside World*. Baltimore: Penguin, 1964.

—— 1954 (1958). "Metapsychological and Clinical Aspects of Regression within the Psycho-Analytical Set-Up," in *Collected Papers*. New York: Basic Books.

—— 1960 (1965). "The Theory of the Parent-Infant Relationship," in *The Maturational Processes and the Facilitating Environment*. New York: International Universities Press. Pp. 37–55.

—— 1963 (1965). "Psychiatric Disorders in Terms of Infantile Maturational Processes," in *The Maturational Processes and the Facilitating Environment*. New York: International Universities Press. Pp. 230–241.

—— 1964. *The Child, the Family and the Outside World*. Baltimore: Penguin Books.

—— 1967. "The Location of Cultural Experience," *International Journal of Psycho-Analysis* 48: 368–372.

Conclusions

In this book, I have studied workplace symbolism and metaphor via countertransference as well as through other more conventional social science "qualitative" methods. I have described and attempted to explain, at least in part, the frightened flight from love and death into the anxious, protective safety of puritanical privatism, corporatism, and globalization. I have come to the conclusion that the ultimate promise of this new wage serfdom is the freedom to disappear after having worked to the hilt. I have questioned our very language of discourse in the boardroom and on the streets. Human beings are, and deserve to be seen as, better than "human capital" or as "human resources" to spend, to use up, and to dispose of as waste.

Human workplaces—like all cultures—are heir to the potentialities and vulnerabilities of growing up in a long-dependent human organism, experienced during childhood as infancy and childhood within a family (La Barre 1951, 1954; de Mause 1974). We bring to work with us the kind of human animal we are. Exploitation of that vulnerability, and regression during adulthood to its frightening experience and ways of experiencing, culminates—to cite one form—in cultures whose members declare with protective schizoid naivete "It's nothing personal, just business." These cultures—always in the form of persons—proceed to assault people's lives in the workplace just as they were once themselves assaulted during that infinitely exploitable universal condition called childhood. What we cannot remember, we repeat as if it were the first time.

Outside conscious awareness, workplaces repeat and further inflict in the present the developmental and organizational pasts. "Transference" is far from limited to the realm of therapy; it largely defines social reality. Projective hatred *of* the workplace fuses with hatred cultivated and unleashed *in* the workplace. What does this landscape of darkness mean for us in organizations? What are the "implications" of this study for the future of workplace life? Does this study commend hope or despair? What needs to happen in order to lift organizations out of their darkness? Despite the official bravado, there is a pervasive sense of pessimism—at least of quiet panic—in business. If we are to "change," do we "change" organizations or do we "change" society? What questions should we be asking? What can be recommended without becoming part of the current "hype"?

Certainly humans are adaptable, resilient beings. The several-million-year-history of the human species commends the fact of human ingenuity in adapting culturally to many natural environmental niches without having to make major genetic changes. The question is: To what should people be *forced* to adapt? It is one matter to change oneself (autoplastic adaptation) or to modify the environment (alloplastic adaptation) in the face of geological, geographical, climatological, and other external realities. But what shall we say of the obligation to adapt to our own creations: culture, ethnic groups, workplaces, and nations? The cultural world to which we adapt is largely spun of our own substance.

Can we recognize that, at least at times, the solution is the problem, the cure is the disease? Is the darkness I have described an instance of what Robert Edgerton (1992) called "sick societies" and what Jules Henry (1963) a generation earlier called "culture against man"? Organizational "darkness" is comprehensible only if there is something else with which to contrast, against which to calibrate, it.

A REDEMPTIVE PHONE CALL

In 1999, I received a telephone call "out of the blue" from a senior hospital administrator in California. She called to tell me that she had just read my 1998 book, *Euphemism, Spin, and the Crisis in Organizational Life,* and to offer her personal testimony to validate the book's questioning of the euphemisms that have guided and ruled workplace life for two decades. My quotation is approximate, but it evokes the spirit of her story to me. She openly used the phrase "spiritual awakening" to characterize her own personal and professional transformation. Earlier in her career, she said, she had herself been a ruthless, bottom-line defending executive who

cut people out like pawns in a chess game. Hundreds of pawns. There were no people, just numbers, in this game. I was good at what I did, one of the best. Nothing mattered except looking good on paper and in PowerPoint presentations for the hospital board. I was of the generation they called Generation X. Nothing mattered except succeeding in your professional life, advancing your career, making more and more money. There wasn't anything else to trust in. You tried to keep ahead of the game. But, all the great things we thought would happen didn't happen. We deluded ourselves into thinking getting rid of all those people, and moving everyone around who remained, would make a big difference in profit and productivity. It killed the spirit of the place. We made ourselves into gods. We didn't have to do it that way. We just believed that we did, and we mowed down anything that stood in our way. After a while, I just couldn't live with myself running a hospital like this. "What kind of life is this?", I asked myself. I started speaking out about the wrong we were doing. Some people started listening. So that when I read your book, I said to myself, "Yes, what we are doing is not good business, but evil. I need to call him and tell him that he's being heard, that at least I heard him. He's not alone."

If I may borrow from John Donne: No observer, no consultant, is an island, sufficient unto himself or herself. If, in the course of the cultural and organizational odyssey that became this book, I have learned to trust myself—my "instincts," my perceptions, my feelings—it is because I have also found others to trust and who trusted me. A dreadful alone-ness and fear of spiritual death in that aloneness—scientific, artistic, ex-istential—drives me to doubt myself, then to despise even myself for this self-doubt.

For a senior executive from the "real" world of business to affirm my experience from a career separate from my own, gives me both confir-mation from a different "data set" and hope that the darkness of orga-nizational life might lift. Subjectivity and objectivity are deeply entwined intersubjective experiences in all science, "natural" and "social."

There is no promise that the type of change my administrator-colleague experienced will be widespread, or that it will be enough. The human damage that has already been done in the last two decades is enormous, and most people refuse to acknowledge it even as "damage" in need of "repair."

The lifting of organizational darkness will not occur by yet another inspection of the accounting spreadsheet, by imaginative "bean count-ing," but by nothing less than a spiritual awakening that redefines for what and to whom we are responsible. In a change of heart, the notion of "stakeholders" is less redefined than transfigured. Our share, our por-tion, becomes entirely different. Everything, even business, becomes per-sonal. Consciously so.

WORK, WORKPLACE, AND THE HUMAN MEASURE

Who and what are we as human beings? What is our measure? With what metaphors and other symbols do we define and recognize ourselves? Can our symbolic worlds—from "business" to "Holocaust"—also be our self-imposed prisons? In our organizational claustrums, could we be jailer and jailed both at once? If we are to be lifted out of our own darkness, if we are to leave the anxious security of that darkness, we must first recognize it *as* darkness. Certainly, there are, structurally speaking, many kinds of organizations, each likely with a different form of that darkness: *Fortune* 500, Internet-based, public administration, community, and so on. But they share a cultural darkness that descends and extends beyond their boundaries. What they have in common is the cultural creation of meaninglessness through the destruction of meaning.

In the late 1990s, I passed around an essay by an ethicist colleague on organizational ethics. One cunning CEO to whom I gave it quipped, "Isn't 'organizational ethics' an oxymoron?" We have created an ethos of organizational power and authority based on a "managerial mystique" (Zaleznik 1989) and an ethical anaesthesia in the service of frightened opportunism. In this stern moral order, any notion of ethics as "the heart of leadership" (Ciulla 1998) must seem both naive and foreign. Yet, that "heart"—rooted in courage and love—is a way out from this darkness. Understandably, heartless expediency and arrogance must trample its own heart as well as others' in order not to know (and feel) what it does.

Clearly, from the varied studies in this book, "business" is far from "just business." Psychodynamic depth psychology, organizational studies, and anthropology (to name but three disciplines and viewpoints) have revealed to us many unwelcome facets of the workplace. But this is not all they have to teach. Business does not have to be defined by destructiveness and self-destructiveness. The beginning of authentic change (in contrast with restless manic change) lies in the recognition that depersonalized globalization, together with its forms of "managed" social change, are part of the *problem* of the flight from feeling and from relatedness to other people who have needs distinct from our own.

From Socrates and Freud, we learn that truth will make us free. An essential ingredient to that truth is the socially binding power of Eros, most broadly conceived. In our isolated work chambers, we often feel "related" only to the "bottom line" and its fickle vicissitudes. We have become little more than our silo's keeper. We are not only not our brother's (or sister's) keeper, but we are not even our brother's (or sister's) brother (or sister). If individualism is a cultural value and obsession, it is also increasingly a condition into which we humans are thrown. We are asked to give our all for the corporate "mission," but we are entitled only to abandonment in return. We harden our hearts and become indifferent. Perhaps, though, we may—then can—imagine alternatives to this frightened survivalism.

Lest I be misunderstood, the direction of my argument is not a call for a (re-) turn to some form of social-ism or commune-ism to replace capitalism. All-encompassing grand ideologies have local variants that change with time. If this book is to be construed as a critique of capitalism, then it is specifically a critique of the *form* and *spirit* capitalism has taken by American culture in the late twentieth century. It is more a cultural critique than a strictly economic one. I have situated economics as an "institution" and "ideology" *within* culture rather than as the primary driving force *of* culture. Any attempt to change "the economy" (or "political economy") and "the workplace" without addressing the human depths that affect them are shortsighted. What is at stake is the assault upon, and the reclamation of, the human spirit everywhere. The realities of globalized, economically liberalized "managed social change" promise—or threaten—a scale of dehumanization and pauperization that will dwarf the inequities and suffering of the early Industrial Revolution. Sweatshops, coal mines, and company towns are cruel enough as past history to avoid commending them as future.

TRANSCENDING OUR DISCONTENTS

In a famous passage that concludes *Civilization and Its Discontents*, Freud (1930) anticipated this predicament.

> The fateful question for the human species seems to me to be whether and to what extent their cultural development will succeed in mastering the disturbance of their communal life by the human instinct of aggression and self-destruction. It may be that in this respect precisely the present time deserves a special interest. Men have gained control over the forces of nature to such an extent that with their help they would have no difficulty in exterminating one another to the last man. They know this, and hence comes a large part of their current unrest, their unhappiness and their mood of anxiety. And now it is to be expected that the other of the two "Heavenly Powers" ["in the eternal struggle between the trends of love and death," p. 133], eternal Eros, will make an effort to assert himself in the struggle with his equally immortal adversary. But who can foresee with what success and with what result? (1930: 145)

One does not, I believe, need to accept classical instinct theory to recognize the dramatic validity of Freud's broad sweep. Freud added the last sentence in 1931, when Hitler's Nazism was already threatening Europe. I likewise temper my wish and hope with an acknowledgment of the stern cultural reality of our time. The voice of human love, of caring, and of relatedness is vulnerable in the face of violence and hatred—even its bloodlessly rationalized forms.

Yet that vulnerable voice will not be entirely silenced. If there is a path out of the organizational and cultural darkness, it is in heeding the persistent voice that could redeem us from the prison of our own making.

REFERENCES

Ciulla, Joanne B. 1998. *Ethics: The Heart of Leadership*. Westport, CT: Quorum.

de Mause, Lloyd, ed. 1974. *The History of Childhood*. New York: Psychohistory Press.

Edgerton, Robert B. 1992. *Sick Societies: Challenging the Myth of Primitive Harmony*. New York: Free Press.

Freud, Sigmund. 1930 (1961). "Civilization and Its Discontents," in *The Standard Edition of the Complete Psychological Works of Sigmund Freud*. Volume 21. London: Hogarth Press. Pp. 64–145.

Henry, Jules. 1963. *Culture Against Man*. New York: Random House.

La Barre, Weston. 1951. "Family and Symbol," in G. Wilbur and W. Muensterberger, eds., *Psychoanalysis and Culture: Essays in Honor of Géza Róheim*. New York: International Universities Press. Pp. 156–167.

———. 1954. *The Human Animal*. Chicago: University of Chicago Press.

Zaleznik, Abraham. 1989. *The Managerial Mystique: Restoring Leadership in Business*. New York: Harper and Row.

Index

Abse, D. Wilfred, 108
Acknowledgment, 139–40
Acting out, 23–24, 138
Adams, Scott, 71
Adler, William, 13
Aggression, loss and, 119, 159. *See also* Violence in the workplace
Allcorn, Seth, 28, 36, 40
Altruistic surrender, 33
Analytic process, 126. *See also* Holding environment
Apology for errors, 139–40
Armstrong, David, 34–35

Balint, Michael, 139, 144
Barondess, Jeremiah, 8
Baum, Howell, 28, 36
Beisel, David, 81
Berlin Wall metaphor, 130
Berman, Morris, 29, 39
Bion, Wilfred R.: catastrophic change, 64; containers, 114; on countertransference, 3, 25, 31, 33–34; fight-flight groups, 141, 146–47
Bollas, Christopher, 53
Bottom line, as justification, 8, 26

Boyer, L. Bryce, 149
Brent, Lucille, 135–36
Brodsky, A., 69–71
Brown, Janet, 122, 134–37
Brutalization in the workplace: demoralized employees, 113–15; demoralized leadership, 112–13; euphemism, 7–10, 15; future of workplace life, 156; the Jew in their midst vignette, 88–90; management by intimidation, 95–97; need for mourning, 102, 128, 132, 138–39, 144; organizational change, 106–11; rectification of names vignette, 90–92. *See also* Violence in the workplace
Bursztajn, Harold, 8, 69, 70, 71
Business organizations: adaptation to a sense of doom, 113–15; cataclysm and memory, 92–95; change-loss-grief triad, 118–19, 128; consultant as listener, 111; darkness in, 156–57; demoralized leadership, 112–13; importance of history, 138–39, 141; letter from former administrator, 82–84; organizational ethics, 158;

spiritual awakenings, 156–57; wishing a subsidiary would disappear, 106–11; xenophobia and nationalism, 87–92
Byrne, John, 13

Case studies. *See* School system case study; Vignettes
Change-loss-grief triad, 118–19, 128
Circling the wagons, 108
Ciulla, Joanne, 13
Civilization and Its Discontents, 142, 159
Coming to Our Senses, 29
Consultants: apology for errors, 139–40; holding environment, 124–29, 131, 133, 141, 146, 148–50; as listeners, 111, 129; roles during retreat, 129–32, 142, 144, 148–50. *See also* Countertransference
Container, consultant as, 124–29, 131, 133, 141, 146, 148–50
Corporate apocalypse, 65
"Corporate Killers," 13
Counteridentification, 95
Countertransference, 21–44; author's vignette, 35–40; concordant and complementary, 30; cultural knowledge, 40, 53–54, 60–63; definition, 22; dissociation, 58–59, 62; embodied versus disembodied knowing, 26, 38; emptied office vignette, 54–56; environmental invalidation and, 3; in fieldwork, 27–31, 34; as foundation to understanding, 25–26, 52, 125; as grounding, 73–74; in group treatment, 33–34; identification with the aggressor, 24, 84; as knowing via the senses, 28–31; MCA example, 115; nurse-educator vignette, 56–60; in organizational methodology, 42–44; policeman versus driver example, 23–24; projective identification, 32–35, 38, 56; in school system retreat, 122, 146, 148, 150
Credibility, 108
Cruelty, 4–5

Csordas, Thomas, 26, 44
Cultural knowledge, 40–42, 53–54, 60–63

Darkness at Noon, 24–25, 43
Death anxiety, 71–73
Death imagery, 110, 143
Demoralization, 109–15
Devereux, George, 31, 43, 125
Diamond, Michael, 13–14, 28, 36–37, 123
Disasters, natural, 4
Dissociation, 58–59, 62
Douglas, Mary, 141
"The Downside of Downsizing," 13
Downsizing: after holiday celebrations, 69; consequences of, 13; dissociation, 58–59, 62; effects on remaining personnel, 93–95; emptied office vignette, 54–56; globalization and, 13; Holocaust analogy, 11, 15–16, 63; hospital longitudinal study, 12, 28, 88; need for mourning, 102; nurse-educator vignette, 56–60; semantics of, 65, 73; statistics, 12; threat of, 95–97; water-bowl analogy, 2–3; wish to disappear, 62–63, 71, 110–11
"The Downsizing of America," 12–13
The Drowned and the Saved, 68
Dundes, Alan, 41

Ebel, Henry, 66, 71, 73
Embodied versus disembodied knowing, 26, 38
Emotion, 42, 147
Emotional responses: in group treatment, 33–34; key to metaphors, 67; as reliable measure of social reality, 25; role of, xx. *See also* Countertransference
Empathy, failure of, 140
Employment, social worth and, 69
Emptied office vignette, 54–56
Enemies, need for, 145–46
Environmental invalidation, 3
Erikson, Erik H., 89, 145
Ethical imperative, 10

Ethnic cleansing metaphor, 69, 95, 101
Ethnicity, 53
Ethnography: countertransference in fieldwork, 28–31; knowing the Other, 41–42; projective identification, 33
Euphemism, xvii, 7–10, 15
Euphemism, Spin, and the Crisis in Organization Life, xv, xvii, 15, 57, 82, 156
Evil, xvi, 71–73, 80–82
Ewing, Katherine P., 145
"Expecting the Barbarians," 101
Experiences in Groups, 146

Faludi, Susan, 14
Family medicine, 97–100
Farming disasters, 4
Fight-flight groups, 141, 146–47
Fornari, Franco, 81
Frank, Hans, 62, 68
Frantz, Paul, 124
Freud, Anna, 32–33
Freud, Sigmund, 22, 31, 34, 72, 142, 159–60
Friedman, David B., 16, 24
From Anxiety to Method in the Behavioral Sciences, 31
"From Countertransference to Social Theory," 82
A Future Perfect, 13

Gay, Peter, 62
Geertz, Clifford, 13, 30, 41
Gilkey, Roderick W., 12
Globalization, 13
Golden Rule, 98
Greenspan, Alan, 2
Grief. *See* Mourning
Grimsley, K. D., 13
Grolnick, Simon, 139
Group dynamics: emotion in, 147; fight-flight, 141, 146–47; in group treatment, 33–34; holding environment, 124–29, 131, 133, 141, 146, 148–50; humiliation, 9; nationalism and xenophobia, 87–92, 101–2; psy-

chogeography, 149; sense of we-ness, 141
Groupthink, 9
Grund, George, 134, 136
Gutheil, T. G., 69

Hammer, Michael, 65
Hart, Gregory, 124
Hatred, need for, 145–46, 156
Health care. *See* Managed health care
Health insurance, 100
Hill, Robert F., 149
Holding environment, 124–29, 131, 133, 141, 146, 148–50
Holmes, Gary, 81
The Holocaust and the Crisis of Human Behavior, 80
Holocaust metaphor: arguments against, 15–16, 58; as evil, 80–82; feelings, 16, 63; from former administrator, 82–85; as metaphor, 10–11, 15–16, 26–27, 39–40, 66, 81–82; origin of word, 80. *See also* Nazis and Jews
Hospital downsizing, 12, 28, 59–60, 88. *See also* MCA example
The HUMAN Cost of a Management Failure, 36
Humiliation, 9, 95–97
Hypernationalism, 87–92

Identity assaults, 62
Implicit culture, 41
Intellectual property of subordinates, 6–7, 89
International diplomacy, 139
Intersubjectivity, 125, 149
Intimidation, 6–7, 14, 24, 92, 95–97
Introjective identification, 32, 62

Janis, Irving, 9
Jew in their midst vignette, 88–90
Johnson, Mark, 40
Jones, Barbara, 134–35

Kabaphes, Konstantinos, 101
Katz, Jay, 8
Kim, David, 99

Klein, Melanie, 31–33, 72, 84
Kleinfield, N. R., 12–13
Knight, Terry, 4
Knowing: cultural knowledge, 40–42, 53–54; embodied versus disembodied, 26, 38; environmental invalidation, 3; otherness, 41–42; projective identification, 32–35, 38, 60–63; resistance to, 5–6, 129; through the senses, 28–31
Koestler, Arthur, 24–25, 43
Kohut, Heinz, 140
Kormos, Harry R., 106
Kren, George, 80

La Barre, Weston, 29
Labeling theory, 43, 91
Lakoff, George, 40
Language: bimodal distribution of, 15; to clarify, 7–10; curse words, 17; of downsizing, 65–67; projective identification, 64–67
Laub, Dori, 5
Lawrence, W. Gordon, 31, 34–35, 39, 64
Levi, Primo, 1–2, 4, 68
Levinson, Harry, 102
Lewis, Jerry, 137–38
Lieberman, Gary R., 12
Lifton, Robert Jay, 29, 84
Listening, 111, 129
Loyalty, 138–39

Maltz, Marc, 35
Managed health care: family medicine, 99–100; industrialization of, 106; Nuremberg Code and, 8, 69–70; nurses' responses to downsizing, 59–60; organizational change and sense of doom, 106–11; triage model, 71
Managed social change, 15
Masculinity, assault on, 14
MCA example, 105–15; adaptation to a sense of doom, 113–15; consultant as listener, 111; effect of demoralized leadership, 111–13; effect of organizational change, 106–11

Meaninglessness, 64
Medical insurance, 100
Medicine, family, 97–100. *See also* Managed health care
Meltzer, Donald, 72
Melville, Herman, 25
Metaphors: Berlin Wall, 130; bimodal distribution of, 15; definition, 14; emotional responses, 67; ethnic cleansing, 69, 95, 101; Holocaust as, 10–11, 15–16, 26–27, 39–40, 63, 81–82; specificity of, 16–17; that we live by, 40; Vietnam War, 15–16, 40, 43
Methodology: definition, 53; emotional responses, xx; importance to understanding, 14–15. *See also* Countertransference
Micklethwait, John, 13
Moby Dick, 25
Modell, Arnold, 30–31, 125–26
Montville, Joseph, 139, 144
Moses, Rafael, 139–40
Mourning: as break in cycle, 102; change-loss-grief triad, 118–19, 128; political, 139; role of unspent grief, 128; scapegoating versus, 132; in school system retreat, 118–19, 122, 138–39, 144, 148

Naming theory, 43, 91
Nationalism, 87–92, 101–2
Nazi death camps, 1, 68
Nazi physicians, 29
Nazis and Jews: soccer games between, 68–69; symbolic, 9, 62, 65–66, 68–69; in the workplace, 84–85. *See also* Holocaust metaphor
Negative capability, 54
Negative identity, 89
Niederland, William G., 149
Niemöller, Martin, 10
Nuremberg Code, 8, 69–70
Nyiszli, Miklos, 68

Object relations conflict, 61
Ochberg, Frank M., 3–5
Ogden, Thomas, 72, 125–27
Organizational ethics, 158

Organizations. *See* Business organizations
Owen, Wilfred, 7, 117

Paranoid ethos, 64
Parsifal, 142
Pascal, Blaise, 29–30
Petschauer, Peter, 66–67
Podell, Daniel, 5
Poetry, xix–xxi
Post-traumatic stress disorder (PTSD),
    xviii, 3–5
Potential space, 148–49
Potlatching, 52
Power, corruption by, 82–84
Preston, Paul, 13
Projective hatred, 156
Projective identification: cultural
    understanding, 60–63; death anxiety
    and, 71–73; *de facto* captivity, 69–71;
    in downsizing, 56, 63; example of,
    61; in group dynamics, 32–35, 38;
    language and, 64–67
"Psychoanalytic Listening to
    Historical Trauma," 5
Psychotherapy, failure of empathy in,
    140

Ramirez, Henry, 134–36
Rappoport, Leon, 80
Rauschmann, Jerry, 124, 135, 137–38
Reality, denial of, xix
Rectification of names vignette, 90–92
The Reenchantment of the World, 29
Reputation, 108
Retreat structure, 114, 118
Rich, Adrienne, 43
Ritual process, 141
Roby, T. B., 147
Role-playing, 131
Roth, William, 13
Rubin, Leigh, 71

Scapegoating, organizational, 39, 132
Schlager, William, 136
School system case study, 117–51; ac-
    knowledgment of errors, 140; assign-
    ment, 120; change-loss-grief triad,

118–19, 128; consultant roles, 129–
32; follow-up, 146; group sense of
we-ness, 141; history, 120–24;
holding environment, 124–29, 131,
133, 141, 146, 148–50; initial mis-
trust, 123; methodology and theory,
124–29; organizational culture, 149;
success of retreat, 143–44; transfigu-
ration scene, 132–38; understanding
the transformation, 138–42
Schwartz, Theodore, 64
Scott-Stevens, Susan, 128
Sensuous Scholarship, 29
Shapiro, Johanna, 99
Shapiro, Roger L., 32
Shore, Karen, 8
Shreck, Carl, 134–37
Smith, Walter, 122, 136
Social dreaming, 34–35, 39
Spiritual awakening, 156–57
Spiro, Melford, 30
Stein, Howard F.: experience of coun-
    tertransference, 35–40, 122, 125, 146,
    148; influence of Jewish back-
    ground, 27; making a holding envi-
    ronment, 127, 131, 133, 141, 146,
    148–50; previous works by, 15, 41,
    57; roles during retreat, 129–32, 142,
    150
Stephens, G. Gayle, 97–99
*Stiffed: The Betrayal of the American
    Man*, 14
Stockholm Syndrome, 4
Stoller, Paul, 28–29, 39
Stuart, Glenn, 124, 133–34
Sutherland, J. D., 147

The Taste of Ethnographic Things, 29
Technology, symbolism of, 149
Therapists. *See* Consultants
Totalism, 145
Transference: definition, 22; parent/
    child, 140; policeman versus driver
    example, 23; social reality, 156;
    workplace intimidation and, 6–7
Traumatization, 3–5, 43
Turner, Victor, 141

Uchitelle, Louis, 12–13
Unruh, Jim, 136
Ute Indians, 4

Victimization, 3–5, 81
Vietnam War metaphor, 15–16, 40, 43
Vignettes: author's, 35–40; from counterculture to Brave New World, 97–100; emptied office, 54–56; the Jew in their midst, 88–90; making too much of something, 93–95; nurse-educator, 56–60; rectification of names, 90–92; why is he here?, 95–97
Violence in folklore, 30, 41
Violence in the workplace: aggression and loss, 119, 159; disparagement of outsiders, 91–92; intimidation, 6–7, 14, 24, 92, 95–97; limitation of term, 9; waterbowl analogy, 2–3. *See also* Brutalization in the workplace
Volkan, Vamik D., 4, 138

Wagner, Richard, 142
Walker, E. Martin, 35
Wall, Nancy, 135–37
Winnicott, Donald, 72, 84, 126–27, 148–49
Wooldridge, Adrian, 13
The Working Life, 13
Workplace organizations. *See* Business organizations

Xenophobia, 87–92, 101–2

Zinner, John, 32

About the Author

HOWARD F. STEIN is a professor in the Department of Family and Preventive Medicine, University of Oklahoma Health Sciences Center, Oklahoma City. A medical and psychoanalytic anthropologist, organizational consultant, political psychologist and psychohistorian, Dr. Stein specializes in teaching clinical behavioral science to residents and graduate students in Family Medicine and in Occupational Medicine. He is a former editor of *The Journal of Psychoanalytic Anthropology*, has published more than 200 articles and chapters in books, and has written and edited more than 20 of his own books, most recently *Euphemism, Spin, and the Crisis in Organizational Life* (Quorum, 1998).

Date Due

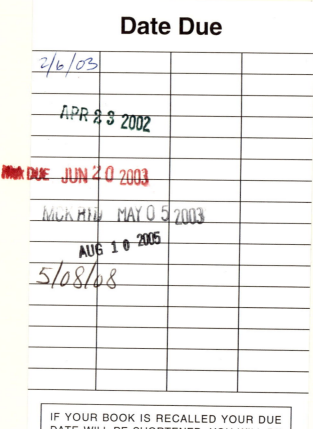

2/6/03			
APR 2 3 2002			
~~MCK DUE~~ JUN 2 0 2003			
MCK RID MAY 0 5 2003			
AUG 1 0 2005			
5/08/08			